THE DOUBLE

To the memory of Bill Nicholson

The Double

The Inside Story of Spurs' Triumphant 1960–61 Season

KEN FERRIS

MAINSTREAM PUBLISHING

EDINBURGH AND LONDON

Reprinted 2008

First published in 1996 by Two Heads

First published in Great Britain in 1999 by
MAINSTREAM PUBLISHING COMPANY (EDINBURGH) LTD
7 Albany Street
Edinburgh EH1 3UG

Reprinted 2001, 2005, 2006

ISBN 9781840182354

A catalogue record for this book is available from the British Library

Typeset in Sabon
Printed and bound in Great Britain by
Cox & Wyman Ltd

Contents

Acknowledgements

THIS BOOK IS about a team who rank among the greatest to have graced a football pitch anywhere in the world. I would like to thank all of them for giving me their time and for sharing their memories of a wonderful season. My heartfelt thanks go to Bill Brown, Ron Henry, Peter Baker, Maurice Norman, Dave Mackay, Terry Dyson, Terry Medwin, Bobby Smith, Cliff Jones, Tony Marchi, Frank Saul and Mel Hopkins. The only player missing is Les Allen who I was unable to track down despite extensive efforts. Sorry Les.

I would also like to thank Bill Nicholson for sparing the time to see me in his office at Tottenham Hotspur. Bill had an aura about him that demanded respect and it was a privilege to meet him. He sadly passed away in October 2004 but as current Tottenham chairman Daniel Levy said, 'He will never be forgotten.'

John White and Danny Blanchflower are also sadly no longer with us but I would like to thank John's widow Sandra (she has since remarried and is now Sandra Hart) and Danny's wife Betty for memories of their husbands and the 'double' season. This book is dedicated as much to them as to John and Danny.

I would also like to thank Alan Leather and Barbara Wallace, who worked in the general office during the 'double' season.

The journalists who helped me with my research include Ian Wooldridge of the *Daily Mail*, Ken Jones of *The Independent*, Kenneth Wolstenholme and BBC radio commentator Ron Jones.

A special mention goes to Andy Porter, the Tottenham historian, whose help in digging up newspaper cuttings, checking facts and reading through the drafts was invaluable; and to Les Gold who read through the manuscripts to check for any errors. The book is more accurate as a result.

I would like to thank my mother, Sadie, who spent countless hours transcribing tapes of my interviews with all the main characters. Her knowledge of football is growing rapidly with each new project I undertake!

My thanks also go to Chris Badcock at the News International library for his help in finding newspaper cuttings and thanks to Ian Middleton at Reuters who provided me with his collection of match programmes for the 1960–61 season.

And finally I must mention Ronnie Massey, a lifelong Spurs fan and very good friend of the family. He is responsible for my love of Tottenham Hotspur and therefore, indirectly, for this book. I accompanied him and my father, Ken, to many games at White Hart Lane as a boy. Without his influence I would have supported West Ham. Thanks Ron.

I hope my endeavours have uncovered little-known facts about the 'double' season and the players who took part in making history. My aim has been to take you back in time to see the season as the players lived it. I hope it's as enjoyable to read as it was to write.

Ken Ferris

Foreword

TOTTENHAM HOTSPUR'S REPUTATION around the world was forged by the great double-winning team fashioned by Bill Nicholson, and every Spurs manager since then has lived in the shadow of the great man's achievements over the course of that amazing 1960–61 season.

The double has been claimed by Arsenal, Liverpool and Manchester United in recent years, but when Tottenham won the league championship and the FA Cup in one season they achieved a feat that was thought to be impossible. Nobody had done it in the twentieth century.

Nicholson's success made White Hart Lane 'the world famous home of the Spurs' and their success was renowned throughout Europe, even more so when they became the first British team to win a European trophy after lifting the Cup-Winners' Cup in 1963.

Sadly, Bill is no longer with us, and the week after his memorial service I was entrusted with carrying on his legacy and trying to build a side that could live up to the great man's achievements. I'd only been at the club four months, but already I loved it.

I knew a lot about English football – having been a midfielder at West Bromwich Albion and Coventry City in the 1980s – when I joined Spurs in July 2004 as coach after a successful career in my native Holland.

I was aware of the esteem in which the fans held Bill Nick and when I attended his memorial service my immediate thought was that it would be marvellous if I could share the same feeling of success he had enjoyed. I knew it was not a minor task, but Spurs are still a massive club.

It was always my ambition to return to England as a manager and now I've been given the chance to put Tottenham back on the map. Football is all about tradition and history, which is why Spurs will always be one of Europe's most respected clubs.

Bill Nicholson made sure of that.

Martin Jol

Preface

I WAS WALKING through New York's Central Park on a glorious summer day in early June wearing a white T-shirt with BLANCH-FLOWER emblazoned across the back in navy blue above the famous number 4. 'Blanchflower – what a player,' said someone with a Lancashire accent walking behind me. I turned to find a balding middle-aged man from Bolton who proceeded to name the entire Spurs 'double' team. 'Brown, Baker, Henry, Blanchflower, Norman, Mackay, Dyson, Allen, Smith, White, Jones. Did I miss anyone?' he asked. 'Medwin played quite a few games that season as well,' I replied. 'Oh yes, so he did,' said the man, glad I'd jogged his memory.

A few weeks earlier a call to Tottenham director Douglas Alexiou elicited the same response: a full rundown of that immortal Spurs team, the first side in the twentieth century to win the 'double'. 'They were a wonderful team to watch with a combination of power and grace. They were irresistible,' said Alexiou. Indeed, they were.

When Spurs began their quest in the summer of 1960 most people believed winning the Championship and the FA Cup in the same season was impossible. Many teams had come close including Manchester United's Busby Babes in '57 and Wolverhampton Wanderers in '60. But still nobody had done it since Aston Villa way back in 1897.

The Spurs team that finally silenced the doubters was full of stars. Of course, there was Danny Blanchflower, captain of Northern Ireland and destined to become Footballer of the Year for the second time at the end of that historic season. But Tottenham also had the rugged Scot Dave Mackay, reckoned by many to be the inspiration behind the 'double' success, and his fellow international John White, nicknamed 'the Ghost'. That midfield trio was one of the greatest the game has ever seen.

Welsh international Cliff Jones was the first-choice wingman who could play on either flank. He was partnered either by Welsh compatriot Terry Medwin on the right wing or the diminutive Terry Dyson on the left, depending on twhich of them was fit and/or in form.

Scottish international Bill Brown was in goal, while the swashbuckling Bobby Smith banged in the goals at centre-forward playing alongside Les Allen. Peter Baker and Ron Henry were rock solid in the full-back positions and big Maurice Norman, known as 'Monty' or 'Swede' to team-mates and supporters alike, was the centre-half at the heart of the defence.

Over 2.5 million people watched Tottenham's League and Cup triumphs that season – more than had seen any other club at any time. The 11 successive wins which opened their campaign is still a record for the First Division (Reading now hold the record for all Divisions with an opening run of 13 wins in the 1985–86 season). Spurs also notched up a record 31 wins in 42 League games and a record 16 away wins out of 21 matches; equalled Arsenal's record of 66 points in a season and 33 from away games; went 16 matches without defeat at the start of the season; and were the first team to reach 50 points from only 29 games. And they did it all with only 17 players – another record (since beaten by Liverpool in 1965–66 and Aston Villa in 1980–81 when they used only 14 players each).

For the first time this book, based on interviews with the players and manager Bill Nicholson, tells the story of that historic 'double' season from the inside.

It takes you behind the scenes to explain why Bobby Smith 'disappeared' on the morning of the FA Cup final; why Cliff Jones was crocked in the first game of the season by one of his mates; why actress Jayne Mansfield was the first woman allowed into the Spurs boardroom; and why Bill Nicholson left the Cup final banquet a disappointed man.

It tells of the players' superstitions; how they trained; how they thought; what they ate; how they passed the time on long journeys to away matches; what they were told in the dressing-room before big games; how they celebrated in a revolutionary new way on the pitch;

what they got up to after matches; the players they admired and those they feared playing against; and how they felt before, during and after the FA Cup final.

This book also follows what happened to the players when the glory years were over, chronicling their successes and failures off the pitch.

Prologue

FOR DANNY BLANCHFLOWER Saturday, 7 March 1959, was a day of personal triumph. It didn't look as if it would turn out that way. The morning rain seemed to have set in for the summer and heavy, black clouds were reflected in the pools of water lying on a saturated White Hart Lane pitch.

Only 30,000 were brave enough to leave the comfort of their homes to come and watch the match against Leicester City, but they were glad they did. This was Blanchflower at his best. Such was his determination that he would probably have performed just as well in an empty stadium or at the local park.

For this was the day when the Irish international orchestrated Tottenham's finest display since they went to Old Trafford on the last day of November 1957 and took two points from the Champions in a thrilling 4-3 win – the first time a London club had won there in 19 years. Blanchflower later rated that victory as one of his best matches and one of Spurs' best performances in all his years with the club.

Against Leicester, Danny played at wing-half, the job he once lost because Spurs wanted someone who could defend. The adventurous Irish genius rewarded the small crowd for their loyal support by giving them a taste of the glory a team can aspire to when driven by one of the greatest attacking wing-halves in the world.

He played like a man possessed, controlling the greasy ball as if it were attached to his boots by a piece of string, stepping over the slippery pitch, spraying the ball around with uncanny accuracy. He won every tackle, every challenge, every fight for possession. He was playing this match for one man: Danny Blanchflower. After all, he had something to prove: to his manager Bill Nicholson, to the fans, and to the Press; most of all he had something to prove to himself. Tottenham scored six perfect goals, including a fifth by Danny himself. But it hadn't always been like this.

Blanchflower had taken an increasingly important role in the team since his arrival at Spurs in 1954. He didn't believe his role as captain was merely to toss up and decide which way to kick. He considered that it gave him the authority to change the side if things were going badly. In those days captains weren't expected to make changes on the field, but Blanchflower was used to doing it. Northern Ireland manager Peter Doherty gave him the authority to change things if he thought alterations were necessary.

Once he made a decisive switch in a Sixth Round FA Cup match against West Ham when Spurs were losing 3-1 with 20 minutes to go. He ordered centre-half Maurice Norman up into the attack and Tottenham earned a replay, which they won 2-1. The directors didn't complain that time because the move worked. But when Blanchflower tried it again in an FA Cup semi-final against Manchester City the gamble failed.

Tottenham were already playing with three centre-forwards that day – Dave Dunmore, Bobby Smith and Len Duquemin. In the 70th minute Blanchflower decided to push Maurice Norman up front. That made four centre-forwards!

The ploy seemed to work when George Robb finally broke through. With City's big German keeper Bert Trautmann sprawled on the ground, Robb had only to put the ball into an empty net. But Trautmann grabbed his legs, the linesman didn't see it and the chance had gone. City won 1-0.

The Spurs players congratulated their rivals and trooped dejectedly off the pitch. As Blanchflower peeled off his shirt in the silent gloom of the dressing-room Jimmy Anderson, the flustered Spurs manager, rushed through the door and slid onto the bench beside him. 'You shouldn't have done that. My directors are up there asking me what you're doing and who gave you the authority to change the team.'

'Jimmy,' he pleaded, 'I'm as disappointed as you and the directors. I tried to win the game by taking a gamble. You think I made a mistake. I think it's better to make a mistake trying something than to accept things and do nothing about them.'

'Well, I'm the manager here and I'll make the changes,' Anderson told him. 'It makes me look silly in front of my directors.'

'I wasn't trying to buck your authority,' replied Blanchflower. 'I was out there and the Cup was slipping away. I took a chance. You should have some confidence in me as the captain.' The row ended when Anderson was suddenly called away.

The Cup defeat had a devastating effect on morale and Spurs soon found themselves struggling against relegation. Some weeks later, with the club languishing near the foot of the First Division and the Cup a distant memory, they found themselves 2-1 down to fellow strugglers Huddersfield.

Tottenham led 1-0 halfway through the second-half and seemed to have the game comfortably in their control. Then Huddersfield sent over a harmless-looking cross. Norman, playing at right-back, headed it back for goalkeeper Ron Reynolds. But he'd come out to catch the cross and could do little but stand and watch helplessly as the ball flew into the net.

Not long afterwards a Huddersfield goal-kick bounced awkwardly past Spurs centre-half Harry Clarke and Huddersfield centre-forward Dave Hickson hurried a shot from well outside the area. Nobody was more surprised than Reynolds when it got past him into the net.

With 15 minutes left, wing-half Tony Marchi pleaded with Blanchflower to let him push forward. 'It wasn't going like we wanted so I shouted across to Danny, "Let me have a go up front",' recalls Marchi. Blanchflower, being a captain who always encouraged players to try something different, agreed. 'OK, try to do what you can,' he told Marchi. He brought Johnny Brooks back to left-half. But it didn't help. 'You have to try these things. But we still lost and Dan got a right rollicking,' says Marchi. It was another bitter disappointment.

Anderson was quick to scold Blanchflower again in the dressing-room. 'You shouldn't have changed the team,' he snapped. His captain said nothing. 'Jimmy, it was my fault we lost the game,' said Reynolds. 'Don't tell me whose fault it was,' barked Anderson, triggering a different argument amid the tension. Blanchflower apologised and told Reynolds not to interfere. 'We'll talk about it later,' Anderson told his captain before leaving.

When the other results came through, Spurs were left needing one point from their two remaining games – away to Cardiff and home to Sheffield United – to escape the drop. 'We should get that on Monday night against Cardiff,' Blanchflower told Reynolds, 'and then I'll hand in the captaincy if I'm not to be allowed some authority on the field.'

After the match Anderson dashed off to Swansea to sign Welsh international winger Terry Medwin for £18,000. The Spurs players were told to report on Monday morning for the journey to Cardiff.

When Blanchflower got to Tottenham on the Monday, little Tommy Harmer was there waiting for him, his face as white as a sheet. 'You're not going,' gasped Harmer, 'you're not on the team sheet'. The surprised Blanchflower tried to take the news in his stride.

When he walked into the dressing-room, Spurs trainer Cecil Poynton was standing there. 'I've left some kit out for you in case you want to do a bit of training,' he told Blanchflower almost apologetically. 'No, Cecil. I'll go for a game of golf,' said the deposed captain. 'OK,' said Poynton, 'I'll leave it to you.'

Before leaving White Hart Lane, Blanchflower phoned Jack Orange, sports editor of the *Evening News*. Blanchflower had been writing a column for the Saturday evening edition and had agreed not to allow his name to be used on articles in other papers. An Irish paper had asked whether they could write a series about him and Blanchflower wanted to clear it with the *News*. Orange wasn't in the office so someone else checked his query with the editor. He returned to tell Blanchflower it was OK.

'How's your injury?' the journalist asked innocently as he was about to hang up. 'What injury?' replied Blanchflower, thinking he'd been mixed up with another player. 'Your injury,' said the reporter with growing interest. 'You're not playing tonight at Cardiff are you?' 'No, I'm not,' said Blanchflower. 'Well, how's the injury then? Is it bad?' 'I'm not injured. How did you get that idea?' 'We were told you were not playing at Cardiff tonight because you were injured.' 'Well, if I'm injured I know nothing about it. As far as I'm concerned I've been dropped from the team for tonight's game.' 'Do you mind if we use that?' said the stunned reporter. 'Not at all because it's the truth to me,' replied an honest, if slightly bemused, Blanchflower.

That night, while Spurs battled for their vital point at Ninian Park,

Cardiff, the story of how their captain had been dropped was plastered across the front page of the *Evening News*.

It was Thursday morning before Blanchflower saw Anderson again. The Spurs manager had spent a few days in Wales finalising Medwin's transfer. Blanchflower sat in front of Anderson's desk in his office. 'That was a dirty trick you did . . .' said Anderson. 'What do you mean?' asked Blanchflower. 'Phoning up the *Evening News* to tell them you weren't injured.' 'Who told you that?' 'Never mind who. I get my information,' snapped Anderson. 'I hope he told you the story accurately,' said Blanchflower who then explained why he'd phoned the paper, making the point that he didn't know Anderson had told the *News* he was injured.

Later Anderson asked if he was certain how he felt over the captaincy. 'I am,' Blanchflower assured him. 'I shall not tell the Press anything about our chat,' said Anderson, 'and I hope you'll be sensible about it.' 'I shall not get in touch with them,' Danny said, 'but if they should ask me I shall give them an honest answer.'

That afternoon Blanchflower met journalist Bernard Joy at a lunch. 'You've been deprived of the captaincy,' said Joy. 'How did you find out?' asked a startled Blanchflower. 'I phoned Tottenham for the team news and when they got to your name they said you had been deprived of the captaincy because they didn't want changes made on the field.' Blanchflower was amazed.

That Saturday he played well against Sheffield United in the final game of the season. The papers said it was because he no longer had so much responsibility on his shoulders. He was amused. He'd played well before he was captain and while he'd been captain and nobody had said before that his form was related to whether he was captain or not. Besides, he wanted the responsibility, he wasn't afraid of it.

Despite the dispute over the captaincy, Blanchflower didn't want to leave Spurs. He liked Tottenham. He was proud of their great football traditions. There was something about the place that had been missing at his former club Aston Villa. He could sense the same feeling at Wolves – particularly at their famous floodlit games – and at Old Trafford, and in a more subdued way at Highbury and Goodison Park, but nowhere else.

The following season, 1956–57, Spurs were in good form until Third Division Bournemouth knocked them out of the Cup in the Fifth Round. The shock defeat affected Tottenham's League form and they lost valuable ground to Manchester United in the title race. The Busby Babes were at their post-war peak – a year before the Munich crash. They eventually won the Championship by eight points. Spurs were second. United also narrowly missed achieving the 'double' when, ironically, they lost to the last 'double' winners, Aston Villa, in controversial circumstances after their keeper Ray Wood was injured. There were no substitutes in those days.

Spurs began the 1957–58 campaign – their 50th in the League and their 75th since they were formed under a lamp post in Tottenham High Road – badly. But they recovered. After losing in the Third Round of the Cup to Sheffield United, they raced up the table and finished third behind Wolves and Preston.

Jimmy Anderson, the Spurs manager, celebrated 50 years with the club, but everyone sensed he wouldn't last much longer. The pressures were getting to him and he was taken ill in October. On the 11th he called coach Bill Nicholson into his office and told him that Fred Wale, the vice-chairman, wanted to see him at his works, Brown's of Tottenham.

'What's it all about, Jim?' asked Nicholson, a member of the great Spurs 'push and run side' which won the League Championship in 1951. 'You go down there,' said Anderson. 'You'll soon find out.'

Nicholson drove to the vice-chairman's firm and was welcomed into the office. 'Jimmy Anderson isn't going to carry on as manager,' said Wale. 'Would you like the job?' There was no suggestion at the time that Anderson was ill but when Nicholson's appointment was made public three days later the club said their manager had retired through ill-health.

Wale didn't offer Nicholson a pay rise or even a contract. Indeed, he never had a contract as manager of Tottenham Hotspur. 'I reasoned that if I was good enough to do the job they'd keep me. If I wasn't good enough to do it they'd sack me. A contract would make no difference,' said Nicholson years later. He told Wale that after four years as coach he'd like to be manager and felt he could do it. 'Fine,' said Wale.

Anderson's reign was over. He'd done almost every job it was possible to do at Tottenham in his 50 years with the club. He'd twice taken over when Rowe was ill and fashioned a team which was good enough to challenge for the title. But his legacy was the shrewd signings he'd made, players like Maurice Norman, Bobby Smith, Cliff Jones and the two Terrys, Dyson and Medwin. They would all go on to play a major role in making Spurs probably the best team the Football League had ever seen.

The club announced Nicholson's appointment on the Saturday morning before a home game with Everton. Spurs were 16th, having taken nine points from their first eleven matches. Everton were in the bottom three. The sun was shining that day – literally. Nicholson's reign began with an amazing 10-4 victory as Spurs celebrated his promotion in style. Bobby Smith got four goals.

Despite the bright start there were already warning signs. Everton had played as if they were desperate to get into the Second Division as quickly as possible – yet they still managed to breach Tottenham's defence four times with Jimmy Harris scoring a hat-trick.

As usual it was Blanchflower, newly restored to the first team, who made the most telling comment in the dressing-room after the match. 'It can only get worse,' he said. And he was right.

Tottenham won their next match away to Leicester 4-3. They then lost their next two games. More worrying was the fact that the defence kept giving away silly goals: in their first four games under Nicholson Spurs conceded 15. After the win over Leicester they won only one of their next 11 games. The new manager had a big problem on his hands right from the start.

He brought in a coach from Italy called Jesse Carver. He arrived at White Hart Lane with quite a reputation, having been coach to the Dutch national team and the Amsterdam club Ajax. He'd also held highly paid jobs with six top Italian sides including Juventus, Inter Milan and Roma, as well as working in the English League with Millwall, West Brom and Coventry.

Nicholson and Carver both tried everything they knew to stop the decline in the club's fortunes. But Spurs remained dangerously close to the relegation zone. Carver's new approach was not paying dividends. 'Carver had a bit of a reputation out in Italy, but when he came here we were disappointed,' recalls Nicholson. 'He was recommended to us but we soon got shot of him. I realised I'd made a boob as soon as he arrived.'

Carver was replaced as assistant manager by Harry Evans. Evans had played for a number of clubs including Southampton and Aldershot. When he finished playing at the age of 32 he became Aldershot's trainer before taking a job as club physio, secretary and finally manager. He got the sack and then joined Spurs.

Evans was the perfect foil for Nicholson. He handled most of the administration leaving Nicholson to do what he loved best: coaching. 'Harry was more of a practical office-type man,' says Nicholson. 'Carver was supposed to be but he wasn't. Harry did a lot of the office work and I could work with the players.'

The obvious weakness in the Tottenham side was at wing-half where Jim Iley and Blanchflower, both attacking wing halves, left enormous gaps in front of the full-backs which no defence could cover. Spurs spent most of the season in the First Division's bottom third.

Nicholson didn't mince his words. He told Blanchflower he was one of the culprits. 'You're taking too many liberties. When the ball is played into our box you're often on your way out looking for a throw from the keeper. You should be in that box marking someone and doing your defensive job.' Nicholson said it was all very well Blanchflower being one of the outstanding attacking midfield players in the country but when a move broke down he had to defend along with the other players.

Nicholson wanted him to concentrate on defence so young Jim Iley could do the foraging and prompting. But Blanchflower was either unable, or unwilling, to respond.

At first, Nicholson was reluctant to apply the obvious remedy and Spurs continued to slide down the table, losing six of the last seven matches of the year. They lost at home to lowly Birmingham; they lost away to West Brom; they lost at home to Preston; and after going down 3-1 at Burnley in early December found themselves sharing bottom place with Leicester and Aston Villa. A double defeat at the hands of West Ham over Christmas left them with only one win in their last eleven games.

Finally, on 3 January 1959 Blanchflower was dropped for the home game against Blackburn and replaced by a young, aggressive lad called Bill Dodge. Nicholson had reasoned that Dodge was a defensive type of player who could balance the team on one flank, while Iley was the better bet as the attacking wing-half on the other side.

Nicholson explained that he was leaving Blanchflower out for three or four matches. Blanchflower accepted it. He knew it wasn't easy for a new young manager to drop such a famous and experienced player. 'I want to tighten up the defence with a more defensive wing-half,' Nicholson told him. 'I might use you as a deep inside-forward later and I would like you to try it in the reserve team.'

Spurs beat Blackburn 3-1, their first home victory in nearly three months, and went on to win their next three matches. The directors breathed a sigh of relief. A humble Blanchflower took the demotion as well as he could and approached this new experience of 'playing with the "stiffs"' – as he called it – with the intention of doing his best and enjoying it.

'At 33, time is running out for me in the football sense,' he was quoted as saying at the time. 'As I see it I have only a few more years in top football and I want to enjoy those . . . I was told I was dropped from the team because I am an attacking wing-half and Mr Nicholson wanted a defensive wing-half. Since I went out of the team Spurs have won their four games so Mr Nicholson's point may be considered to be proved.'

Blanchflower thought the Spurs boss had decided he didn't need him and maybe even thought he was past it. He asked for a transfer, mainly to clear the air. Blanchflower wanted to know what Nicholson thought of him. They didn't know one another that well or have the respect and confidence in each other that would come later.

Nicholson wasn't very pleased to receive Blanchflower's transfer request, but he took it well. 'I'm sorry that you should ask and I'll put it before the board,' he said. 'But I'll tell you right now that I will strongly insist they do not let you go. The club cannot afford to, the position we are in. But later on, if you still want to go, we will reconsider it.' Blanchflower respected Nicholson's candour.

The following week the directors turned down his transfer request, but there was no ill-feeling. Nicholson knew Blanchflower was one player he could have a rational discussion with and still remain friends. In fact, once Blanchflower's position with the club was made clear he forgot the idea of a transfer altogether. He decided he could get along with the manager after all.

Nicholson's mistake in dropping Blanchflower became obvious when, on successive Saturdays, Arsenal and Manchester United both won at White Hart Lane and then Norwich came in the FA Cup and were unlucky to go home with just a draw.

Blanchflower was drafted back into the team for the Fifth Round Cup replay against Norwich, though he was disappointed to be playing inside-forward. Nevertheless, he might have won the match with a number of brilliant touches including a scissors-kick that sent winger Cliff Jones away early in the game. Another inspired run through the midfield ended with a chip over the Norwich defence but Bobby Smith headed wide.

Smith was filling in as captain but didn't like the job. 'I was captain only because Bill and Danny had a row,' says Smith. 'No one wanted it so I said I'll take it until you get somebody.' Nicholson was also unhappy about having his striker as captain. He knew Smith was out of touch with what was going on around him. He needed a midfield player to do the job.

Meanwhile, Blanchflower was clearly unhappy in his new position and Iley and Dodge were struggling to direct the play behind him. But he was at inside-forward again in a 4-4 draw against bottom-of-the-table Portsmouth. It was a relegation struggle in the White Hart Lane mud. Spurs scraped a draw with a last-minute goal.

Blanchflower was on the team sheet at inside-forward again the following week at Everton but played at wing-half after some last-minute changes.

The following Monday, 2 March, Spurs played Wolves at Molineux. Wolves were heading for their second successive Championship, while Tottenham were moving in the opposite direction. Nicholson didn't travel up with the team and the players had to wait for his arrival to hear who was playing. Smith had a slight injury and was doubtful.

At about six o'clock Nicholson addressed the team in their private room at a Wolverhampton hotel. Blanchflower was back at right-half and Nicholson told him he had also decided to appoint him as club captain. The players would respect his position. 'We'll talk about it later,' he told Blanchflower as the meeting broke up. Spurs played well and snatched a point from the Champions in a 1-1 draw.

When Tottenham entertained Leicester at White Hart Lane on 7 March, Blanchflower had thus been restored to his rightful place not only as right-half but as captain. As journalist Julian Holland put it: 'The mainspring had been put back; now, at last, the clock might tick again.'

The 6-0 thrashing of Leicester removed the threat of relegation from the minds of the players, though Spurs weren't yet safe. But they won four, lost three and drew three of their remaining games to secure their position in the top flight. Their total of 36 points put them six ahead of Aston Villa and 15 in front of Portsmouth, the two relegated teams.

The Leicester match heralded the start of a great new partnership in football combining two of the game's best talents. From that day, Nicholson and Blanchflower worked ceaselessly, one off the field, the other on, to take Tottenham to the pinnacle of British soccer. Manager and captain, would take Spurs from the bottom of the First Division to within a whisker of the top in one season. The glory years were about to begin.

CHAPTER 1
Blanchflower's Promise

'WE'LL WIN THE "double" for you this year – the League and the Cup,' Tottenham captain Danny Blanchflower told the club's elderly but respected chairman Fred Bearman before the start of the 1960–61 season. The distinguished Mr Bearman always visited the training ground at the beginning of the campaign and had made it his custom to ask how the team would do. But this was the first time Blanchflower promised him what most people thought was impossible: the League Championship and the FA Cup.

Blanchflower had answered instinctively without thinking too much about what he was saying. He had replied quietly and confidently. He wasn't timid, but he wasn't boasting either. 'All right, my boy,' said the Spurs chairman, 'I believe you will . . .'

Many years later Bill Nicholson was still not convinced the story was true. After all, he knew Blanchflower was something of a romancer who could tell a good tale. But it wasn't the first time the genial Irish genius had raised the prospect of Spurs doing the elusive 'double'.

In the summer of 1958 Blanchflower had captained Northern Ireland to their finest moments at the World Cup in Sweden. The Irish qualified for the finals by beating Italy 2-1 and advanced to the later stages of the competition from a group which included Czechoslovakia, Germany and Argentina after an extra-time play-off win over the Czechs. It was a very tired Irish side that eventually went down 4-0 to France.

But Blanchflower had learned much that would help the development of his club side. That World Cup gave him the experience that was to be invaluable in the years to come. The man he respected more than any other in football, Northern Ireland manager Peter Doherty, gave his captain what he craved more than anything else: total authority on the field. Danny was only too pleased to run the show. Looking back he remarked: 'It was not the greatest team in the world but this worked for us.'

The tricks that the great sides unveiled on the world stage in Sweden would one day be used by Spurs and it was Blanchflower who showed the way. 'In the build-up to those finals we had beaten both Portugal and Italy,' recalled Danny. 'We used to do things that nobody else had thought of. We had to because they were better sides.'

'In Italy in 1957 we put up the first wall at a free kick. The Italians couldn't believe their eyes. We just stood 10 yards from the kick. It had taken them long enough to get out of their own half. It did have its teething problems though. The referee had never seen it before either, so when the Italian picked up the ball and moved it five yards away from the wall and shot into the net he gave a goal!'

At the finals in Sweden, Northern Ireland's quarter-final opponents France had done their homework to beat the wall. 'They curled the ball round the wall so we had to make sure that it was lined up properly. Jimmy McIlroy did the job. As the inside-forward he would stand behind the kick and line the wall up, but he got booked for holding the game up.'

'We then used the full-back and that led to everyone being played onside. Finally we ended up with the last man on the wall lining it up. It sounds a simple thing but it showed the planning and the work that went into everything. That was the sort of thinking that we took back to our clubs. It became commonplace. At the time though it was revolutionary.'

Each innovation broadened the possibilities on the pitch, and Blanchflower thought constantly about how to overcome the problems these new tactics raised. 'We used to call our ploys moving plays – not set pieces. It showed though what sort of damage and dangers could be created. The Tottenham team were just starting to get together and I realised what we could achieve. I knew that Tottenham had better players than Northern Ireland. They were really a bit like a Great Britain side and with the right direction would be outstanding.'

It was late summer when a British European Airways plane carrying the heroes of Northern Ireland's World Cup squad rose into the sky above Sweden. The England team was also on board for the journey back to London. Joe Mercer sat next to Stan Cullis, the Wolves star whose team had just missed out on the 'double' the previous season despite winning the League by five clear points.

The impossible 'double' was a much more common football topic than it had been 30 years before or would be 20 years later. That was mainly because Manchester United in 1957 and Wolves the following year had both come close to achieving the dream.

On board the aircraft Blanchflower turned to Mercer and said simply: 'Tottenham are going to win the "double" within the next few years.' He could talk of little else and the discussion went on in the taxi from Heathrow. 'He told us over and over again' recalled Mercer. "And we'll be the ones to do it," he had promised.'

Blanchflower was sure that neither Mercer nor Cullis believed him, but his own faith in the 'double' dream was unshakeable. He repeated his conviction many times over, perhaps to convince himself as much as anyone else that the impossible could be achieved.

Bill Nicholson made no such confident predictions at the start of the season. He was far too modest and wary for that. He knew Spurs had a good squad of players and felt they'd have a successful season. But he also knew luck played a big part. 'We could be drawn away in the Third Round of the FA Cup on a wet and windy day in early January and find ourselves out of the competition at the first hurdle,' he said.

The 'double' had only been done twice before. In 1889 Preston's 'Invincibles' won the first-ever Championship without losing a match and the FA Cup without conceding a goal. But they only played 27 games, including five rounds of the Cup in which they didn't meet a League side until the semi-final.

Aston Villa repeated the feat in 1897, playing 37 matches (the League only comprised a total of 22 clubs after the First World War), including six rounds of the Cup culminating in a tough FA Cup final against Everton at Crystal Palace.

But the twentieth century had brought a new era of tougher competition. Clubs like Kettering, Newton Heath, Heanor Town, Stockton, Burton Swifts, Glossop North End and Small Heath, who all took part in the FA Cup in 1897, had disappeared or were outside the Football League. Every year since Villa's 'double' season it had become more difficult to win both the First Division Championship and the FA Cup.

Many thought the 'double' was impossible. Blanchflower's boast had to contend with the greater strain, the longer and more arduous season, the existence of more top-class clubs and all the tension, drama and agony that faced every team which thought the 'double' was even slightly within their grasp.

On Easter Saturday, 1957, Manchester United were crowned Champions and ended the season with an eight-point lead. They also reached the FA Cup final where their opponents were, ironically, an indifferent Aston Villa – the last 'double' winners. Everyone thought it was a certainty the great 'Busby Babes', soon to be tragically decimated by the Munich air crash, would win the Cup and the glorious 'double'.

But Nicholson's view that luck plays such a big part in the Cup was to be borne out in the Final. The Wembley jinx struck United when, for the third time in five years, a serious injury to a player effectively reduced one of the teams to 10 men and turned English football's most prestigious occasion into a farce. This time it was United keeper Ray Wood who was controversially fouled by Villa forward Peter McParland. Just six minutes had gone when McParland crashed into Wood as he stood four yards from goal after collecting the Irish international's header. He went off with a fractured cheek-bone before returning in the 33rd minute to limp along the right wing. Jackie Blanchflower, Danny's brother, went in goal with Duncan Edwards moving to centre-half. Ironically, the FA had discussed the use of substitutes just 24 hours before the final and rejected the idea.

The rearranged United team held out for almost an hour before McParland, of all people, scored twice in the 61st and 75th minutes. Tommy Taylor headed home a corner from Edwards with seven minutes left and, as United gambled everything to try to pull level, Wood returned in goal. But they couldn't score the vital equaliser. The dream had died for another season and Villa preserved their status as the last 'double' winners. They also broke another record by winning the FA Cup for the seventh time.

Almost 40 years later Jackie Blanchflower was still bitter about that Cup Final defeat. 'We were robbed only because of the injury to Ray Wood. The referee didn't send players off in those days and the keeper didn't get any favours. There had to be a really bad challenge for someone to get sent off. Really, we should have been the first team of the century to win the "double".' Fate had ruled otherwise.

His brother Danny watched the Final and, after seeing United beat Spurs to the title, had fancied them to overcome Aston Villa. Although they lost, United had convinced the Spurs captain that the 'double' was possible; very difficult, maybe, but possible. He felt it couldn't be done with a weak heart and that the team which might do it would have to really believe they could.

'We can do the "double",' he said to one or two players. 'Yes,' they said, as if they didn't disbelieve him. Blanchflower mentioned it to Nicholson. The Spurs manager looked at him cautiously; he might have been thinking the same. According to Blanchflower, Nicholson replied: 'I think it can be done too.'

Nicholson insists he never made predictions. '. . . it wasn't my job to. And it's not a thing I'd lend myself to, the game is so fickle. If Danny liked to say it . . . well, that was Danny. He should have known by then that teams often win games they don't deserve to win.'

But Nicholson also thought all the players would have to believe in the 'double' to do it and that they must create the right atmosphere. Tottenham were about to try to achieve the 'impossible'.

CHAPTER 2
The Russian Tour

MOSCOW WAS THE unlikely setting to which Spurs really began to lay the foundations of a great side. It was May 1959 and the club had arranged a 'prestige-tour' of the USSR. Bill Nicholson felt he was building a side that could win a trophy and he wanted to create the right spirit among the players. He was an expert on Russian football at the time and he used the tour as part of the build-up for the coming season.

As the team prepared to leave, Danny Blanchflower also began to realise they had the makings of a very good team.

Welsh international winger Cliff Jones had joined the club in February 1958 for a record £35,000. He was fast and could score goals. Jones had taken some time to settle down at Spurs and had only returned to the first team the previous December after breaking his leg in training. Although the side was struggling he scored 20 goals in 38 games which Nicholson thought was a commendable record for a winger. Hopefully, his teething troubles behind him, Jones would now show his true potential.

He would be helped by having Dave Mackay playing just behind him at left-half. The rugged Scottish international had been signed from Hearts just before Easter 1959 for £30,000 to partner Blanchflower in midfield. He was to become Nicholson's best-ever signing.

Both had strengthened the squad and helped to foster the mood of optimism developing among the players as they prepared for their trip.

It was with mixed feelings of excitement and curiosity that the Spurs party boarded a giant Russian T.U. 104A jet on Monday 25 May for the club's first trip to Russia. They would fly 6,000 miles and visit cities which had been just names on a map until now. The flight to Moscow was the first stage of a 12-day tour behind the Iron Curtain.

The plane took off just after 10 o'clock and was soon flying over Northern Europe at 30,000 feet. Although they were travelling at more than 500 miles per hour, the players had no sensation of how fast they were moving. The noise was a different matter. It took some getting used to despite the pressurised cabins.

They landed at Moscow Airport in the early evening to be welcomed by a customary floral greeting organised by representatives of the USSR Football Section and the Torpedo Club, Spurs' first opponents. A 30-minute coach journey took them to the Metropole Hotel right in the heart of Moscow near the famous Red Square.

The Spurs and Russian officials discussed the details of the tour and toasted each decision with vodka. By midnight everything was settled. Meanwhile, the players had spent a quiet evening getting used to their new surroundings.

Nicholson was determined to create a good atmosphere among the players he thought were capable of winning a trophy in the coming season. Dave Mackay had only been with the club for a few months and he found the tour invaluable in getting to know his new colleagues both on and off the pitch.

'For reasons I can never understand – except that we get on – I shared a room with Cliff Jones,' says Mackay. 'Cliff is so Welsh, and I'm so Scottish, I guess we couldn't understand each other, which may account for the fact we never argued.'

The players trained every day and Nicholson organised the morning sessions as though they were still at home. By 10.30 the day after they arrived the players were being put through a strenuous routine on one of the many pitches surrounding the massive Lenin Stadium. They were determined to play well and trained hard.

After training, the team was given a conducted tour of the Torpedo Motor Works – the largest in the Soviet Union employing some 40,000 men and women. It was a colossal place, almost a town in itself. The factory had a representative side in the National League, but also fielded 60 other teams every week. The tour was followed by a reception where the players had their first, and last, taste of vodka before visiting the Oriental Circus in the evening.

'There wasn't much to do except go to the circus,' recalls Mackay. 'The circus'. . . after a while those words almost drove him mad because a visit to see the horses, the acrobats and the trapeze artistes seemed to be the only entertainment, apart from the ballet. 'Even the biggest circus enthusiast can have too much of a good thing.'

He was also struck by the fact that, after reading so much about Russian circus performers, all the circuses they visited claimed to be everything but Russian.

On the Wednesday morning a one-hour workout was followed by a rest before the first match against Torpedo. The weather had been dull and rainy and the players were worried about the pitch. They shouldn't have been. The playing surface at the Lenin Stadium had been covered by two huge plastic squares to protect it from the rain. By the time Spurs arrived the covers had been removed and the ground was perfectly dry.

Another surprise awaited the team when they entered the dressing-room. It was large and carpeted and furnished with easy chairs. Vases of flowers decorated the whole room. It was very different from the changing-rooms at White Hart Lane. The players were also intrigued to see their names in Russian in the match programme. They had to look at their positions to tell who was who.

Nicholson made one major change to the team on the Russian tour which was to transform the defence: he switched Maurice Norman from right-back to centre-half and brought Peter Baker into the side in the full-back position. It was an inspired tactical change. Norman would no longer be embarrassed by speedy wingers who could catch him on the turn. He was to become the rock at the heart of the Tottenham defence.

Fifty thousand people were packed into the Lenin Stadium and the Spurs players were a little nervous as they took to the field. But after the usual pre-match ceremonies the tension eased as the game got under way. Although it was still raining, Tottenham got off to a bright start. They scored after only five minutes when Welsh international winger Terry Medwin latched onto a Blanchflower free-kick.

Spurs were on top for most of the first-half and unlucky not to increase their lead. The second period was a different story as their defence took a hammering and keeper Johnnie Hollowbread had to make three difficult saves. As is customary in Russia, a massive gong was sounded five minutes before the end of the match. When the final whistle went there was relief all around the team. They'd started with a win. It was a happy group of players who relaxed in the luxurious dressing room that night.

The next day the squad took in some sightseeing and shopping. They were told to be careful about where they went and what they did in Communist Russia. They visited the city's landmarks in two large groups accompanied by a couple of Russian officials. 'You could wander on your own, but it was commonsense to stay together,' said Medwin. 'They were a bit nervous because of the way the country was being run.'

The Spurs players were amazed at the size of Russia and were also struck by the seemingly endless rows of 40-storey flats. The bombardment of Moscow during the Second World War meant there was plenty of room to build a lot more. Hollowbread was surprised at how hard the women worked. 'We saw a lot of women doing heavy work such as working pneumatic drills, labouring on building-sites, sweeping streets, and driving buses and taxis.' He also noticed that, while the people were quite friendly, their clothes were drab and poor-looking. Compared to most of the population the Russian footballers didn't do too badly.

The players visited the People's Museum, where they had to wear slippers to protect the polished floors, and the Kremlin. They also queued in Red Square to see Lenin and Stalin lying in state at the Mausoleum. The long procession passing the bodies of the two famous leaders was impressive, but it was also very morbid. Terry Medwin remembers the visit vividly. 'They'd been injected to preserve them. They were sitting and you could see the bodies from the waist up. It was the first time I'd seen anybody dead.'

They were also invited to see the famous Russian dancer Nureyev perform at the Bolshoi ballet. Most didn't fancy it, but Nicholson forced them to accept the invitation saying: 'If you don't go you'll regret it'.

In the end about half the party attended and were thoroughly impressed. Some of the players were in a box facing the stage while the others sat at the side.

Jones and Medwin were among those who appreciated the cultural experience. 'It was about the fall of St Petersburg, and Nureyev was brilliant, magnificent,' says Medwin. 'I had respect for his fitness.' However, some of the others struggled to come to terms with this new brand of sophisticated entertainment. 'I remember Jim Iley coming down to us from the back,' recalls Jones, "What's up, Jim?" I asked him. "I can't hear what they're saying," he told me. "What are you talking about?" I said. "It's a ballet. They don't say anything".'

At the interval the players went into the foyer. They were amazed to find the Russians walking round and round in pairs. 'What's going on?' asked Peter Baker. 'Don't worry, it's the custom. We stand, they walk,' said the interpreter.

The players returned to the hotel talking enthusiastically about what they'd seen. Nicholson thought they appreciated the affinity between ballet and football. Hollowbread put it more simply: 'All the lads agreed it was very good and the best show we'd seen on the tour.' They were a little concerned though that Nicholson might want them to become as fit as Nureyev!

The facilities in Russia were basic and the food was 'awful' according to Nicholson. The players took some time to get used to it. The hotel tried to give them 'English food' but wasn't very successful. Mealtimes did raise a few laughs though, especially when it came to ordering. Nicholson spent most of his time working out menus with the hotel catering manager. He described it as like 'negotiating a wage deal with a trade union'. Every item had to be bargained for and even then they'd come back and say: 'We have none of that. Can you order something else?' Food of all kinds was in short supply.

Once Nicholson ordered tea and toast. The tea arrived without milk or sugar (Russians usually drink it with lemon) and there was no jam or butter for the toast. 'Where is it?' demanded the Spurs manager. 'You didn't order it,' he was told. 'You only ordered tea and toast!' The tea was so weak that Nicholson ended up making it himself. The next day he asked for rice pudding before a match; it came in cold slabs and the players couldn't eat it.

Eventually a system was devised to find out whether the local food could be eaten by players who rarely strayed from a limited menu at home. Tottenham's Assistant Secretary Alan Leather, a late addition to the tour because director Douglas Deacock had to pull out after his wife broke her arm, was appointed as the official food taster. He ordered from the Russian menu and if he thought a dish was all right he'd tell Nicholson. Unfortunately, none of the Spurs party took his advice.

The food aside, the players were impressed with Moscow. 'It was a lovely place,' says full-back Ron Henry. 'I can remember going to the underground in Russia with Tony Marchi. We went up to the top of the steps and a soldier saluted us. He took us down to the train and we went about four stops, crossed over the platform and came back. He stood to attention and saluted us again before he left. We enjoyed that.'

On the Friday morning the Spurs party left Moscow and flew south to Kiev, capital of the Ukraine. After the disappointing weather in the Russian capital they were more than happy to arrive on a wonderful sunny day. The players were confidently told that the good weather would last throughout their stay and the visit to Kiev turned out to be the highlight of the tour.

The people in the sun-drenched city seemed more relaxed than those in Moscow and the extensive beaches stretching along the banks of the River Dnieper were crowded with sunbathers. 'They were a different sort of people,' recalls Medwin. 'They weren't near Moscow and so didn't feel the same pressure. It was a different way of life there. They enjoyed themselves and it looked a bit more glamorous.'

When the players weren't training they spent many hours on or around the beautiful river which was over a mile wide near Kiev. The team was impressed by the quality of their hotel, especially the rooms which came with their own bathroom and toilets.

On Saturday and Sunday morning they trained in the splendid Kruschev Stadium. After training on the Sunday they spent a couple of hours on the River Dnieper in speedboats – five to a boat – and were entertained in the evening . . . by a circus.

Meanwhile, interest in the first-ever Anglo-Russian match to be played in Kiev was mounting. All 60,000 tickets for the Monday night game against local side Dynamo Kiev had been sold days in advance.

Ron Henry was left out of the side which beat Moscow Torpedo in the first match and didn't rate his chances of playing too highly because of the form of Welsh international defender Mel Hopkins. Henry had been at Spurs since 1954, turning professional in January 1955. But his appearances had been limited to covering for Hopkins when he was away on international duty. 'I thought to myself I've come all this way to Russia and I'm not going to get into the side,' said Henry. But to his surprise he was picked to play alongside Peter Baker against Kiev.

Out on the pitch in front of a capacity crowd each player was presented with a bouquet of flowers and was cheered loudly in turn when, by tradition, the gifts were thrown to the fans. The hard dusty pitch made ball control difficult but, as in Moscow, Spurs had the advantage of an early goal, this time scored by Johnny Brooks. But Kiev fought back and deservedly equalised just before half-time when their outside-right cracked the ball into the far corner of the Tottenham net. At the break the home side were confident they would win.

Spurs came out with even more determination in the second-half and gradually got on top as the game progressed. A wonderful flowing movement ended with Brooks scoring his second goal of the game and Tottenham eventually ran out worthy winners. They had enjoyed Kiev and were sorry to leave, especially as the weather in the ancient city of Leningrad, their next port of call many miles to the north, had been very bad with almost a month of continuous rain.

In the event, the Spurs party was again pleasantly surprised to be greeted by warm, sunny weather – and also to learn that the Thursday night match was a 100,000 sell-out. The players were by now getting a little tired from all the travelling but, as in Kiev, they trained on the pitch in the impressive Kirov Stadium every day – including the day of the match. Their stay in Leningrad was shorter than in either Moscow or Kiev but after training the players found time to go shopping.

Although tiredness was creeping in, the Spurs team was very keen to win their last match. The Kirov Stadium, a vast concrete bowl on the outskirts of Leningrad, was bathed in evening sunshine as they attempted to preserve their 100 per cent record. Their opponents were billed as a 'Select XI' and it was only just before the game that Tottenham discovered they would probably be facing the Russian Olympic team.

The Russians played in front of their fanatical fans as though their lives depended on the result and some of their tactics were less than 'friendly'. At one point, the Russian full-back pulled Jones's shorts down and threw them into the crowd. 'He did that for a laugh, but also to stop him playing,' recalls Henry.

Spurs Vice-Chairman Fred Wale chose his words carefully when he summed up the match. '. . . although they won, deservedly, many of the referee's decisions and the defensive tactics employed left us all rather bewildered.' But Dave Mackay had no complaints. 'They were tough, rugged and always fair, but the football made no impression on us.'

Spurs put everything into the game for the full 90 minutes and were not disgraced despite losing 3-1, Brooks scoring again. The local fans had been a special part of Tottenham's Russian experience. Over an hour after the final whistle the players left the stadium to be greeted by a large crowd which had stayed behind to give them a rousing send-off.

Despite the fact that Spurs lost their last match Mackay didn't hold the Russians in high regard. 'As a football education the tour was not a marked success,' he says. 'As footballers the Russians had little to commend them.'

In fact, Mackay had mixed feelings about the whole trip. 'As a tour it was neither an education nor an adventure, but as a special occasion it was a tremendous success and in Kiev, Moscow and other parts behind the Iron Curtain, I shall always believe we laid the foundation of the team spirit and genuine friendship which has since played a notable part in the success of Tottenham Hotspur Football Club.'

The other players could also tell that something special was being created. 'That's where we first saw the signs,' says Cliff Jones. 'That's when we really started to play.' 'It all came together in Russia,' says Ron Henry.

The Russian tour had accomplished Nicholson's goal of bringing the players closer. 'I was glad of the opportunity of getting the players together. I had said that we would go to see what it was like there. "It's a lot different," I had told the boys. I cannot overstate the value of the trip in terms of getting things together. And we still had a very enjoyable time, very enjoyable.'

The question now was whether Nicholson's team was good enough to win a trophy?

CHAPTER 3
'Push and Run'

TOTTENHAM HOTSPUR HAVE always been a footballing side. Throughout their history, even when they were a struggling Second Division team, they've tried to play football. At times, when there weren't enough skilful players available, it would have been easier to resort to the long-ball game then being played by most teams. But that's not Spurs' style. Winning isn't enough either; it's the way you win that's important.

When Arthur Rowe took over as manager in 1949 he introduced a completely new style of football for the first time since Herbert Chapman's days in charge of Huddersfield and then Arsenal in the 1930s. The game Rowe's team played was perfectly suited to Tottenham's purist traditions and was dubbed 'push and run'. It was based on keeping possession through quick, short, accurate passes.

Rowe, an attacking centre-half, played for Spurs between 1929 and 1939. Like Bill Nicholson he gained just one England cap. But Rowe had a vision about the game summed up by the catch phrase: 'Make it simple, make it quick.' Nicholson, a member of the 'push and run' team, learned a lot from his coaching and, like Rowe, later used his own slogans to remind players what they should be doing.

Rowe was a bit short for a centre-half, but he was strong and very good in the air. A native of Tottenham, the place was in his blood. Like Blanchflower, one of Rowe's last signings, he was a passionate talker and thinker about the game. He'd worked in Hungary where his ideas helped shape the great Hungarian team of Puskas. When Rowe returned to England he mixed the ball-playing traditions of Tottenham and the short-passing game of the Hungarians.

His 'push and run' demanded great skill, especially movement of the ball, and Spurs were fortunate to have the players who could adopt the style effectively. It demanded absolute fitness since if just one player was not 100 per cent fit he could unravel the whole system. But when it worked, and most of the time it did, 'push and run' was attractive and successful.

Rowe's gospel was that if a team is to demand and make use of a greater share of the ball there can be no elaborate play and little dribbling. The ball had to be moved swiftly to create space. The emphasis was on speed and finding the shortest passing route to goal. The ball was rarely held, seldom even trapped. It was passed around first time giving opponents no chance to make a tackle. Players were always running into space, either to collect a pass or decoy a defender, and constantly switching positions.

The result was the greatest football team Britain had seen for years. The side had many star players including goalkeeper Ted Ditchburn, full-back Alf Ramsey, wing-half Ron Burgess, Nicholson and his future coach Eddie Baily. Bennett, Duquemin and Walters with Willis or Withers, and Clarke, completed a line-up packed with talent.

Under Rowe, Spurs won the Second Divison title in 1950 with 61 points having used only 18 players. The average attendance that season was a record 54,405. The following year they were First Division Champions with 66 points and the average gate rose to 55,486. And, in 1952, the 'push and run' side challenged for the title again, this time coming runners-up to Manchester United.

Their style was summed up by Ralph Finn of *The People*. 'Here was fluid football. An integrated flowing patternwork of football that sent opponents dizzy trying to counter its precise, deadly advances, its merciless accuracy, its devastating beauty. Lovely it was to watch and suicide to play against.'

But the 'push and run' team stayed at the top for only three years. The glory days were soon over. Their flame had flickered briefly because the style was difficult to adopt – which explains why few others tried to copy it. When the players lost the edge to their fitness or their form, the system failed.

So 'push and run' faded away. But Nicholson didn't forget the basic philosophy and his Spurs team would adopt a similar style of play when he became manager. Nicholson's system was to be more

controlled, a little slower, but even more deadly. It was based on the traditional Tottenham formula of accurate passing and creating space. Arthur Rowe had been his mentor; Nicholson couldn't have asked for a better one.

CHAPTER 4
Danny Blanchflower

THE DECLINE OF Rowe's 'push and run' side had a major impact on his health. By the end of 1953 Spurs were near the bottom of the First Division and Rowe was very sick in hospital. He took the gradual break-up of his ageing team to heart and suffered more than anybody realised for the players who'd brought him so much glory but were now on their way out.

Spurs' shock defeat in a Fifth Round FA Cup tie away to Third Division York in 1955 was the final blow. He had a second breakdown and never returned to White Hart Lane. But before Rowe handed over to long-serving trainer Jimmy Anderson and his new coach Bill Nicholson, he made probably the most significant signing of his managerial career: Danny Blanchflower. The Irish genius was the link between Rowe's fading 'push and run' side and Nicholson's glorious team of the early '60s.

Blanchflower was born on 10 February 1926 in his grandparents' terraced house in a quiet street in the Bloomfield district of East Belfast, Northern Ireland. It was a Protestant working-class ghetto.

He showed the first signs of his passion for football at the age of two. His mother Selina had hit him and sent him to his room after some act of mischief, but the unusual silence that followed puzzled her. She thought that perhaps she'd hurt him and quietly climbed the stairs to his bedroom. On carefully opening his door she was shocked to find her young son precariously balanced on the open window sill watching some local kids playing football.

Selina was herself keen on football and played inside-right for the Belfast Ropeworks ladies team. Women's football was much more popular then than it is today. 'You'd get crowds of up to 25,000 watching them play,' remembers Danny's brother Jackie. Selina could often be found out in the streets kicking a ball around with her kids. She was proud of her gold medal and the fading photograph of her ladies team. Whatever instinct young Danny and Jackie had for competitive sports was probably inherited from her.

But their lives could have turned out very differently if their father's plans to emigrate to America had worked out. He sold the family home and got ready to embark on a new life but, after failing a medical, mistakenly as it turned out, he was prevented from joining his fellow Irish emigrants on one of the packed ships bound for the New World.

The Blanchflowers thus remained in the Belfast area, though they moved around a lot. Danny was eventually joined in three-yearly intervals by two sisters and two brothers. Jackie was destined for stardom and tragedy in equal measure at Manchester United. But everything continued to revolve around Danny.

His first real football team was the 19th Belfast Wolf Cub eleven. The first week he was a reserve but somebody couldn't play and young Blanchflower turned out at inside-right. He scored three times in a pair of borrowed boots. They won 10-0 and obviously couldn't change a winning team after that result.

The Cubs sometimes went for a week's camping on a farm near a little town called Donaghadee. Once they made a special journey to the town's cinema where they saw a brief newsreel flash of Manchester City in a cup tie. The cubs liked City because their hero Peter Doherty played for them.

It was as a kid growing up in Belfast that Danny Blanchflower first heard the name Tottenham Hotspur. 'There was something special about them,' he recalled. 'They were not just City, United or Rovers. They were one of a small bunch with more appealing names like Forest, Villa, North End and Argyle. They were like far away planets to me – out there somewhere, where distance lends enchantment.'

When he was about ten years old Danny started playing for his school team on Saturday mornings, but he still turned out for the Cubs in the afternoon. Later, when he was too old for the Cubs, he joined the Boys' Brigade because they had a team and he could still play twice on Saturdays. But he wasn't really old enough for the Boys'

Brigade. The game was too fast and the other players were too strong. After one match he was 'dead-legged' and could hardly walk for a week.

Danny's mother encouraged her sons to play football. 'She did us proud and wanted things done the right way,' says Jackie. In those days boys bought their football boots a size smaller so they'd fit like a glove. But the heavy boots, made of thick leather, needed softening up. Unlike most mothers, Selina allowed Danny and Jackie to sit on the edge of the bath with their boots on so they could soak the leather and mould them to their feet. That chipped enamel bath became her pride and joy.

Danny began at outside-right for his school before moving to inside-forward. In later years, as captain, he was sometimes picked as a roving centre-half. The school was small and couldn't always put out a full side so Danny tried to improvise for the missing players from his centre-half position. They usually lost by six or seven goals even with a full team!

But Danny's enthusiasm for football was undiminished and his desire to succeed almost obsessive. He was naturally thin and bony but that didn't stop him being a fitness fanatic.

Danny was also Jackie's mentor: 'I remember when I was about 18 years old going to see him play for his school team,' remembered Danny. 'I was impressed with his ability: he was outstanding . . . with his graceful style and timing.'

Danny had been what Jackie calls 'a thinker' even as a young child. He was very bright and won a scholarship to the Belfast College of Technology. Danny played for the college at inside-right. He started a three-year course in general education which led to an examination for University Matriculation, but his father was working hard in the shipyards to provide for his family and university was out of the question for Danny.

After a year at college an uncle got him a job as an apprentice electrician at the Gallahers factory. It was a big place with all kinds of electrically operated equipment such as packing machines, air-conditioners and lifts which explained why they needed electricians.

When the Second World War started in September 1939 his father was sent to France. Belfast had become a target for German bombers so the rest of the family was evacuated to the country. It was difficult to play organised football since most of the junior competitions were suspended. But that didn't stop Danny. He bought a set of shirts for 10 shillings and formed a team called Bloomfield United. The players were drawn from his mates at the factory and neighbourhood friends. But they needed more than players and a kit. They had to find teams to play, grounds to play on and referees.

Sometimes they'd walk around the town on a Friday night looking for replacements for their own team. But gradually other sides were formed and a keenly contested league was started. At around this time Danny was spotted by scouts from the local professional club Glentoran. Bob Harpur, then a Glentoran director but later a successful scout for Matt Busby at Manchester United, invited Danny to sign professional forms. He wasn't quite 16 and was too slight for that class of football. Eventually, Danny drifted away to play for other teams more suited to his ability.

His mother and the family got tired of evacuation and returned to Belfast, while his father was released from the Army because of his age, his family and the fact that his skills as a tradesman were being wasted. Meanwhile, Danny was impressed by the exploits of the RAF fighter-pilots and joined the Air Training Corps and then the Air Force as a trainee navigator. He won a special scholarship to St Andrews University in Scotland where he'd go for a year before starting his aircrew training. The RAF promised he could return to St Andrews after the war to finish his studies. He took maths, physics and applied kinetics, described as the science of moving bodies over spheres. He also played for the University football team and was awarded colours – an honour bestowed on those who represented the first eleven.

The town of St Andrews, surrounded on three sides by the sea, had an old-world charm about it. The place fostered in Danny a feeling of 'the measured concept of life'. St Andrews left a deep and lasting impression on him. It was formed from the wearing of the scarlet gown, the adult approach and pursuit of knowledge, and the casually accepted respect for honoured customs, both riotous and hallowed.

Danny got a rude awakening when he moved from the tranquillity of St Andrews to Torquay in Devon with the RAF. For six weeks he was up before the crack of dawn polishing boots and buttons, queuing for hash meals and putting his body through its paces under orders from a mad NCO and a fanatical physical training instructor.

More training followed at a variety of camps in the Midlands and a navigation school in Canada. Then, just a week before Danny was to 'pass out' and sent to the Far East after his aircrew training, the Japanese surrendered. To reduce costs the RAF immediately abandoned the flying training and he was shipped back to England.

Danny ended up in an isolated camp at Docking, near King's Lynn. There wasn't much to do, but the football team trained hard and at least the actor Richard Burton, one of his hut-mates, kept everyone entertained.

The concentration on football helped Danny's game. He was very fit and playing well for the station team. On returning to Belfast he was asked by Glentoran if he'd like to play for their reserves. Danny accepted the offer and did well. He was put into the first team for a Christmas match against Belfast Celtic. He heard his name on the radio for the first time after that match when a critic on the regional sports round-up programme said he'd shown great promise as an inside-forward in his first senior game.

That night Bob Harpur, the Glentoran director who'd shown interest in him as a lad of 15, and manager Frank Thompson tried to convince Danny to become a professional footballer. He didn't want to commit himself and was reluctant to sign. Besides he hoped to go back to St Andrews. But they were very persuasive and countered all his objections with 'goodwill compromise'. They'd played this game before. Danny's parents seemed pleased that a club wanted to sign him but left the decision to their son.

Danny was offered £50 to sign and £3 a match. He was assured it was a good offer, though he didn't know if it was or not and he wasn't bold enough to negotiate a better deal. They embarrassed him and made him feel he was being unreasonable in not letting them pay him £3 a match for playing a game he already enjoyed playing for nothing. Danny eventually signed though he didn't understand the contract at all. Only later, when he heard some players got £500 and £10 to sign, did he realise how naive he'd been. Glentoran had not been slow to take advantage of him.

Danny went back to the RAF in England where he 'guested' for

Swindon. The following April he was released long before the age group with which he'd attended university. St Andrews was packed with older students returning from the war and Danny had to wait until the group he'd been returned with could attend. He went back to Gallahers to finish his apprenticeship as an electrician and played part-time football.

It was near the end of the season when Glentoran welcomed him back. He trained on Tuesday and Thursday nights with the other part-timers. They ran around the pitch. He was amazed at the 'sloppiness' of the training, but was too young to say anything. It would not be the first time in his career that he felt a club's training methods left a lot to be desired.

Blanchflower used to get up early in the morning to train before work and sometimes hauled his brother Jackie out of bed to help him. 'He used to get me up at five or six o'clock in the morning to go training when we lived in Belfast with our parents,' says Jackie. 'But when you're only 14 or 15 years old you're not that enthusiastic.'

He started the 1946–47 season at inside-right in the reserves but was soon moved to right-half. In mid-September both first team wing-halves were injured and Danny became the regular right-half. Glentoran had a good season; he got more in bonuses than in wages.

In February 1947 he was picked at right-half for the Irish League against the Football League at Goodison Park. After scrounging ration coupons from relatives and friends he ordered his first made-to-measure suit and joined the squad on the boat bound for Liverpool. The English papers reckoned the Irish League would lose by anything up to ten goals, while the Irish Press baulked at a scoreline above six or seven. The Football League won 4-2 on a frosty pitch. 'It was, of course, another moral victory for the Irish,' according to Danny.

They were overjoyed at the result, but Danny was disappointed. He didn't play well. The way Wilf Mannion, Jimmy Hagan and Tommy Lawton played the game both bewildered and fascinated the young Blanchflower. '. . . the way they flitted and changed positions behind my back, as I concentrated on the ball, was strange to me,' he recalled. 'The pattern of the game, the picture that I do not see but somehow fell in my mind's eye, was fluttering and slipping like a badly adjusted television set.'

The experience opened his mind to new thoughts about football as he began to stumble upon its secrets. Failure led him to the beginnings of a new understanding of the game. He noticed that patterns of play in the Irish League were entirely different from the English style and that he could no sooner adopt that style to any real benefit in Irish football than he could try the Irish way in English football.

Danny wanted to improve and harboured ambitions of playing in England where he felt he'd benefit from full-time training and the experience of competing with the Mannions and Hagans. He wanted an English club to buy him. The local paper occasionally reported that an English manager liked his play, but most didn't think he was strong enough to adapt himself to the English game.

His first full season with Glentoran was successful and the following year he became more consistent. His reputation was growing and there was some transfer speculation. Danny's form improved with the growing experience of another season and the papers increasingly wrote about his possible departure to English soccer.

In April 1949 he drifted closer to Tottenham Hotspur, although the connection didn't occur to him at the time. It was just after the Easter matches when he was asked to join the Glentoran officials in the Grand Hotel, Belfast. He was introduced to Barnsley manager Angus Seed who said he was impressed by Blanchflower's play and would like him to join Barnsley. Danny readily agreed and was sold for £6,000. 'You'll not be sorry to join our club,' Seed told him.

Danny had often told Jackie that when he went to England he'd take his younger brother with him. 'As it turned out I went a week before him,' recalls Jackie. 'I went to [Manchester] United; he went to Barnsley.' Danny was 23 when he joined Barnsley, while Jackie was just 16 years old when he left Belfast for Old Trafford. The younger Blanchflower had to have a legal guardian to leave Ireland. Matt Busby signed the papers.

Jackie, intelligent and articulate like Danny, was one of the first of the new kids to arrive in Manchester. 'It seemed like I'd got a better deal than Danny at the time, but not later on,' says Jackie reflecting on the 1958 Munich air disaster which ended his playing career.

Meanwhile, Danny was on his way to Barnsley. As he sat alone in a train compartment trundling through the slag heaps from Leeds to

Barnsley he kept turning over in his head the words, 'You'll not be sorry to join our club' which his new manager had left him with the day he agreed to sign. 'I thought he was joking as I tried to resist the feeling that I was tumbling down a coal mine into some football oblivion,' he recalled. But Seed was right and Barnsley was to be the start of what Blanchflower himself called 'The Yellow Brick Road' that was to lead him to White Hart Lane.

If his dreams before Barnsley had come true then Glentoran would have transferred him to Wolves, or Arsenal, or another of the top English teams of the day and he might never have made it as a professional footballer. He had to learn the tricks of the trade and his nature demanded that he learned them thoroughly.

'I needed time and opportunity because, first, you must find the right questions before you find the right answers. And opportunity leads you to mistakes and mistakes hurt and hustle you to find the right way to do it. Then more time and opportunity will help you do it right. They call it trial and error.'

The top teams of the day might not have suffered him through all his trials and tribulations. He could have been discarded. At Barnsley, on the other hand, he could hold his own for a few years. They wanted him no more than he needed them.

Indeed, Danny even found the training rigorous. There were long road walks, exercises, skipping, throwing the medicine ball and lapping the pitch. He thought circling the pitch was aimless and boring. Danny wanted the running to be linked to ball play and teamwork to make it more thought-provoking and interesting.

Barnsley started the 1949–50 season well. But fate was to deny him something special. Injury and international duty kept him out of Barnsley's two League encounters with a stylish Spurs team and he was to miss seeing the champions of the Second Divison that year. Some of his team-mates talked about the Tottenham style, but they hadn't recognised its details; it remained a mystery to them. And even more so to Blanchflower. He wondered what it was like as Spurs soared up into the First Division.

Danny was picked to play for Northern Ireland against Scotland at Windsor Park in early October that year. He was overjoyed, though the training was little better than at Barnsley. The players were told to run around the pitch for 20 minutes and then they took shots at the keeper. Somebody suggested a five-a-side game, but the trainer didn't want any injuries. Blanchflower thought the whole affair was a shambles.

The local papers favoured the Scots and doubted Blanchflower could cope. He also thought that barring a miracle Scotland would win and it would be all his fault. The Irish captain Jack Vernon gave Danny specific instructions. 'And you don't be going on any of your excursions today. Keep in close to me and don't be letting them past.'

He took Vernon's comments on board, but once he got out on the pitch he didn't know what he did. Ireland lost 8-0 and Danny had a terrible game. His mind was a daze and he seemed to have no control over his play. Nerves had affected him and he just wasn't good enough for that class of football. But against Wales in his next international the following March he played much better in a goalless draw.

By now, Danny had established himself at Barnsley and was happy. But when he returned for pre-season training in July 1950 the monotonous routines were getting to him. There was little ball work since the players enjoyed that and they weren't supposed to enjoy training. 'The result was that we finished up fit and strong enough – but it was a condition estranged from good football simply because we had neglected to match the advancing degrees of skill and speed with the ball with the advancing degree of our physical fitness,' recalled Danny.

Some of the mysterious clouds surrounding Tottenham Hotspur began to evaporate in the 1950–51 season at least in young Danny's eyes. Spurs were heading for their first League Championship; they were the big stars of radio and the words 'push and run' were introduced to football.

'The commentators tried to explain it, but they were talking through their hats,' remembered Danny. 'With television, a young pro might have been able to see the magic ingredients, but in a way radio was better than TV. Radio did not show you just the camera's angle to reduce the argument. It left a touch of mystery about the style and television does not know that all style must have a sense of mystery.'

Although he'd not yet seen it for himself, 'push and run' was magic to Blanchflower and had a distant influence on him while he was learning the trade at Barnsley.

In October he played for Ireland against England in Belfast. The Irish lost 4-1 and he had another bad game. His failure at international level was a big disappointment to him but at least his reputation was spreading. When Barnsley played away he was described in the local papers as one of the club's stars and an Irish international.

Meanwhile, the training routine was still frustrating. When the team played badly Seed ordered them back to the ground in the afternoons – not to train but to make sure the fans didn't see the players in the local snooker halls. Instead, they played snooker at the club. Danny wasn't much of a snooker player and wanted to practise his ball skills, but Seed thought he'd take too much out of himself. The compromise was that he could practise in the mornings after lapping the track.

His brother Jackie was having a much better time at Manchester United where Matt Busby's Babes were given ample opportunity to hone their ball skills on the training pitch. Busby was one of the first managers to go out in a tracksuit and train with his players. Most managers wore suits and raincoats and shiny dress shoes. They directed training from the side of the pitch, often using a megaphone so the players could hear their instructions. 'Danny was quite envious. We were playing with the ball all day while they never saw it until Saturday afternoon,' remembers Jackie.

Danny's situation was becoming untenable. 'If you get the ball the others will want it,' Seed argued, as if it was a bad thing. But Danny insisted that he needed to practise with the ball to improve. 'I don't believe in that sort of practice,' said Seed. 'If you don't see the ball during the week you'll be more keen to get it on Saturdays.' 'But if I don't get some practice I won't know what to do with it when I do get it on Saturdays,' said Danny.

Danny didn't enjoy this conflict. Seed had been like a father figure to him and he liked the Barnsley manager. He'd had faith in Danny's ability to cope with Second Division football when he bought him from Glentoran while other managers said he was too weak and too slow. But Danny was soon back in Seed's office again. 'I could not forsake my own faith, the things I thought and believed,' he said. Another showdown loomed.

'The trouble with you is that you think this club is not good enough for you,' said Seed. 'You're right,' said Danny. 'If you deny ball practice the club's not good enough for anyone.' He said that maybe he'd better have a transfer to another club where he could practise. Seed told him to put his request to the board of directors which he did. Surprisingly, they didn't ask why he wanted to leave but just agreed to a transfer. The directors told the Press they didn't want to keep an unhappy player at the club, but Danny thought later that they must have wanted the transfer fee.

The days rolled by with no news of a transfer until one night in March when Barnsley chairman Joe Richards called to see Danny. 'Do you still want a transfer?' he asked. 'Yes I do.' 'Well, then I'll pick you up at 10 o'clock in the morning.' 'Where am I going to?' asked Danny. 'Take my word for it, you're going to one of the most famous clubs in the country.' And so on Thursday, 15 March 1951 Danny Blanchflower discovered he was being sold to Aston Villa.

Danny was introduced to his new employers at a Derby hotel: Mr F.H. Normansell, the chairman, and Mr George Martin, the recently appointed manager. Martin talked enthusiastically about his plans to take Villa from the depths of the First Division to 'some impregnable point of glory in the highest heavens,' recalled Danny. 'I was young and naive enough to believe him.'

'There is something I want to clear up before I agree to sign for you,' said Danny. They looked dismayed. They probably thought he was going to ask for an under-the-counter payment. 'What's that my boy?' asked the Villa chairman. 'I want your word that I can train with a ball as much as I like when I have finished whatever other training routine you expect of me.' They looked amazed. 'Sure, son,' grinned Martin, 'you can have the ball as much as you like.' That was music to Danny's ears and he readily agreed to sign.

There was one more thing. How much were Villa paying for him? He asked Martin. 'I could see the question embarrassed him,' remembered Danny. 'He looked startled for a moment, cast a furtive glance in either direction, then flashed the fingers and thumb of one hand – deaf and dumb style – three times to intimate the sum.' The fee was £15,000.

At first Martin seemed likely to deliver on his promises. When Danny joined Villa they hadn't won a game for a long time and were bottom of the First Division. Then things started to pick up. An inside-forward called Tommy Thompson arrived from Newcastle and when Danny came into the side they only lost one match during the rest of the season to avoid relegation. He'd finished the campaign on a high note and took pride in his position as an established wing-half with a famous First Division club.

By the following September, Villa were on top of the First division for the first time in many years, but their early form faded and with it their hopes of sustaining a title challenge. But he did come face to face with Tottenham both at White Hart Lane and Villa Park. 'They were very good indeed and appealed to me more than any other team I had seen at the time. They beat us 2-0 in London and 3-0 in Birmingham.'

The next season Blanchflower played against Spurs again. But by now they'd lost their edge. Other teams were learning how to stop them and some of the vital links in the team were ageing. 'It is easier to stop something good than to create it,' said Blanchflower. 'The rise and decline of 'push and run', the lesson that good things come to an end, was part of my education of football at the time.'

Meanwhile, things gradually got worse at Villa Park and the annual struggle against relegation claimed manager George Martin as its victim. He was replaced by Eric Houghton but Villa failed to improve. Things got so bad that Danny was called before the board and asked what team he would pick to get the club out of trouble!

At Barnsley he had learned old tricks of the game from Raich Carter, Peter Doherty and Jimmy Hagan who were all in the Yorkshire area at the time. Then he'd been transferred into a long-ball game at Villa Park, learning its strengths and weaknesses in a team which always preferred to play the long ball. And playing against Tottenham's shorter 'push and run' game had given him something else to think about.

All these thoughts were playing on his mind during the 1953–54 season. How could he mix them up and apply them successfully? He tried to persuade some of the Villa players to co-operate in training with him, but they felt no urge to change. Why should they? They were regular first-team players, comfortable with their own familiar way of playing football. And Villa were one of the all-time greats, a big club with famous traditions. 'Just being at Villa was a privilege itself. I was a banana case wanting to change things; a round peg in a square hole.'

He wondered whether he was out of order or whether it was Villa's lack of ambition that was to blame for the way he felt. Danny sat in the huge Villa dressing-room thinking about that and wondering what the old giants of the past had been like. Then he wandered down the corridors peering at the old framed pictures on the walls, sniffing the ghosts of yesterday. And then, reluctantly, he realised he was living in the past – somebody else's past.

Finally, he could take no more. In September 1954 he decided it was time to try his luck somewhere else. 'I was 28 years old and a soccer career is a short one. I wanted to be part of something progressive, to belong to a club that was striving to achieve something, a club that thought in terms of good constructive football, a club that was keen and vital.'

He wrote a transfer request and put it in an envelope. No one would take it from him. The manager, the secretary, the assistant secretary all kept their hands behind their backs. They knew what was in the envelope and nobody wanted to be the bearer of bad news. In the end, Blanchflower had to post it.

The chairman wasn't feeling too well and said he'd appreciate it if Blanchflower didn't mention the matter until he was well enough to see him. But he'd already told a few of the players about his letter to the board and the story soon got around. A few days later a *Birmingham Mail* reporter rang to ask if it was true. Blanchflower told him he didn't want to say anything for the moment. The paper broke the story that night. Like it or not, his impending departure had become the hot sports story. One of the longest transfer sagas of all time had begun.

CHAPTER 5
Blanchflower Joins Spurs

THE ASTON VILLA board tried to persuade Blanchflower to stay, but he was determined to leave. He told the chairman it wasn't a question of his treatment at Villa Park; it was his desire to achieve success in his short career. He didn't think he'd do that with Villa.

The board eventually decided to let Blanchflower go. They wanted £40,000. It was a lot of money to ask for a 29-year-old wing-half, even if he was the captain of Northern Ireland. The story was big news and made the front pages. The record transfer fee at the time was the £34,000 Sheffield Wednesday had paid Notts County for Jackie Sewell. Villa wanted not far short of 20 per cent more than that.

The newspapers reported that both Arsenal and Tottenham were interested. But neither club was willing to pay anywhere near the asking price. They wanted no part in any auction and the respective managers, Tom Whittaker of Arsenal and Arthur Rowe of Spurs, struck a gentleman's agreement that they wouldn't offer more than £30,000. If they both bid the same then Blanchflower would have to choose between them. They agreed to hold the fee to about £28,000 and to stay in touch.

The following morning Blanchflower was summoned to the Villa offices. He was told that Whittaker was waiting at the home of the Villa chairman to see him. Whittaker told him that the fee was ridiculous. 'But you needn't worry about that. They'll come to their senses and whatever anybody else bids we'll bid a little higher.' Blanchflower agreed with him about the fee and Whittaker was so assured and confident in speaking of the terms of the transfer that Blanchflower had already begun to think of himself as an Arsenal player.

Whittaker gave him his telephone number and said that if he had any problems over the transfer he should let him know. Blanchflower was sure Whittaker felt the same as he did, that it was merely a matter of a few days before the deal was clinched.

The next day Blanchflower was called to the offices again. He was told that Spurs manager Arthur Rowe had been given permission to approach him. He would arrive that afternoon. Although Blanchflower thought he was to become an Arsenal player he saw no harm in meeting Rowe.

Rowe was well respected in the game. His 'push and run' philosophy and the way he'd guided the great Tottenham team of the late '40s and early '50s had been a great source of inspiration to many of the young hopeful players Blanchflower knew. He'd spoken to Rowe briefly before an international match against Wales at Swansea the previous season and had been very impressed.

But Spurs' fortunes were wilting as their great team aged and there was a certain suspicion about the club. They were not as famous or well known as their North London rivals and there were rumours within the game that they were inclined to be mean. Also, Rowe had suffered a breakdown at the club. All of this tended to make Blanchflower a little cautious about Tottenham's approach.

Rowe had travelled up to Villa by car and was still wearing his overcoat and hat when he met Blanchflower in the players' billiard room. Blanchflower liked Rowe's direct, honest approach. 'Well, my boy, how about it?' said Rowe. Blanchflower told him about his meeting with Whittaker and what the Arsenal manager had said about outbidding other clubs. 'That's fair enough, but we're not out of it yet,' said Rowe.

Rowe seemed impressed with Blanchflower's attitude. He struck him as the kind of player he was looking for. He wanted players who would fight for themselves and what they believed in because if they didn't want to fight for themselves they wouldn't want to fight for him.

Blanchflower said it seemed certain he'd go to Arsenal. He'd promised Mr Whittaker he'd go to Highbury. They argued about the pros and cons of the two clubs. Despite the intense rivalry of their teams, Rowe and Whittaker were good friends and had a great professional respect for each other. Rowe said Arsenal were a fine club and he couldn't honestly advise Blanchflower against joining them. But he still hoped the Irishman might come to Tottenham because they could do big things together.

Rowe said he had some good young players and wanted an experienced wing-half to help. He also wanted Blanchflower to take over the captaincy when Alf Ramsey retired. He knew Blanchflower would like the thriving atmosphere of good football for the sake of it at Tottenham. Blanchflower said he liked Spurs' style of play better than any other club. He told Rowe he respected him very much and liked the thought of Tottenham with him in charge. But he also mentioned the little superstitions about the club's reputation and wondered how strong Rowe's position was as manager.

Rowe answered his doubts very clearly and candidly. He'd heard the rumours about the club and he and the board were trying to deal with them. He admitted people might have some misgivings about the way Spurs went about things, but no more than they would have about most other clubs in football. He claimed Arsenal had always made good publicity out of their good deeds and managed to keep their bad ones quiet. Tottenham had been the victims of their own bad deeds and their good ones rarely saw the light. He said he was fairly established at the club himself but he wouldn't like to promise anything. A manager could never be certain how strong he was but if Blanchflower joined him he'd be stronger since a manager is as strong as his team.

Rowe's sincerity and honesty opened Blanchflower's mind a good deal regarding his transfer. He won him over by talking more about football than transfer details. Blanchflower thought Rowe was very down to earth, sincere and honest, too modest to expect anyone to call him anything but Arthur. 'You will like it at Spurs,' he told Blanchflower, 'where it's still football for football's sake. I just want to know if you will come to Spurs if we beat Arsenal to a deal with Villa?' Blanchflower said he would. When Rowe left for London Blanchflower still felt he'd be going to Highbury, but he wasn't nearly so certain about it; after all, Rowe had erased most of the doubts he had about Tottenham.

The days passed and Blanchflower's expected transfer to Arsenal failed to materialise. He took up Whittaker's invitation to phone him if anything went wrong and asked about the prospects of joining Arsenal. 'We're stuck for the moment, my boy,' said Whittaker. 'We can't agree on the fee. But don't you worry, I'm working on that. Keep in touch.'

The passage of time and more phone calls revealed that it wasn't working out the way he wanted. 'My directors have stopped me. They won't let me go higher than £28,500. I'm trying to move them, but it's going to be difficult.'

Blanchflower phoned Whittaker about three times and the Arsenal man seemed to grow sadder each time he spoke. Gone was the assured air with which he'd told Blanchflower that Arsenal would outbid the rest. Blanchflower thought it was as if Whittaker was losing faith in himself and the thing he loved most – Arsenal.

Blanchflower began to lose faith in Arsenal too. 'I had always thought of them as big time. They had always seemed to do things the big way. But there was something in the sadness of Tom Whittaker's voice that suggested to me they were cutting down on the big times and the big ways. I didn't like the idea, either, of Tom Whittaker trying to move the directors and not being able to do so. Why didn't they respect his advice? Were Arsenal not so wealthy or so big time as they appeared? Was Tom Whittaker the manager in name only? Were the directors not big enough to keep up with and expand the traditions of the club? Was the empire beginning to crumble as had the one at Villa Park?'

These doubts were building up in Blanchflower's mind. He also thought the delay was just a smart way of pushing down the price, but that didn't account for the sadness in Whittaker's voice and Blanchflower grew uneasy about Arsenal. The papers claimed that other clubs, including Wolves, were becoming interested because of the delay.

The transfer saga took a twist in early November when Blanchflower was badly injured playing against Scotland at Hampden Park. He now had plenty of time to think. Blanchflower gradually became less sure about Arsenal and had the uneasy feeling they were about to slip. He liked Tottenham's traditions and style of football and there was a strange appeal in their name. (The Hotspur part came from a

Shakespeare character called Harry Hotspur.) He was convinced their style of play was more in keeping with the future than Arsenal's.

Spurs were well supported and it was claimed they were the wealthiest club in the country. Blanchflower thought that perhaps their past thriftiness had set them solid foundations to face the future. And perhaps the mood of the club was changing to face the new demands of a changing football world. Tottenham had never been known for spending big on players, but here they were in a bidding war for Blanchflower.

His feelings were swinging towards Tottenham. But he decided to first see which club came to an agreement with Villa about the fee. Gradually his injury healed and his confidence grew. After five weeks he was back in the first team again for a match against Cardiff at Villa Park. His knee still hurt a little at times but all was well. He was ready to be transferred.

Rowe badly wanted the classic wing-half skills of the cultured Blanchflower and needed his leadership as captain when Alf Ramsey moved on. Rowe told the Tottenham directors that Blanchflower was a one-off, a midfield thinker without parallel in the twentieth century. He argued his case well and the board allowed him to raise his offer by £2,000 to the £30,000 ceiling he'd agreed with Whittaker.

Rowe phoned Whittaker to tell him the position. If Arsenal matched Tottenham's bid of £30,000 it would be up to Blanchflower which club he joined. But Arsenal stuck on £28,000 and Blanchflower would have to take what he'd originally decided was his second choice.

On the Wednesday after the Cardiff match Northern Ireland were due to play the Army at Highbury. Blanchflower had been unfit when the team was picked but he was invited to lunch with the party in their London hotel and to attend the match. He travelled down from Birmingham to meet them with no thought of the pending transfer in his head.

Meanwhile, his younger brother Jackie was in the hotel preparing for the match when he was paged: 'Mr Blanchflower wanted on the telephone.' He answered the call and the voice at the other end said: 'Eric here . . . you've been transferred to Tottenham.'

Jackie realised it was Villa's manager Eric Houghton. 'I'm sorry

Eric, you've got the wrong one [Blanchflower],' he told him, trying to explain the mistake. 'Oh, no. Arsenal wouldn't agree to meet our price,' exclaimed Houghton, thinking Jackie was Danny and that the 'wrong one' meant the wrong club. Eventually they sorted out the confusion and Houghton asked Jackie to tell Danny that Villa and Tottenham had agreed on a price and that Arthur Rowe would be contacting him at the hotel.

When Danny arrived around lunchtime Jackie greeted him with a smile. 'Hey kid,' he grinned, 'you've been transferred to Tottenham.' It didn't give Danny much time to think about his transfer. Whittaker had not kept his promise to outbid any opposition, nor had he explained the situation to him. Arthur Rowe had been right. Spurs were not out of it.

Rowe phoned and asked Danny to be ready to hop into his taxi when he arrived. The Spurs manager wanted to avoid the Press until they'd talked over the details. In the back of the taxi, Rowe told Blanchflower Arsenal would not go beyond £28,000. Spurs had agreed to pay £30,000. Rowe had persuaded his board that a future captain was worth another £2,000.

'There was not the slightest thought of Arsenal in my mind: perhaps what my brother Jackie had told me earlier about Eric Houghton saying that they had not agreed to meet Villa's price had cast away all thought of them,' wrote Danny later. 'As I drove around in the taxi with Arthur Rowe my feeling of wanting to become a Spur was complete.'

Then Rowe was a bit hesitant. 'Would you mind having that injured knee examined by our specialist?' he asked. Blanchflower didn't mind.

They ended up at the offices of Headlam & Sims, a boot, shoe and sporting goods manufacturer in Newman Street, London W1. The company, mutual friends of both Rowe and Blanchflower, had made a popular football boot endorsed by Rowe. As the taxi took them in that direction they thought it would be a quiet place where they would both be welcomed and at ease and where they they could sign the necessary documents in peace. Also, Rowe could use the phone to tell his directors and others waiting for the news. It was there that Danny Blanchflower signed the forms to become a

Tottenham player. He was the most expensive half-back in football history.

He played his first game for Tottenham on 11 December 1954 against Manchester City at Maine Road. It was a good game in wet, muddy conditions and Spurs collected a valuable point in a 0-0 draw. 'The first time for weeks that I was able to sit back with confidence and enjoy the match,' Rowe said afterwards.

Tottenham had struggled near the bottom of the First Division all season and, although Blanchflower's new club were in much the same position as his old one, there seemed to be more hope playing for Spurs. 'There was an altogether different feeling about their style of play . . . the sense of a more definite rhythm in the game: as if the players were more related to one another and that collectively they were trying to control the game and direct the course of play instead of, as it had seemed at Villa, dashing determinedly after it in the hope of keeping up with it and perhaps finishing in front.'

His first impressions were borne out in training. During the morning five-a-side practices at White Hart Lane he was pleasantly surprised at the habits of 'push and run', the great degree of combined play that stood out for the unaccustomed eye to see, and the speed and skill with which it was accomplished in that small area of play.

On first sight Blanchflower didn't think White Hart Lane was as imposing as Villa Park. It was concealed by houses, shops, pubs, churches and the passing traffic along Tottenham High Road. The club offices conveyed the same sense of age as the ones at Villa Park, but there seemed to be more of an air of respect and vitality.

There wasn't the same sense of space inside the stadium as at Villa Park, but the space was ample and all of it has been used wisely. Blanchflower decided White Hart Lane was 'a grand, compact soccer oasis in the heart of a heavily built-up area'.

He enjoyed playing there from the start. Covered on all sides, it conveyed a sense of theatre, particularly in floodlit games. From the pitch the sea of surrounding faces looked uniform and comfortably housed. The crowd played their part to perfection; they were neither too near nor too far from the pitch and, with a roof over their head, created just the right atmosphere. Danny Blanchflower felt at home.

The Tottenham directors soon discovered that Blanchflower was no ordinary footballer. He'd written a weekly column in the *Birmingham Argus* and had agreed to write a similar column for a Fleet Street paper. He had a feel for words and was a good writer.

The FA reminded Tottenham that players were not allowed to write in newspapers and the directors asked him to stop. Blanchflower was nothing if not independent and refused. Eventually a compromise was reached whereby Spurs agreed to vet his articles. 'As far as I knew no one at the club ever saw them before they went into print,' says Bill Nicholson.

CHAPTER 6
Bill Nicholson

IRONICALLY, BLANCHFLOWER WAS bought to replace Bill Nicholson who was coming to the end of his playing days. Neither of them knew it at the time but in their respective future roles as captain and manager of Tottenham Hotspur Football Club they were to become one of the greatest partnerships in the history of British club football.

Nicholson was born in Scarborough on 26 January 1919 at number 15 Vine Street. The rented house was part of a livery stable. At the time he was the youngest of eight children, but another one followed making a total of five boys and four girls. There was an impressive archway in front of the houses. The stables stood behind.

His father Joe worked with horses for a hansom-cab company. In the winter he was a groom and in the summer he drove a horse-drawn carriage along the Scarborough seafront. But he didn't make enough money to keep the family, so Bill's mother, Edith, worked as a cleaning lady as well as running the house and bringing up nine children.

Money was tight and the kids didn't have much. There was one scooter between them and they all had to line up at the front gate to wait their turn while one went round the block.

But for someone in Joe Nicholson's position the house in Vine Street was imposing. It had four bedrooms, a scullery and a front room which was only used on Sundays. Bill's upbringing was straightforward with the emphasis on hard work and self-reliance.

He took advantage of living near one of the best beaches on that part of the coast. But his parents never bought the boys swimming trunks so they went to the beach in short trousers. Bill never did learn to swim, something he later regretted.

His father Joe was lame, having been born with a limp, but nobody ever talked to him about it. 'Yorkshire people in those days were private folk,' says Bill. 'It was looked on as bad manners to discuss other people's ages or their disabilities.'

Bill was seven years old before he kicked his first football. Before then he had no interest in the game which was to dominate his life. There were so many other things to do in the lively seaside resort of Scarborough.

Young Bill shared his father's love of horses. He used to go out with him on the horse and carriage when he was very young. Every Sunday Joe's hansom cab took people to church in their best clothes, and during the summer it paraded up and down the promenade taking customers backwards and forwards from the station.

Bill oiled the horse's hooves and polished the brass on the harness. It was hard work but he enjoyed it. He liked the horse but was frightened of falling off when placed in the saddle and never managed to ride it. Sadly, when cars became popular, demand for the service offered by Joe Nicholson fell away.

At the age of seven Bill was given a rubber football by a relative as a present. 'Having your own football in those days – it was 1926, the year of the General Strike – made you a king, and I didn't have to search far to find enough boys to make up a scratch game,' recalls Bill. 'We would pick up a stone, put it in a clenched fist behind our backs and invite the opposing captain to nominate which hand covered the stone.'

'Winning the toss and having first choice of a dozen or so players usually meant kicking down the hill, because most of the spare bits of ground we played on in Scarborough were hilly. Often we played in the streets. If the ball went over a wall, you climbed over and collected it. We played every day in the holidays and most nights in school time until it was dark. There was no organised football for boys of that age, so we played our own games with our own rules.'

Although Bill, by his own admission, was no academic he gained a scholarship to attend the Scarborough Boys' High School. He was the only one of the nine Nicholson children to pass the scholarship exam. Many of the pupils were fee-paying, most the sons of local businessmen. But Bill Nicholson never felt excluded in any way.

He was only 11 years old when he arrived but went straight into the Under-14 team. Bill played centre-half and, though small, could outjump most opponents. His attendance at the High School meant he wasn't allowed to play for the district side – Scarborough High thought its students were above such common things! But he represented his school at places like Hull, York, Whitby and Malton. It took him outside Scarborough for the first time in his life.

The players had to pay their own fare on these trips and some days young Bill was so embarrassed at having to ask his mother for half-a-crown, which she couldn't afford to give him, that he told the master, a Mr C.H. Bradley, that he couldn't play. 'He soon found out the reason and somehow wangled me onto the trip without charging the fare,' recalls Bill. Bradley was a remarkable man who played a prominent role in the establishment of boys' clubs in England.

By this time Bill was getting up at five o'clock to do a paper round for six shillings a week to supplement the family income. The extra money enabled him to buy his own pair of boots. He repaired them with the last and hammer his father used in the stables.

Bill stayed at Scarborough High School until he was nearly 16 years old, past the usual school-leaving age of 14. But he wasn't that interested in his studies, with the exception of geography, and didn't matriculate. Finding a career was a problem. But just before he turned 16 he got a job in the Alexandra Laundry through one of his brothers who already worked there. He helped dry the clothes on a hydro-drying machine for £2 a week. It wasn't much of a job but in the midst of depression he was lucky to have one.

On Saturdays he played for a local league side, the Young Liberals. 'I wasn't involved in politics but I suppose if I supported a party at the time it was the Liberals, the yellows,' says Bill. The team was run by a dentist called Jones. Football was his hobby. It was through a friend of his in York called Nelson who had connections with Tottenham that Bill was first introduced to the club.

'One day I received a letter from Tottenham asking me to accept a month's trial at White Hart Lane. I was amazed: I had no idea how they had come to hear of me,' says Bill.

'When the letter came no one knew what to do. We weren't even sure exactly where Tottenham was. My mother and father had never once seen me play football. They knew I was keen, but they had no idea whether I was any good or not.'

He'd never thought of a career as a footballer. Scarborough was an out-of-the-way place and no one from the town had ever become a star player. 'I honestly had no idea what the world of professional football was about,' says Nicholson. 'Our heroes were the local Midland League side – none of my friends had even been to see Hull or York.'

Bill was given instructions to meet the local Spurs scout based in York who would travel down to London with him on the night train. At King's Cross they caught an underground train to Manor House and then a bus. It was Bill's first experience of the capital and a completely different world from Scarborough.

His first match in the Midweek League against West Ham made him feel more at home. The pitch was almost as sandy as the South bay at Scarborough! His performance earned him a job as a ground staff boy. 'That's what they used to call them,' he says. His wages were £2 a week. 'We were cheap labour really,' he says. The club found digs for him close to White Hart Lane at 23 Farningham Road where his landlady was a Mrs Lawrence.

Bill played for the Spurs nursery team, Northfleet United, on Saturdays, but during the week there wasn't much time for football. He worked from eight o'clock until five with a short lunch break. Training was restricted to Tuesday and Thursday afternoons, but even that was only after the boys had done almost a full day's work. If they had a spare moment they'd have a kickabout under the stands with a bundle of old cloth tied into a ball. They didn't have much energy left for anything else.

Nicholson spent most of his two years as a ground staff boy working on the pitch, sweeping up, and painting the stands. 'I dreaded having to paint the girders of the stands because I had no head for heights. I nearly fell off once. I painted every one of those girders in all four stands before I became a professional. Though I disliked painting, I developed an affinity with those old stands and was sad when the wooden one on the High Road side was pulled down. The wood was warm and homely and people could sit without being squashed.'

One of Bill's jobs as a teenager was to pull the fly roller across the pitch to flatten it after matches. The roller was in a wooden frame and almost six feet wide. 'It took some heaving to move it across the squelchy mud,' says Bill. By the end of the season the pitch was usually bare and the boys joined the ground staff men to help re-seed it. All 18 of them would line up along the touchline and then slowly move across the pitch, putting down new seeds and raking them. 'I had blisters on my hand with doing it,' says Bill. He also used the carpentry skills he'd picked up at school to build a shooting box for the professional players.

The ground staff lads weren't allowed near the dressing-rooms and the professionals rarely spoke to them. 'But it wasn't all bad,' says Bill. 'I remember that Willie Hall, who was club captain at the time, was very kind and always took a great interest.'

Bill was eventually signed by Spurs as a professional in 1938, though he still wasn't confident about his future in the game. He made his first team debut at Ewood Park against Blackburn Rovers later that year at the age of 19. He was fortunate to get the chance since Spurs had 54 players on their staff, 46 professionals and the eight ground staff boys. His chance came only because of an injury to regular left-back Billy Whatley.

Meanwhile, he'd started going out with someone who could almost be described as the girl next door. Her name was Grace and she lived just a few houses along from Bill's digs, at 17 Farningham Road. She was his first and only girlfriend and would become his wife.

'I must confess I was more attracted to her elder sister Winnie when I was first introduced to the family. Grace's twin sister Ivy was nicknamed "Fairy" within the family because she was light-skinned, while Grace was called "Darkie". Ivy's nickname soon disappeared, however, because she didn't like it, but my wife is still "Darkie" as she detests the name Grace.'

'I had a job understanding Bill at first,' Darkie told Hunter Davies in his classic book *The Glory Game*. 'He came to our house practically every night as he didn't know anyone else in London. My father had a billiards table and he often used to come and play.'

Darkie was very proud to have a Spurs player as her boyfriend. Football wasn't a glamorous profession back then, but Bill was still considered quite a catch. 'He talked a lot about it being an insecure job, he might not make it, he might break a leg one day and that would be it, but I never worried.'

In October 1939, only three games into the season, Bill was called up by the Army. Most of his six and a half years in the Forces were spent in Britain as an instructor, first in infantry training, which he knew little about, and then in the Army Physical Training Corps at Brancepeth.

He worked with several hundred troops on 16-week courses. It was a punishing schedule. There was no time to play much football except for the odd 'guest' appearances for Newcastle, Sunderland, Darlington and some of the local clubs based in the north of England.

In 1942 Bill married Darkie. They set up home in two attic rooms in Farningham Road before moving to Commonwealth Road, next door to Spurs goalkeeper Ted Ditchburn. Bill didn't have a car then and Ted used to give him a lift in his exotic American 'Dillinger'. 'It had running boards and needed some handling. Ted hadn't passed his driving test at the time!' he recalls.

Bill was 26 years old when the war ended in 1945. He was sent to join the headquarters of the Central Mediterranean Forces in Udini, Italy. His task was to teach coaches in various sports. 'I had to do everything concerned with football, learning the laws of the game and passing it on to all these different people in the Army who went back to their units and did what I was doing with their troops.' While in Italy he met Geoff Dyson who later became an AAA athletics coach. Dyson was a fantastic organiser and lecturer and probably had more to do with Bill becoming a coach than anyone else.

After the war Bill returned to Tottenham and went straight into the first team at centre-half. He'd been away from the professional game for six years, but then so had everybody else. There was no risk of losing your place to a young player because there hadn't been any proper football for them to play during the war.

He'd probably lost half his playing career, but it was those wartime experiences which set him up to be a coach. 'It was invaluable. What I did for six years in the Army taught me how to handle people and how to talk to people. It deviously taught me how to get players fit, and I began to think about coaching routines – not in a very organised way, but how it could be done.'

Bill's Army experience as a coach and PE instructor encouraged him to become a qualified coach. 'I was a coach almost as soon as I came out of the Army. One of our players said: "You've not got a coaching certificate." I said: "No, but I fancy going in for one would you come with me?"'

They went to the Football Association and started attending FA coaching courses at Birmingham University. They were founded by England coach Walter Winterbottom. He encouraged the young coaches to think up new methods and routines. They learned from each other. Former Manchester City and England manager Joe Mercer was one of the fledgling coaches putting forward his ideas.

Bill's Army experience also helped him pass his Full Badge at the first attempt. He found the course 'fairly easy' but admits it's much more difficult these days. One of the main requirements for a coach is to be able to put ideas across and Bill was used to addressing a large number of men.

Winterbottom encouraged Bill to take up coaching. He did a lot of coaching in his spare time while playing for Spurs. For a year or two he travelled up to Cambridge each week to coach the university team. 'Being intelligent young men, the Varsity players were receptive to ideas and I enjoyed my time with them,' says Bill.

In 1949 Bill played at right-half in Arthur Rowe's developing 'push and run' team alongside such greats as former England manager Alf Ramsey, Alf's great friend Eddie Baily, Ron Burgess, Les Medley and Ted Ditchburn. He learnt a lot from them all. He was known for his consistency based on strong tackling and careful distribution.

Bill was a member of the Spurs side which won the Second Division Championship in 1950 and the club's first-ever League Championship in 1951. Tottenham dominated their home matches. They attacked so much that centre-half Harry Clarke felt redundant. 'I only touched the ball nine times,' he would say to Bill in the dressing-room after games. 'I didn't get a kick, or a header. You're mopping everything up on one side and Ron Burgess on the other. I'm doing nothing.'

Bill's growing reputation earned him an England call-up and he was first selected for the squad on 16 May 1948 for a match against Italy in Turin. He travelled with the England party 23 times, but played just once in a 5-2 win over Portugal at Goodison Park in May 1951. He scored with his first touch 19 seconds after the kick-off. The ball was rolled back to him just outside the penalty area and he knew as soon as he'd struck it that the keeper was beaten. It's still the fastest goal ever scored by an England player on his debut. The game was played at Everton because in those days the FA took the less important matches to provincial grounds.

His wife Darkie was at Goodison Park that day, one of the few matches she ever saw him play. She was disappointed he only got the one chance to play for England. Bill was considered unlucky not to get more than one full cap. The reason was the presence of Billy Wright. Nicholson didn't think he'd played well against Portugal, despite the goal, and wasn't surprised when Wright was recalled for the next match against France in October. But he didn't worry about not being picked again. He was just pleased to be involved.

Meanwhile, the great 'push and run' team had seen its moments of glory and, after finishing the 1951–52 campaign as runners-up to Manchester United, went into decline. Bill had also seen better days – as a player at least. Towards the end of the 1953–54 season he told Arthur Rowe: 'I'm not as fit as I used to be. Perhaps it's time you put someone else in my place.' Bill had been lucky with injuries throughout his career but one of his knees had been causing him problems towards the end of thc season. He saw a specialist who recommended an operation to remove some foreign bodies.

Bill knew that Rowe, who he describes as 'a compassionate, decent man', was unlikely to leave him out. He was loyal to the players who had won the Championship. 'That was one of the reasons the team was breaking up. He kept in some of the older players when we knew he should have brought in new ones. By speaking up, I was making it easier for him. I felt it was an honest way of going about it.'

Bill was appointed club coach and still played in the reserves or the 'A' team. But he never again travelled with the first team as a player. In those days only the manager and the physiotherapist did that. He'd have to wait until he too took over the reins in October 1958.

CHAPTER 7
The Team Takes Shape

IT WAS DURING the 1959–60 season that a truly great Spurs side began to emerge from the legacy of the 'push and run' era.

Maurice Norman had been switched from right-back to his natural position at centre-half. Scottish international keeper Bill Brown was signed from Dundee for £16,500 and was to prove one of Bill Nicholson's best signings. And former Spurs star Tony Marchi was recaptured from Juventus of Italy for £20,000.

Tottenham started the new season with a 5-1 win at Newcastle and were unbeaten for the first 12 games. The team was Bill Brown; Peter Baker; Mel Hopkins; Danny Blanchflower; Maurice Norman; Dave Mackay; Terry Medwin; Tommy Harmer; Bobby Smith; Johnny Brooks and Cliff Jones, with forward Dave Dunmore and half-back Tony Marchi making the occasional appearance. The side was taking shape.

Nicholson knew the sort of football he wanted his team to play. 'It was a question of getting the right players,' he says. 'It's not always easy. Players came in with a certain way of playing the game. But I'd go for a player who had what I liked. That's what I tried to do. Even if they needed to learn that little bit extra.'

He'd read a lot about a player called John White of Falkirk and was also hearing good reports about him. He asked Dave Mackay for his impressions. 'What's this lad like?' 'Not bad, Bill,' replied Mackay. 'He plays for Scotland.' 'Well, that doesn't make him a good player!' said Nicholson. After all, Spurs already had some very good players.

Nicholson decided to watch White in a League match. He didn't make one bad pass. The Spurs manager was becoming increasingly excited about the prospect of signing him. Falkirk were short of money and both Leicester and Chelsea had made offers. Nicholson was told that Leicester had bid £13,000 and were close to reaching agreement with the Scottish club.

In October Danny Blanchflower played for Northern Ireland against Scotland at Windsor Park in Belfast. The Scots won comfortably by 4-0 with a number of new young players in their side. Among them was the slim, pale figure of John White who scored one of the goals. Blanchflower particularly liked White. 'I had read somewhere that Spurs were interested in him but I had not paid much attention to it,' he said.

Nicholson's view that he had to sign White was reinforced when he met Blanchflower, Mackay and Brown in the Tottenham car park on their return from Belfast. 'What's this fellow White like?' he asked Blanchflower. 'I liked him very much. Seems to have a wonderful sense of position and good control of the ball in a quiet smooth way. He would suit in our team,' said the Spurs captain. 'I like him too,' said Nicholson. 'I can get him for £20,000.' 'Fly up right away and don't waste time,' urged Blanchflower.

Nicholson had one reservation: White's stamina. The Tottenham manager thought he looked too lightweight. 'We had had problems with Tommy Harmer's physique; we didn't want another player with a similar drawback.' Mackay tried to reassure him. 'He's a cross-country runner,' he told Nicholson.

White was in the Army and the Spurs boss phoned the sports officer at his unit. 'When I got in touch with this bloke in the Army he said: "I know what you're phoning for but you won't get him this week,"' recalls Nicholson. "Why not?" I asked.

"Because he's in the cross country team."

"Is he a cross-country runner then?"

"Yes," he said. "He's so good that he won't be playing football this coming Saturday because he'll be running for the Scottish command." Nicholson thought, 'That's all I want to know.'

He immediately phoned Falkirk manager Tommy Younger, the former Scotland, Hibernian and Liverpool star, and offered him £20,000. Younger accepted and the next morning he was in Nicholson's office with White. 'He [White] had become a luxury for us because he was thinking two and three moves ahead and his passes were not being picked up,' recalled the Falkirk boss.

After introducing the young Scottish international Younger noticed that Nicholson wasn't happy with the progress being made in his talks with White. He took the youngster aside and asked him what was holding up the deal. 'I'm not good enough for here,' said a distraught White, 'I'll never fit in with these players.' Younger had never known a player with a worse inferiority complex.

White's Tottenham debut was at Hillsborough against a powerful Sheffield Wednesday team. Spurs were missing three regulars – Mel Hopkins, Cliff Jones and Terry Medwin – who were all playing for Wales. White scored but did little else and Tottenham lost 2-1. It was their first defeat of the season in their 13th League match.

After that White and Tommy Harmer became the inside-forwards and Spurs continued to head the League table. But at times they became a little goal-shy and didn't win games as comfortably as they should have done. Some people claimed that Harmer and White were too similar in style and that the fabric of the team wasn't complete.

In November, Mel Hopkins broke his nose in a horrific collision with Ian St John while playing against Scotland. But young Ron Henry had stepped in and was showing great promise at left-back.

In December 1959 Nicholson strengthened the squad by exchanging Johnny Brooks for Les Allen of Chelsea. He hoped Allen would provide more goals. Some Spurs fans were surprised they'd recruited Allen because he was in Chelsea's reserves and didn't seem to compare to some of the club's other signings. But Nicholson thought Allen was vastly under-rated. 'He was good at sniffing out goalscoring positions and was a sound finisher. His only weakness was that he was on the slow side.'

Actually, Nicholson didn't set out to sign Allen. One day Chelsea manager Ted Drake, the former England centre-forward, came to Nicholson's office and said: 'Billy, I need Johnny Brooks.' Chelsea were in the relegation zone and Nicholson said: 'What do you want him for? He's not the kind of player to get you out of a hole.' Brooks had a lot of skill but Nicholson believed he was inconsistent. 'He was a better player in a winning side than a losing one.'

Nothing came of Nicholson's conversation with Drake but a few weeks later the Chelsea boss was round again. 'Look, Billy,' he said, 'I must have Brooksey.' Nicholson had seen Allen play in Chelsea's reserves and liked his style. 'All right. I'll let you have him if you give me Les Allen in exchange.' Drake looked pleased. 'But how much money will you give me?' Nicholson was annoyed. 'The lad's in your reserves and you want money? It's not on is it?' Eventually Drake agreed that no money would be involved.

Allen came into the side at inside-left with White moving to outside-right. Blanchflower was now even more encouraged because he could see the team branching out. Once again he began telling people Tottenham could do the 'double'. Allen made his debut at Elland Road against Leeds on Boxing Day scoring two goals in a 4-2 win which took Spurs back to the top of the First Division. But two days later Leeds came to White Hart Lane and thrashed Tottenham 4-1. They needed to be more consistent to become a great side.

In the Cup, Spurs had beaten Newport County in the Third Round and were now drawn away to Fourth Division Crewe.

One morning at Tottenham, Bernard Joy of the *Evening Standard* approached Blanchflower. 'You really think the "double" can be done?' he asked. 'I do and I think we can do it,' Blanchflower told him. But it didn't look like they were capable of winning the Cup, let alone the League, when they visited Crewe the following Saturday.

The little town was buzzing with excitement as Spurs arrived. People packed the pavements and hung out of windows. They were convinced their team could humble the mighty Tottenham. 'It was like entering a beehive to steal the honey only to find that all the bees were waiting for you,' said Blanchflower. 'We had an uneasy feeling we might get stung.'

There was a record 20,000 crowd at Gresty Road. Spurs played too cautiously and drew 2-2. If a Crewe shot which hit the post had gone in, Spurs would have been out of the Cup. That was how close the underdogs came to upsetting their mighty First Division opponents.

A massive crowd of more than 64,000 turned up at White Hart Lane for the replay. It was to be a different story from the first game. Crewe were like lambs to the slaughter. Tottenham led 10-1 at half-time and eventually won 13-2. That scoreline remains their record victory. Crewe had arrived at London's Euston station on platform 2 – and they left from platform 13!

Spurs were drawn to play Blackburn in the Fifth Round. Rovers, a capable team with plenty of talent, clicked and won 3-1. Spurs were out of the Cup, and the 'double' was something the players could only continue to talk about as being possible.

The title looked like going to Wolves who had also reached the Cup final. The 'double' was in their sights when Tottenham went to Molineux on Saturday 23 April. Wolves were odds-on favourites to equal the hat-trick of Championships won by Huddersfield and Arsenal. They were four points clear of Burnley and three ahead of Spurs. If they beat Tottenham they only had to overcome Chelsea and the title was theirs. If Burnley didn't get maximum points then beating Spurs would do it for Wolves.

But Tottenham were relaxed. Their own chance of winning the League had virtually gone. Blanchflower held his team talk in the middle of the pitch rather than in the dressing-room. Fifty-five thousand fans were packed into Molineux on a warm, sunny day. But the home fans were to be disappointed. Within two minutes Spurs were ahead and went on to beat Wolves 3-1. Tottenham still had a slight chance of winning the title.

The following Saturday Spurs beat Blackpool at home, but when the other results came through, Wolves, who beat Chelsea 5-1, were a point in front of them. Burnley could take the title if they won their last game the following Monday night. Burnley scraped home against Manchester City to win the League, while Wolves beat Blackburn to lift the Cup. The possibility of achieving the 'double' was again clear.

Meanwhile, Spurs finished third, just two points behind Burnley and with a better goal average. They'd scored 86 goals, a total only bettered by Wolves and Manchester United, and conceded 50, the lowest number in the First Division. Their rise from 18th in the table the previous season to third was a great improvement. So was the performance of the defence which conceded 45 goals fewer than in the last campaign.

The defence had often let Tottenham down in the past. Now, with Bill Brown behind such sound defenders as Peter Baker, Maurice Norman, Dave Mackay and Ron Henry, Nicholson felt they had a strong enough squad to win the title. He was optimistic.

'The third in the League table was a boost. We were getting it together, getting the team working and playing for one another and getting to know each other. Ron Henry for Mel Hopkins at left-back was an important change. Then Terry Dyson came in for Terry Medwin. I felt that we would have a good shout in the League, but in the Cup . . . well, who knows about the Cup? One afternoon on a strange pitch, an awkward ground, one or two little things going the opposite way and bingo! You're gone. It's different again, the Cup.'

CHAPTER 8
Getting It Right

WHEN THE PLAYERS reported for pre-season training on a Thursday morning in July 1960 Danny Blanchflower was convinced the season ahead would be one of destiny. Bill Nicholson also believed his team was on the verge of greatness. 'I felt in 1960 that I had a side well prepared to do something. You cannot put it into words; it's a feeling you get. And I had this strong feeling around that time.'

As the players sat on the grass before their first training session the talk was all about how they'd lost out to Burnley in the Championship race the season before. Danny Blanchflower may have later promised Spurs chairman Fred Bearman that they could win the 'double' in the coming season, but that elusive prize wasn't mentioned on the first day. The target was the First Division title and a place in the European Cup.

Nicholson began with his welcome-back talk. He was brief, as usual, and got straight to the point. 'I want to congratulate you on last season. I think you did very well. But I know you can do much better. Our target is the League title. It's time it came back to White Hart Lane – and it's time we had a crack at the European Cup.

'I naturally feel disappointed we didn't win the Championship last season after such a fine run, but the defence did extremely well. We gave away fewer goals than anyone else. Now I hope the forwards will get more goals and it is up to us all to see that they do. Work is the key to success at soccer – and we're going to work. And, once again, I must tell you that team selection will be strictly on merit.'

Nicholson and his players mapped out in the minutest detail how the Championship could be won. If they were able to clinch the 'double' by winning the FA Cup as well, then so be it. But that would rest as much on luck as on judgement.

During the season, training usually finished by about half past one, but for the four weeks of pre-season their Cheshunt training ground became more of a camp. The players spent the whole day there training, playing and talking football. Nicholson liked to start pre-season training on a Thursday. He could give the players a fairly easy time for the first couple of days and then they had the weekend to get any stiffness out.

They worked hard in that summer of 1960. Roles were allotted, skills perfected, moves practised and techniques honed. 'We worked particularly hard in the first week,' recalls Nicholson.

At that time most British clubs concentrated on getting players fit. At Tottenham the emphasis was on competitive training, tactical exercises and ball skills. The Spurs players worked as hard on fitness as any team in the country, but Nicholson always made sure there was a balance between conditioning training and that aimed at improving ability.

One of the main ways of conditioning the players was the long-distance road race. It became known as 'Bill's road run', but was really a very fast walk. 'We did a lot of road walking,' says Nicholson. 'We'd do five or six miles walking and let them run the last mile if they wanted to. They could please themselves but had to wait until I told them to go.'

Nicholson always took the walks himself. He led from the front because he didn't want players running past him. The leaders would stay close to him, while the rest struggled to keep up. The Spurs manager had always been good at road walks. He was as quick as any of his players and faster than most.

Once Nicholson gave the signal to run, Blanchflower, sweating in his number eight training shirt, would race away. He always maintained the ever-increasing pace and usually came home first. Blanchflower was 34 years old, but he felt as fit and as strong as ever. He felt he'd withstood the tough training routine no worse for wear than the younger players.

Unlike Blanchflower, John White wasn't a good walker. The man who was to become known as 'the Ghost' because of his blind side runs, preferred sprinting. But Nicholson believed road work was good for footballers because it got the muscles going without too much strain.

The Spurs manager mingled with his players in training like one of the squad. Only full-backs Peter Baker and Mel Hopkins, reserve wing-half Tony Marchi and winger Terry Dyson had played with him in the mid-'50s. But Nicholson was close to his players and they responded to him with genuine enthusiasm. 'I'd been a player all my life. I knew the players. When I was the coach most of them were here so I knew what they could or couldn't do,' he says.

Pre-season training at Tottenham focused on tactics and strategy. The players did more work in this area in a day than they'd cover in a week during the season. They played lopsided matches, where the pitch was divided into three and they weren't allowed into certain areas. It was designed to make them support the man on the ball without making it too easy for him. They went through varied routines related to the game. 'We didn't just make them run for running's sake,' says Nicholson.

Statistics had shown that between a third and a half of all goals came from situations like corners, free-kicks or throw-ins. Spurs spent hours rehearsing their 'dead ball' tactics. They were the only drills they followed. Tottenham were one of the first clubs, possibly the first, to put a marker on an opponent taking a throw-in. They also worked on five or six free-kick routines with each player knowing his role precisely. Nicholson thought one of the best was the chip over the wall for a player on the end to turn, run onto and shoot.

Tottenham were also one of the first clubs to send their centre-backs up into the penalty area for corners. And when they conceded a corner Nicholson insisted his two full-backs stood about two yards in from either post so the keeper could see the ball if it was coming straight at him. If it was a short corner the defender could move out quickly to challenge; if it was long, he was able to get back and cover his keeper.

Many hours of training were also spent on throw-ins and corners. Dave Mackay's long throw was a very useful weapon in the right circumstances. He practised throwing the ball onto Bobby Smith's head so he could flick it back to Dyson, White, Allen or Jones in the centre. On corners, White practised hitting a long ball over the defenders' heads to Jones on the far edge of the penalty area.

Another unique aspect of Tottenham's training regimen was what became known as 'ghost football'. The first team faced the second team on the training pitch, but they didn't play each other. Instead, with Nicholson in charge of the first team, and his assistant Harry Evans controlling the reserves, each side created their own moves and tried to finish them off against the opposing goalkeeper.

'The idea may sound a little off-beat,' says Cliff Jones, 'but I can assure you it built up rhythm, helped us improvise and enabled us to work out 101 little routines without the formality of having to beat or bypass an opponent. It was all about knowing where the positions were. There was lots of ball work in twos and threes, going through movements so they were automatic to us when we got on the pitch. This was also the time when we worked out our drills for corners, free-kicks and throw-ins.'

Nicholson was both stern and critical in training. He knew the weaknesses of all his players and he exposed them so their team-mates could help to cover them in matches.

He was also fond of slogans: 'The man without the ball makes the play.' 'Time equals space.' He used them to get his players to do certain things.

Spurs' whole game was based on space – the creation and use of open gaps. Nicholson wanted his players to run in all directions during matches so the man in possession had options in almost any part of the pitch. This meant opposing defenders could never relax. One player unmarked waiting for a pass was all right, two was good, but three, or even four, was much better. Everyone had to think and run all the time. But Nicholson felt it was particularly important that the forwards kept moving and turning up in unexpected positions.

'During our pre-season preparations Bill Nicholson had us working overtime developing this type of forward play,' says Dave Mackay. 'It was hard drill, but our manager kept it so interesting that no one lost concentration. And as we began to perfect this technique, interest developed into enthusiasm for an idea. We could hardly wait for the start of the season so that we could try and put into practice the theories we had seen work out in trial games.'

Once the season began, Nicholson would put away the tactics board for another year. He knew it wouldn't help his players in the heat of battle. What they hadn't learnt in pre-season training they wouldn't remember out on the pitch in front of a roaring crowd. He trusted his players to take control and to improvise. The basics had been instilled in his squad; they were now free to build on them as they wished.

'It's important that a team does not take the field with preconceived plans, for there is always the opposition to be borne in mind,' says Mackay. 'This was a point we at Tottenham understood, so the moves we worked out were not part of a plan. The moves we developed after a time became automatic, and fitted into the pattern of any game, and in no way did we allow ourselves to be mastered by tactical plans.'

Blanchflower was impressed with the team that summer: its individual ability, teamwork and whole personality. 'Of course, there were the little doubts and uncertainties – but where else in the soccer world was there not. Where I looked for a reason for success I seemed to find one.'

Even the fates seemed to favour Spurs. They'd won the Cup in 1901 and 1921; there was no competition in 1941. They just had to be favourites in 1961. They were League Champions in 1951, another year ending in one, so why not the League title in 1961?

Blanchflower was not blindly superstitious, but he believed that when people thought a thing was likely to happen they were liable to make it happen, particularly when the team was good enough. Only time would tell.

CHAPTER 9
Quest for Glory

SPURS BEGAN THEIR quest for glory on the threshold of the Swinging Sixties. Elvis Presley was in the charts along with Cliff Richard, the Everley Brothers and Johnny Kidd & the Pirates. Rock & roll was still all the rage, though it would soon be challenged by the Beatles and the rest of the Merseybeat bands.

On the football pitch Burnley were the team to beat. They'd stolen the title away from Wolves and Tottenham the previous season by winning their final game and were among the favourites to retain their crown. The pretenders to the throne included Sheffield Wednesday, Wolves, Everton, Leicester, Manchester United, West Brom, Bolton and, of course, Spurs.

Sheffield Wednesday were among the other contenders. They were a dour team fashioned by manager Harry Catterick with defenders of the class of Peter Swan, Tony Kay and Don Megson. In goal was the brilliant England keeper Ron Springett.

Wolves favoured the long ball under manager Stan Cullis. Their style was a mixture of strength and finesse. Few teams had a better post-war record. They had talented players like defenders Ron Flowers, Bill Slater and Eddie Clamp, all England internationals. The attack was also experienced with outside-right Norman Deeley, inside-left Peter Broadbent and centre-forward Jimmy Murray a threat to any defence.

Footballers in the early '60s had a comfortable life, but they were poor by today's standards. When Spurs began their League campaign in 1960 the maximum wage was still in force. It restricted players' earnings to £20 a week during the season and £17 in the summer. This arrangement had once drawn a classic line from a young Jimmy

Armfield at Blackpool. When he asked why he wasn't paid the same money as the legendary Stanley Matthews, Armfield was told he wasn't as good as the 'Wizard of the Dribble'. 'But I am in the summer,' he quipped.

The maximum wage meant footballers weren't in the top income bracket like today. They certainly earned more than the average supporter on the terraces, especially if they played for a successful side and earned win bonuses on top of the basic salary, but the gap wasn't enormous.

Most players, certainly the married ones, couldn't afford a car. Their houses were also usually fairly modest and in nearly all cases owned by their clubs to whom they paid rent.

These economic conditions shaped the relationship between player and fan. The 'stars' of the day were more accessible. Most clubs didn't have a players lounge which supporters could only get into with a special pass. After a game the players drank in the same pubs near the ground as the fans.

Les Gold, a lifelong Tottenham supporter, was 20 years old at the start of the 1960–61 campaign. A regular on the 'Shelf' at White Hart Lane, he recalls that players had a different attitude towards supporters in those days. They seemed to be kinder and had more time.

'In our day you were a people's player,' recalls Tony Marchi. 'Not many players had cars so we'd get on a bus to go training. You were lucky if the conductor knew you because he'd let you off the fare – you could save threepence. You met people as you walked along the street and you'd talk to them. Along Tottenham High Road people would say hello to you and of course you'd say hello back.'

The players were certainly idolised by the fans. Les Gold remembers being 'King of the School' for a day if he picked up a bus ticket dropped by one of Tottenham's players. But there was more mutual respect between player and fan.

It was an age when clubs had very little commercial income. Sponsorship was unheard of and, though some clubs carried adverts in their programmes, Tottenham weren't among them. So it was the supporters handing over their hard-earned cash at the gate who paid the players' wages. Bill Nicholson never let them forget it.

'The most important people in this club are not the players, or the board of directors, or the management, but the supporters. They pay our wages. They come through the turnstiles. They work 40 hours a week. So you've got to give them value for money.'

Nicholson made sure that if any local boys club wanted a player to give out prizes, then someone had to do it. It was a way of giving something back to the fans.

'That's leadership,' says Cliff Jones. 'He made you aware of your responsibility to the community because the football club is part of that community and the lives of the supporters. A player may only be loyal to a club because he's getting paid. That's not true of the supporters. And at Spurs they were the best.'

The gate receipts at the successful clubs were huge. Tottenham would draw an average crowd of around 50,000 in 1960–61. Little of that money went into the players pockets, though a lot found its way to the taxman. The only way the players could earn a fortune was to move abroad.

It was more of a trickle than an exodus, but when Leeds United sold centre-forward John Charles to Juventus in April 1957 the shock waves reverberated through English football. The wealthy Italian club paid an astonishing £70,000 for Charles – more than double the British transfer record. He received a £10,000 signing-on fee and was paid £60 a week, four times the maximum wage in England.

Some wondered whether this had opened the floodgates and would be followed by a rush for the lire in which English football would lose its most talented players. Others anticipated spiralling wage demands in the Football League. What happened was a little of both.

Other stars, like Jimmy Greaves, Denis Law, Joe Baker, Gerry Hitchens and Tony Marchi were to try their luck in Italy with only modest success. Juventus first showed an interest in Marchi after Tottenham's close season tour of the United States at the end of the 1956–57 season. 'I was on holiday at the time so I didn't know much about it at first. But then this Italian agent Gigi Peronace was at my house every day.' Everyone told Marchi he'd be crazy not to go.

Marchi was a local boy born in Edmonton and brought up almost in the shadow of White Hart Lane. He'd lived in the area with his parents and younger sister nearly all his life. But he was of Italian descent. His grandparents had come to England in the early 1900s. That made him more of a target for the Italian clubs.

Marchi went to Raynham Road School in Edmonton and, with the Spurs ground so near, quickly showed an interest in football. His uncle, George Dorling, had once played for Tottenham and Marchi was a keen fan. He was also a good player and was soon representing Edmonton Schoolboys as well as being capped four times for the England Schoolboys team.

Marchi signed for Spurs when he left school in 1948, after turning down Arsenal. In May 1950, at the age of 17, he turned professional. Marchi was fortunate to be coached by two of Spurs' great half-backs: Arthur Rowe and Bill Nicholson. But he established himself in the Tottenham team with his own style of play.

Marchi made his debut in place of Ron Burgess, one of the finest left-halves of all time, in the 1949–50 Second Division Championship team, but had to bide his time as an understudy to Burgess until he left at the start of the 1954–55 season.

After that Marchi established himself at left-half and became an influential member of the Spurs team. In 1957 he became captain and was selected for the England 'B' team. When Juventus signed him for £42,000 he was Tottenham's longest-serving player with more than 100 appearances and was on the verge of a full England cap.

The Tottenham fans were sorry to see him go, but they realised he'd been made an offer he couldn't refuse. Marchi received a signing-on fee of £7,000, an enormous sum in those days, and was paid £20 a week – double his wages at Spurs. The Italian clubs also paid big bonuses and players at a successful team could clear a total of £50 a week. The stars at Juventus were taking home up to £100 a week – a colossal amount in the late 1950s.

Despite his pedigree at Spurs, Marchi found himself surplus to requirements almost immediately at Juventus. 'In those days the Italians only allowed one foreign player in each team,' he recalls. 'But the big clubs were buying as many as they could and farming them out to other teams. They thought the ruling was going to change and they could bring them all in but it didn't happen.'

Marchi was first loaned out to Vicenza, then known as Lanerossi Vicenza after the wool firm that sponsored the club. They transferred him to Torino. 'The football was more defensive in Italy,' recalls Marchi. 'I went there playing like I did at Tottenham and they said: "No, you can't play that way." Wing-halves weren't allowed over the halfway line.

'I didn't like the way they played. It wasn't an open game like in England. They played with a five-man defence all the time and had another two players who always came back. The football was like it is today in that you could do what you liked without too much tackling until you got to the edge of the 18-yard box. Then it was like a war zone.

'In the end they played me in front of the back five and said I could defend and go on the attack. Basically, I could go where I wanted.'

Marchi noticed that the training wasn't as strenuous since the Italian teams didn't put so much emphasis on stamina as Tottenham. They concentrated more on ball control and tactics. Some of the juggling was quite fantastic.

There were no supporters clubs in Italy in those days, but that didn't stop the fans. They were football fanatics and much noisier than in England. They dressed up and paraded with bands and banners at the big games.

While Marchi was coming to grips with Italian football, Spurs were struggling to play the English game. During Marchi's second year in Italy, Danny Blanchflower was running out for Tottenham's reserves. Nicholson thought Blanchflower's career was coming to an end so he paid a visit to his former captain in Italy.

He wanted to re-sign Marchi immediately. Juventus wouldn't let him go. 'Bill told me he wanted me back at the end of my contract. I thought about the way Juventus kept farming me out from one team to another and I decided that it just wasn't on. So I told Bill, "OK".'

Meanwhile, Spurs went from bad to worse. Nicholson knew something had to be done. He needed to sign a player as the club entered the '60s.

Nicholson first noticed Hearts Scottish international half-back Dave Mackay when he was assistant manager and coach at Tottenham. England manager Walter Winterbottom had asked him to take the Under-23 team to play Scotland. Nicholson didn't watch much of the game because of a serious injury to one of the England players. But he saw enough to convince him that Mackay was a player he'd want in his side.

Nicholson's views were confirmed when he saw Mackay mark the great Johnny Haynes out of a game at Ibrox. Ironically, Mackay rates Haynes as the most difficult opponent he's ever played against. Nicholson saw in Mackay another Ronnie Burgess, a half-back who was quick and could both attack and defend. To be compared with Burgess was the highest compliment any half-back could receive.

But Mackay had already been given as great a compliment by Matt Busby who'd been trying to build a new Scottish team around him. Mackay was made captain of his country for a match against Wales in 1958 – and missed a penalty within 30 seconds of the kick-off!

When Nicholson took over as manager at Spurs he put Mackay's name on his list of possible signings. He asked Hearts manager Tommy Walker about him and was told he wasn't available. But Swansea were prepared to sell Mel Charles, younger brother of the famous John Charles.

Nicholson travelled to South Wales to see Charles, though he wasn't that excited. His best position was centre-half, though he could also play centre-forward. Spurs already had Maurice Norman and Bobby Smith in those positions. Nicholson hoped Charles would tell him he'd like to play in other positions, but he didn't.

The Welshman promised to give Nicholson his answer by Saturday night. He rang to say he was sorry but he was joining Arsenal. Nicholson was relieved. 'OK, son,' he said. 'Thanks for ringing and I wish you all the best of luck with Arsenal.' Charles wasn't too successful at Highbury and soon returned to Wales.

Meanwhile, Nicholson hadn't given up hope of signing Mackay. He again rang Hearts manager Tommy Walker in Edinburgh. 'Our deadline is Monday, Tommy. Can you let me have him?' he asked. 'I don't want to lose him,' replied Walker. 'Look I'm sure we can agree on a transfer fee,' persisted Nicholson. 'Can I ring you tomorrow morning?' Walker agreed.

The next day was a Sunday. This time Walker was more interested in doing business. 'Before I come up would you mind popping round to see him to find out if he wants to come to Tottenham, otherwise I'm wasting my time,' said Nicholson. He wasn't sure that Walker, a religious man, would see Mackay on a Sunday, but he did.

Dave was having tea at his mother's house in Edinburgh on that sunny day in March 1959. The Mackay clan usually got together on Sunday mornings to talk football. Dave had been injured in midweek and hadn't played for Hearts against Motherwell the previous day. But there was still plenty to say about the match.

The phone rang. It was Walker. The Hearts boss wasn't a talkative man, though when he said something it was usually to the point. It was vitally urgent he met Mackay at once. But he wouldn't discuss the matter on the phone. They arranged to meet at Mackay's mother's house.

Mackay waited in agony. He kept going over what had happened to him in the last few days. Had he broken any club regulations? Why did Walker want to see him on a matter so urgent that he couldn't discuss it on the phone? Within half an hour Walker arrived and Mackay soon had the answer.

'Tottenham Hotspur have asked us whether we will agree to transfer you,' said the Hearts boss. 'You may have certain views on the matter and I am not asking you to go, for we think a lot of you. Still, please think the matter over and call into my office around 10 o'clock in the morning and let me know your decision.' He told Mackay that Spurs manager Bill Nicholson planned to travel up to Edinburgh the next day.

Mackay's parents were shocked at the thought of him leaving Scotland. He had his own house nearby and many friends in the area. He seemed to be in an ideal situation. His wife was open-minded. 'If you want to go south and play in English football it's entirely up to you,' she told him.

Mackay had often talked to other Scottish players about their careers in England but, contrary to some reports, he'd never asked for a move. The first time a transfer was mentioned by Hearts or Mackay was when Nicholson approached the club.

Dave thought about the excitement of playing in English football; he remembered teams he'd seen play like Arsenal, Manchester United and Spurs – the only three clubs he'd consider uprooting himself from Scotland to join. Since Spurs were anxious to sign him he told Walker he'd see Nicholson.

Walker phoned the Tottenham boss. 'If we can agree terms and you can agree with him, he'd like to sign for you,' Walker said.

Nicholson wasted no time and immediately caught the night train. When he arrived in Walker's office early the next morning Mackay was already there waiting. 'I've watched you play and sincerely believe you would fit into our scheme of things at Tottenham,' said Nicholson. 'I can promise you that the football we try to play will give you the utmost satisfaction.'

He added that Mackay would be on top wages and he outlined the club's bonus scheme of £2 for a win and £1 for a draw. Nicholson also offered him a house and said Tottenham would, of course, pay his moving expenses. 'Now,' he smiled, 'will you join us?'

Mackay didn't hesitate since he'd already talked over the move with his family. 'I thought, "Hearts are more or less saying to me they're willing to take the money" and so I decided to leave,' says Mackay. 'I actually took a pay cut to go to Spurs, but I knew the maximum wage was going to be lifted within a year. It was all the talk back then. I knew it was going to happen at any time.'

Mackay was on good money at Hearts, including bonuses, since there were no restrictions on players' wages in Scotland. The Scottish clubs tried to keep wages in line with their English counterparts, but some of the Hearts players earned more than the £20 a week maximum wage paid south of the border. At one time Mackay and the other Hearts players were on a bonus of £1 for every goal the team scored and if they won the League or the Cup they got an extra £200.

Nicholson offered Hearts £32,000 for Mackay – a record for a half-back, eclipsing the £30,000 Spurs had paid Aston Villa for Blanchflower. Walker phoned his directors for permission and the deal was completed 12 hours before the deadline.

Mackay was 'elated', especially as Spurs agreed he could live in Edinburgh and train with Hearts until the start of the following season. He didn't know it at the time but he was moving south to join a club which would field one of the most talked-about teams the game has ever known.

Walker took Nicholson to lunch at a local hotel and then to the station to catch the express train to London. The platform was virtually deserted except for the station master in his top hat. He recognised Walker who introduced Nicholson as the manager of Tottenham Hotspur. 'Oh, and what might you be doing here?' he asked. 'Hearts have just sold Dave Mackay to us,' said Nicholson. The station master was shocked. At that moment Nicholson realised how much Mackay meant to the Hearts fans. It must have hurt them to lose such a good player. That made him feel good.

When the news got out that Tottenham had signed Mackay it was one of the biggest surprises of that or any other season. Nobody had suspected Hearts would part with their captain. The less well-informed employees in the Spurs administration office seemed to be the only sceptics.

'It was all built up in the Press that Mel Charles was going to sign for Tottenham and we were disappointed when he went to Arsenal,' remembers assistant secretary Alan Leather. 'Bill was away when we read in the papers that Spurs had signed Mackay. We thought: "Who is this Mackay?" It was Charles who was supposed to set the club alight so when we heard all this we got depressed. The rest is history. Mel did nothing at Arsenal and Mackay became a legend.'

Meanwhile, Mackay's 'elation' at moving to Spurs soon disappeared when he hurt his right foot during training at Tynecastle. He'd already broken it three times and it was getting more painful. The Scottish papers were full of speculation about his injury and the reason Hearts had let their best player go when the club had insisted he wasn't for sale. The rumour was that maybe he'd been sold because of his injury.

When Mackay boarded the train for London to start his career with Spurs he hoped the rest would do him good. But his foot seemed to hurt even more. He stayed in the capital with Arsenal's Tommy Docherty – a friend and team-mate of Mackay's from the Scotland team.

Mackay reported at Tottenham and was asked to join in a kick-about with the 'A' team. Foolishly he said nothing about his injury and played – badly. 'The thought that Spurs had handed £30,000 for me, and I'd crocked myself, never seemed to leave me,' he remembers.

Nicholson clearly recalls Mackay hobbling into his office. But, despite the injury, he knew from the start that Mackay was a mighty player, powerful in the tackle and very fair. 'I will always remember the first day he arrived at our training ground. The other players were shaken by his commitment and drive. They looked at each other as if to say: "What's happening here?" At the time we had a collection of seasoned professionals, most of them internationals, and Mackay was able to stir them all up.'

Cliff Jones had played with Mackay in the Army and knew all about his tremendous ability. But even he was surprised at the difference the rugged Scotsman made. 'He helped give the side the one thing it needed more than any other – spirit. He was the dynamo that made us begin to hum. I'm not going to say that without him we would not have done well, but he made all the difference between a good side and a very good side.'

Mackay impressed his new team-mates in other ways too. 'When I came down in my Jaguar everybody thought I was a millionaire,' says Mackay. 'Very few people had a car in those days, though Blanchflower had one. Everybody in the club used my Jag. It was on hire for nothing. But the first time they saw it they must have thought, "Who's this?"' They were soon to find out.

CHAPTER 10
Dave Mackay

Dave Mackay was born on 12 November 1934 at 18 Glendevon Park, Edinburgh. He was the second child in a family that would eventually grow to four – all boys and all madly keen on football.

His father worked as a linotype operator at the famous newspaper *The Scotsman* where he earned enough money to provide his family with a comfortable life.

When the war started he was called up and like millions of other families the Mackays suddenly found life much harder. The little luxuries began to disappear, though there was always enough food.

At the age of five Dave attended the Balgreen Primary School. He soon took an interest in football and played with his brothers on a stretch of road they called 'our pitch'. He was quite small and often found himself playing against much bigger boys. 'Our generation didn't have the TV set to entertain us. It was a case of football or nothing and I don't think we suffered unduly because the telly hadn't yet arrived.'

Since money was tight during the war years Dave helped his brother Tommy with a milk round in the morning and a paper round after school. In this way 'The Mackay Brothers Organisation' was able to pay 10 shillings a week to help the family finances.

The Mackays became bored with their deliveries very quickly and decided to make the jobs more interesting by taking a tennis ball with them. As Tommy worked one side of the street and Dave the other they developed little competitions.

'One of the most popular was to glide the ball across the road, rush up the garden path to deliver the milk at some houses and be back in time to stop the return "pass" from hitting the kerb,' recalls Dave. 'It was great fun.'

The games helped the boys to improve their ability to pass accurately and quickly. They didn't know it at the time, but they were laying the foundation for their future careers. Both would play for Hearts.

Dave was small for his age but that didn't stop him tackling hard and accurately. 'I stood four feet six inches, weighed less than a jockey, and on a football pitch looked so tiny that it was often suggested that I should have a label pinned on my back to read "fragile",' he says.

Dave was not only tough, he was also very skilful and could kick a ball well with both feet. He was chosen to play centre-half for his primary school. By the time he moved to the Carrickvale Secondary Modern School at the age of 11 he knew in his heart that he was beginning to know a little about the game of football. Dave was picked to play at left-half and enjoyed the challenge of tackling bigger and tougher boys. His passing was also impressive. Dave was soon picked for the Edinburgh Under-15 team and the Scottish Schools' FA's Under-14 side; he went on to captain the Scottish Schools' team.

Mackay supported Hearts and was delighted when they invited him and the other boys to be coached at Tynecastle. The courses had helped many young players to become professionals. Coach Bobby Flavell asked Mackay what he wanted to do when he left school. 'I want to play for Hearts and for Scotland,' replied the confident youngster. 'Good luck,' said Flavell, adding with a smile, 'and there's nothing like ambition.'

When Mackay left school his uncle got him a job at the company he worked for as an apprentice joiner. Mackay tried his best at Lawrence McIntosh Ltd. but he was only really happy playing football for Slateford Athletic, an Under-17 Edinburgh junior team. The Hearts groundsman Matt Chalmers was on the club's committee.

Mackay's performances for Slateford Athletic attracted the attention of leading junior side Newtongrange Star. A new pair of boots and a kit were enough to persuade him to sign and play at a higher grade.

Scottish junior football was full of skilful, ambitious young players as well as ex-professionals. Mackay had a tough apprenticeship. He had to cope with shocking pitches, a sending-off after losing his temper and the hard knocks that came with playing against experienced League players who were now on their way out. It was hard but fair.

Mackay worked hard at his game and the big clubs began to notice. Hibernian made an approach and so did Hearts. In 1952 he signed for the Midlothian club as a part-timer and had turned professional by the end of the season.

Mackay was immediately struck by the gap between junior and first-class football. The training was much harder and the club's whole approach to the game was more professional. There was a lot more to being a top-class footballer than Mackay had realised. He was slightly overawed.

He made his debut for the reserves against Montrose on a day 'so hot the ice-cream man was doing his best business of the year, the 3,000 spectators were down to their vests and not one of them had a word of sympathy for the 22 players belting the living daylights out of themselves as they chased a football when it would really have been more sensible to sit back in the garden in a deck-chair and relax'.

Hearts played well and won 6-2 but Mackay was terrible. 'I played like a schoolboy, had about as much stamina as a retired carthorse and at half-time I was literally out on my feet. How I finished the match I'll never know.'

Mackay was too scared to tell the trainer how the heat and the pace of the game had affected him. After all, Hearts had signed him as a professional. He decided to put in double-training to reach the level of fitness of his team-mates.

The next Wednesday he made his home debut for the reserves against East Fife. Hearts won 2-1. Mackay 'disappeared' after 35 minutes. It was the same story. He was exhausted. His legs felt like lead weights. He had to do something. The solution was to seek advice.

After speaking to his team-mates and coaches Mackay realised it wasn't his fitness that was the problem, though he was determined to train even harder, but he was using up too much energy chasing lost causes. He was running after players and passes he could never catch. He was using up enough energy in the first-half to last for three matches.

Hearts trainer John Harvey prescribed a course of training to reduce the extra weight Mackay was carrying around his hips and to speed him up. The exercises were hard enough to take it out of players who were fitter than Mackay. But he was given extra time off by his boss, a keen Hearts fan who'd once told him he'd never make the grade.

In those early days at Hearts, Mackay didn't realise how long it took a young player to improve his game even slightly when playing at a higher level. But he was improving with every match and, helped by tips on positional play from his coaches, things began to come more naturally.

Mackay began to position himself to intercept a cross or a chip instead of chasing every pass. He learned how to use his head to save his legs. He was becoming a solid attacking wing-half.

The reserves won the Scottish Cup in Mackay's first season, beating Rangers 2-1 in the semi-final. He scored both goals, including a penalty. 'I knew in my heart that I'd put up quite a good show,' says Mackay, 'but what tickled me most was that I'd twice beaten Bobby Brown, the Scottish international keeper who for so long had been among my heroes.'

In the 1953–54 season he made his full debut against Clyde. Hearts lost 2-1 and Mackay was awful. It was no surprise when he was dropped. 'I wouldn't have blamed them if they'd placed me on the transfer list, so shoddy was my performance,' he says.

This time he knew he couldn't automatically step up a grade without teething problems. He needed time to adapt his game to a higher standard. What he didn't realise was that part of the problem was that he wasn't in full-time training. He was still working as a joiner and wasn't fit enough to last 90 minutes because he was working when he should have been training.

After his disastrous debut he thought about giving up League football. The part-time training was getting him down. After a hard day's work he was exhausted. He wanted to go to bed rather than train.

Then suddenly his fortunes changed. One evening, after a particularly hard day at work, he went to watch Hearts play Hamilton in a League match. The club had a rule that every player, even if he wasn't down to play, had to report to the ground on the day of a match.

Mackay was walking across the old tennis courts in his overalls with his football gear over his shoulder when a team-mate told him trainer John Harvey was looking for him. Mackay found Harvey immediately. 'You've been chosen to play tonight, Davie, so you'd better get ready,' Harvey told him.

Hearts, beaten the previous Saturday, returned to top form and won 6-3. Mackay had played well and he knew it. He never again lost his first-team place – and he finished his five-year apprenticeship as a joiner.

Mackay was called up by the War Office in 1955 and reported for duty with the Royal Engineers. He was posted to Worcester. Mackay lived for the weekends when he flew back to Edinburgh to play for Hearts. But the Army did teach him to appreciate the value of planning and discipline.

He played in the Army side with Maurice Setters, Cliff Jones, Duncan Edwards and Eddie Coleman. Edwards and Coleman would perish in Munich along with most of the Manchester United side a few years later. Mackay had lost half a stone and picked up the nickname 'Craggy'. An excellent season was capped with a 3-1 win over Celtic in the Scottish Cup final while he was still in the Army.

When Mackay was demobbed in 1957 he signed as a full-time professional for Hearts at £16 a week plus bonuses. At one time the bonus was a pound a goal. If Hearts won the League or the Cup the players got £200 each. During Mackay's time at the club they won the League twice and the Cup so he did well financially.

His performances for Hearts soon got him international recognition. He had already played for the Scottish Under-23 team when he was selected for a Scottish FA tour in 1957. Once again it was a baptism of fire. He made his debut against Spain, one of the greatest teams in the world at the time. 'Being thrown to the lions was child's play compared with me, keen but inexperienced, being asked to show what little skill I possessed against the ball-playing maestros whose monthly pay cheque read like a telephone number.'

Mackay, known for his hard sliding tackles, was warned that such tactics would be asking for trouble. 'Keep on your feet all the time, Dave,' he was told. But in front of 100,000 Spaniards he forgot all about the advice and had a very poor game.

'I couldn't have tackled a hot dinner on that showing. The Spaniards, as they tip-tapped the ball to one another with the lightness of ballet dancers, made me feel – and probably look – like a pensioned-off carthorse. I tried hard and put my whole heart into the game, but against magnificent footballers of their calibre it just wasn't good enough.'

Just after half-time Mackay received a knock on his right ankle which virtually put him out of the game. 'I'd have been better off the field for all the good I was on it,' he remembers. Scotland lost 4-1. Mackay went to bed that night feeling sick, weary and sure he would never play for Scotland again. But he did.

Mackay played against France in the 1958 World Cup in Sweden and in all Scotland's internationals the following year. He had become their key player.

When Mackay joined Tottenham he found himself in a struggling team. In fact, they were trying to steer clear of relegation and had signed him to help them stay up. 'When I went to Spurs they were second or third from bottom of the League. They didn't have a team good enough to win anything,' says Mackay. 'They bought me originally to save them from relegation.'

He was relieved when Saturday came and he could make his debut against Manchester City at home. None of the other players thought it strange when Mackay tightly bandaged his injured right foot before the game. 'The genial atmosphere in the Spurs dressing-room seemed to ease my fears for when Danny Blanchflower finally grabbed a ball and said, "Let's go, fellows – and the best of luck Dave," for the first time in a week I was anxious to get down to business,' recalls Mackay.

Tommy Docherty and some of Mackay's other friends had warned him that he'd find English football much quicker than that in Scotland. This was partly because Scotland had so many part-time professionals. Full-time training provided the English players with a vital edge.

But in his first match everything went right for Mackay. 'If I went for the ball in a tackle I invariably seemed to win it. When I jumped into the air the ball seemed to make contact with my forehead. Even when I twice wildly kicked clear, the ball flew across the field to Terry Medwin, our right-winger, and appeared to be a perfect pass. The ball ran for me in that match more than I have ever known it run for any other footballer. Even mistakes, and there were many, seemed to react in my favour.' The morning papers were full of praise for Mackay. When he saw them he allowed himself a wry smile. It had been a fantastic debut – even if a lot of it was down to luck.

'I've missed some games because of my foot and I'm not quite match fit,' Mackay told Blanchflower afterwards. 'But wait until next season.' Mackay had been bought to partner Blanchflower in the other wing-half position. 'The understanding that developed between these two giants was immediate,' wrote Julian Holland in his book *Spurs – The Double*. 'Mackay seemed to interpret Blanchflower as though they had played together as boys or, in a previous life, on some wild Celtic field. Mackay's earthy sensibilities provided a perfect foil to Blanchflower's other-worldly inspirations.'

Mackay was quick to cover Blanchflower when he embarked on his regular sorties upfield. For the first time since he came to Tottenham, Blanchflower could concentrate on attack without having to worry constantly about defending as well. When Mackay was drawn into attack, Blanchflower returned the compliment. Inside-forward Tommy Harmer was reborn and Cliff Jones, completely recovered from his broken leg, began to show why he was thought of as the most exciting winger in Britain.

Spurs took twelve points from their last seven games at White Hart Lane – more than they'd picked up at home all season until then. They didn't lose one of the eight games remaining when Mackay joined them, though he only played in four because of injury. Tottenham had finally turned the corner.

The change in their fortunes was timely. It not only ensured their First Division survival. Just as importantly, they'd got their confidence back. Their form towards the end of the 1958–59 season held out great hope for the future.

CHAPTER 11
A Safe Pair of Hands

In the close season Bill Nicholson decided he wanted to sign another goalkeeper. 'We already had two goalkeepers in Ron Reynolds and John Hollowbread, but neither was good enough in my opinion,' he says. 'I wanted an international-class goalkeeper who was going to help us win the Championship.'

Reynolds had proved himself through the years but had been unlucky with injuries at critical times. A few kicks around the head had not helped his eyes and he had to wear contact lenses. Johnnie Hollowbread was a very capable deputy and some people thought he was unlucky to be dropped. But Nicholson could not afford the slightest suspicion of cover for any vital position and had decided that three goalkeepers were better than two.

The Spurs boss liked Dundee's Bill Brown and went to watch him play for Scotland against England at Wembley in April 1959. 'I didn't like the way he brought the ball down, but he was agile and a good stopper of shots,' said Nicholson. 'I thought he improved as the game went on. He is quite a good goalkeeper.' Some thought his modest assessment was designed to hold down the fee.

Nicholson agreed to pay Dundee £16,500 for Brown and then caught the overnight train – one of his regular pastimes when it came to finalising transfer deals. The Scottish international keeper signed for Spurs early the next morning and Nicholson was heading back to London by lunchtime. Brown was to prove one of his best signings.

Brown was born in Arbroath and was an only child. His father worked as a dairy specialist dealing in milking machines and other dairy apparatus. Bill went to the Arbroath High School and soon became known for his football skills – but as a left-winger rather than a goalkeeper! He even played on the wing in a trial game for the Scottish Schoolboys. He switched to goalkeeping after an injury to the regular keeper during a match. The biggest player was asked to take over and that was Bill. He'd been a keeper ever since.

He became an apprentice electrician after leaving school and joined a team called Carnoustie Juveniles before progressing to Carnoustie Panmuire. In September 1949, at the age of 17, he signed for Dundee. He was to be there for eight years.

Brown also played for Scotland, though he was the understudy to George Younger more than 20 times before he got his first cap in a World Cup match against France in 1958 alongside Dave Mackay. But Brown eventually replaced Younger as Scotland's number one.

Despite his international status he had a tough job when he arrived at Tottenham. It wasn't Johnnie Hollowbread, the keeper he was replacing, whose memory Brown had to eclipse but the Spurs legend who'd kept goal before him: Ted Ditchburn.

Hollowbread had done his best between Ditchburn's departure and Brown's arrival. He was a solid performer, but not quite accomplished enough to make the first-team spot his own.

Hollowbread was also an only child. He was born in Enfield and joined Spurs from his local non-League club in 1952. His father was a keeper too and actually played for Tottenham's nursery club Northfleet before joining the Enfield Fire Service.

His son John had to wait six years before making his debut in August 1958 when Ditchburn broke a finger. He kept his place for the rest of the season with a series of impressive displays and got a reputation for bravery because of his courage in diving at the feet of opposing forwards.

But although he did well, Hollowbread was really never more than a stop-gap keeper. He even took a part-time job as a salesman for a firm of wholesale tobacconists and confectioners. When Brown arrived, Hollowbread's position was clear and for the next five seasons he would graciously accept a role in the reserves.

Meanwhile, Brown was battling to win over the White Hart Lane crowd. They still remembered the great Ditchburn – a magnificent goalkeeper and a firm favourite with the home fans. The sight of him leaping acrobatically to grab and hold the ball in mid-air was spectacular. But Ditchburn also made saves no other keeper could possibly make; incredible saves, impossible saves; he was a truly extraordinary man.

Brown was a complete contrast to Ditchburn in both build and in style. Ditchburn was a huge man with big hands, while Brown was tall and thin. The Scottish international just didn't conform to the popular conception of what a goalkeeper should look like.

'He was tall, sure enough, but where the majority of top custodians boasted immense, muscular frames suggestive of barrier-like impregnability, Bill was lean and stringy and seemingly insubstantial; every line of the Brown figure was angular, an effect heightened by his aquiline features,' wrote Ivan Ponting in his book *Tottenham Hotspur – Player-by-Player*.

His physique seemed to defy the laws of calories. 'Bill is one of the biggest eaters I've met,' says Dave Mackay, 'but even if he had a double helping of everything he would remain the same sinewy character who has become the despair of opposing forwards.'

Brown also played the game quietly, without any fuss or trimmings. Unlike Ditchburn, he couldn't do the impossible. In fact, Brown went unnoticed for most of the game. He was a very safe keeper who knew when to come and when to stay on his line. The one occasional weakness in his game was collecting crosses so, usually, he stayed, happy to let his more-than-capable defence cope with the opposing forwards.

Not for Brown the full-blooded rush into a crowd of players on the edge of the 18-yard box to punch or catch the ball spectacularly. The head of Norman, interceptions of Henry or rescuing boot of Baker could deal with the crisis. But when he did come off his line he invariably made the ball his. And when the defence had been breached he was the best man to have waiting behind to tidy up any dangerous attacks by the opposition.

Brown was agile and like lightning around his goal. He was a superb shot-stopper with razor-sharp reflexes. He'd move from one side of his goal to the other in a flash to block a shot with any part of his body. He seemed to make saves as often with an outstretched leg or some other part of his body as he did with his hands, safe as they were.

To develop his reactions Brown didn't play in defence during the six-a-side practice matches at White Hart Lane. He preferred to play centre-forward where his anticipation brought him goals by the dozen. The other Spurs players playfully resented their keeper's killer instinct in front of goal and insisted he was nothing more than a 'poacher'.

Brown's goalkeeping was efficient rather than spectacular, more intelligent than demonstrative, calm rather than brilliant. It took some time for the supporters to appreciate his talents. The fact that he made saves look easy didn't really help him with the fans. They didn't know how good he was. But they could see that his positioning was outstanding. And they became aware of how difficult some of his 'easy' saves were.

Brown also had unparalleled powers of concentration, a vital attribute on those days when Spurs dominated matches, leaving their keeper isolated for long periods. The fans could rest assured that while all the action was at the other end of the pitch, Brown would be there between his posts, half-crouching, totally involved with the match.

Dave Mackay had plenty of opportunity to watch Brown and knew what made him tick. 'I have studied him from the grandstand, from a place behind the goal, and as a team-mate in front of him. Without any argument, the basis of his success is concentration.'

When Brown was on the pitch he pushed everything out of his mind except the game. He was 'in the game' all the time, though even he admits that it was sometimes difficult to concentrate when he had no saves to make. Brown found it particularly difficult to stay focused when it was a cold, blustery day.

But he always used his powers of concentration as best he could. When a forward kicked the ball on the halfway line, Bill was himself kicking that ball and receiving it. He played hard for the full 90 minutes even if the ball was far away from him.

'Such concentration can be wearying,' says Mackay, 'and I've seen Bill, after what should have been an easy game for him, return to the dressing-room after a match looking as tired as if our opponents had been peppering him all afternoon.'

Brown's ability to concentrate was taken for granted at Spurs and when he played for Scotland, but he himself knew that concentration was a skill like anything else and needed to be worked at. One way he honed his mental capacity was by playing golf. He had a handicap of just five.

Mackay knew all about Brown's abilities on the golf course. 'He's the hardest man I've ever met. He doesn't concede an inch; every game demands from him the same concentration he would give if he reached the final of the Open Championship.'

Brown also had an ice-cool temperament and believed that every match should be enjoyed. He refused to get flustered about anything. His consistent approach to even the most important matches spread through the dressing-room and helped to calm the other players' nerves. Brown's unruffled presence was something money couldn't buy.

Unlike most keepers, who were content to boot the ball aimlessly upfield, Brown always tried to find a team-mate. Even his goalkicks usually found the head or boot of a Spurs player because he could place the ball very accurately. So many moves began with Brown. His ability to always find a colleague was an integral part of the team's possession football.

Eventually, Brown became a favourite on the terraces at White Hart Lane. He knew they'd taken him into their hearts the day they started chanting 'Hovis, Hovis, Hovis'. It was a reference to the famous brown bread and a send up of their keeper's surname. 'If the game was going well that's what they'd chant,' remembers Brown. 'It's just one of those things that happened. Londoners are always trying to find you a nickname.'

Nicholson also swooped again during that close season of 1959 to add another fine player to his developing team. This time it was a familiar face who was brought back to Tottenham: Tony Marchi. He returned from his Italian exile in July for £20,000 – less than half what Juventus had paid just two years before.

Italian agent Gigi Peronace again helped to negotiate the deal and when Nicholson told him Spurs couldn't go above £20,000 Peronace was shocked. 'That's too little,' he said. 'Agnelli [the Juventus President] will never accept that.' But he did. Peronace was on 10 per cent! 'They got me back at a bargain price,' says Marchi. 'Bill was a bit tight in those days but I didn't regret going to Italy. It was good for me financially and the experience helped my game.'

Marchi was made vice-captain on his return. His finest days in the white shirt of Tottenham seemed to lie ahead of him, but it didn't work out that way. 'I thought I'd be replacing Danny, but I found myself competing with Dave Mackay. I got back into the side at the start of the 1959–60 season. But then Danny suddenly hit form and I was piggy in the middle. Dave and Danny were brilliant players. I just couldn't get in the side.'

Marchi was consigned to the reserves hoping he'd get a chance to play in the first team at some point. He was to become known as the finest reserve in League football.

CHAPTER 12
The Season Begins

THE 1960–61 SEASON began dreadfully for Tottenham, despite all the hard work the players had put in on the training pitch. The annual pre-season public trial match, watched by 11,000 fans, was a dismal failure. The Blues, or reserves, held the Whites, made up of first-team players, to a 4-4 draw after being 4-1 down.

It was the worst trial game Nicholson had ever seen. 'If there had been no crowd, we would have stopped it,' he said. The one consolation was that the gate receipts went to charity!

On the Friday before the first League game, at home to Everton, Nicholson announced the team: Brown, Baker, Henry, Blanchflower, Norman, Mackay, Dyson, White, Smith, Allen and Jones. Cliff Jones had been chosen to play in an unfamiliar position on the right wing and there was thus no place for Welsh outside-right Terry Medwin.

It was a lean spell by Medwin towards the end of the previous season that resulted in this tactical change. Spurs had lost their knack of scoring goals and, with the Championship having already virtually slipped from their grasp, Nicholson decided to experiment to find a more potent forward line.

Medwin had been dropped for the penultimate match against Wolves and Jones was switched to the right wing, with Dyson coming in on the left. Jones was sure his manager considered the change to be a temporary measure and was certain Medwin would be back in form by the start of the new season.

But things worked out even better than Nicholson had expected in those last two games of the season. Jones scored in both and Dyson's play reached astonishing heights. The switch had set Nicholson's mind thinking. Perhaps he should stick with the new formation and try Jones on the right wing for the start of the season.

After announcing the team for the first League game, Nicholson pulled Jones to one side. 'I'm going to give you a run on the right because that's where we need you at the moment. I think you can do just as well on that side of the field; in fact you might be able to do better for yourself. But if, at any time, you don't feel happy about the position, come and have another talk with me and we'll see if we can sort it out.'

Until then Jones had thought it was a purely temporary step, but because he knew it was in the interests of the team he decided to put everything he had into making a go of things on the right. He knew he could always switch back to the left wing if things didn't work out smoothly. It was to be another inspired decision by Nicholson.

Blanchflower, of course, had spotted the potential benefits of a Jones wing switch even before his manager. When Jones had first joined Spurs he had a tendency to run the ball straight into the players facing him. Blanchflower told *The People*'s Ralph Finn that he thought this fault would be cured if Jones went to outside-right. And it was.

On 20 August, after all the training and the build-up at the club and in the media, the new season finally began. A crowd of more than 50,000 filed through the White Hart Lane turnstiles to see whether Spurs could kick-start their campaign with a win.

The first match programme of the season was upbeat: 'We could hardly have wished for a more attractive fixture with which to open the season than a visit from Everton,' it said. But the game failed to live up to expectations and Spurs didn't look like potential Champions.

The Tottenham team that had been carefully constructed and fine-tuned on the training ground was still running in. The midfield played the same fast-paced fluent football the home fans had come to expect the previous season. But the forward-line was anxious and firing blanks.

Early in the second-half, Jones was caught by a crunching tackle from Everton right-back Alex Parker. 'I was having a nice time,' he remembers. 'I went past the wing-half and Alex is coming at me. I had

John White inside me and I gave him the ball. Then I went outside. I thought Alex was out of the game, but he just kept on coming.'

Jones had played with Parker in the Army and considered him a good pal. 'Alex, I thought we were mates,' said Jones. 'Nay, laddie, not today,' replied Parker. Jones thought he'd broken his leg again. Instead he'd badly damaged his ankle ligaments and would be out of action for a month.

Substitutes were not allowed then so Jones stayed on the pitch. But he could barely limp along the left touchline. He was a virtual passenger reduced to nuisance value.

Both sides were evenly matched and a draw seemed inevitable. But five minutes from time Smith was dragged down inside the 18-yard box. While he screamed for a penalty, the referee played the advantage. Allen latched onto the loose ball and scored. In the 87th minute Smith sank to his knees to head a second goal from a precise chip by White who hadn't put a foot wrong all afternoon.

Spurs weren't brilliant. But there were some hopeful signs. Chances had come their way and they'd have sewn the game up earlier if it wasn't for Everton keeper Albert Dunlop. Baker and Henry performed solidly, Norman blotted out the threat of Everton centre-forward Harris, and Blanchflower, White and Mackay inspired most of the attacks.

But it was Blanchflower who really shone. He covered every inch of the pitch; probed repeatedly for vital openings; and helped his defence with a series of interceptions. He looked precisely what he was: a cultured, classy, stylish footballer.

Those last five minutes against Everton signalled the start of probably the finest season by a club side in English football history. 'In retrospect, it seems merely that they started the season 85 minutes late,' wrote Julian Holland in *Spurs – The Double*.

After their spluttering start Tottenham took off 'like a house on fire' according to Danny Blanchflower borrowing a quote from Robb Wilton. Even Nicholson, the archetypal, dour Yorkshireman was satisfied. '. . . we settled down and played some impressive football,' he said. Coming from the Spurs boss it was praise indeed.

The next game the following Monday night was up on the north-west coast against Stanley Matthews' Blackpool. At 45 Stan wasn't the wizard of old, but he had plenty of magic left in his ageing limbs. He could still slow the game down when necessary and mesmerise opponents with his skills. Even Mackay once backed away hesitantly from the famous shuffle. But even Matthews couldn't save the Seasiders.

Ron Henry, Tottenham's unspectacular but rock-steady full-back, always had a good game against Stan. Henry's secret weapon was preparation. 'We used to study the players we thought we'd be marking. We did that for every game,' he says. 'There was no video playback then, but I used to think about the way they'd played against me the last time. "What does he like? What doesn't he like?"'

'I noticed that everyone watched Stan's body which he'd throw slightly to unbalance you. But the ball was still in the same position. He used to put his leg over the ball and as soon as he did that I'd go for it and usually get it too. You have to study these things in your own mind. I don't think players do that today. I used to say to Jonesy: "When Stan's got the ball I'll hold him there and you come and chase him." At the end of the game Stan would say: "Why don't you bugger off, Jones, you're a nuisance."'

Jones was missing for the Blackpool game but that didn't stop Tottenham putting on a fine display. It was the night they were dubbed 'super' for the first, but by no means last, time in an amazing season. *The Daily Mirror*'s Frank McGhee opened his report with the immortal words: 'Super Spurs!'. He wrote: 'Tottenham . . . appear to have found that essential quality of success – Determination.'

The goals came from the wingers. Dyson got two and Medwin, standing in for Jones, grabbed the other in a 3-1 win. White was devastating. Spurs had threatened to score in every attack.

Blackburn were the next victims. They'd upset Tottenham 3-1 in the Cup at White Hart Lane the previous February on a mudheap of a pitch. But Spurs had been without Mackay that day. He returned the following week and they destroyed Rovers 4-1 at Ewood Park in a League match. Could they do it again this season?

Only 17 minutes had gone when they'd provided the answer with three goals. The fourth two minutes after half-time completely demoralised the previously unbeaten Rovers team. Brown made a series of fine saves to preserve Tottenham's lead, but the game was over almost before it had begun. John Oakley of the *Evening News* described it as 'a dazzling display which would have overpowered any team in the country.' When the League tables were made up for the first time that night Spurs were top.

CHAPTER 13

Smith Breaks a Record

BOBBY SMITH HAD scored one goal against Everton on the opening day of the season at White Hart Lane; he struck twice against Blackburn at Ewood Park; and in between he failed to find the net against Blackpool at Bloomfield Road. On Wednesday 31 August he set the record straight with a hat-trick against the Seasiders. It made him the highest goalscorer in the club's history.

Smith joined Tottenham from Chelsea in December 1955 for £18,000. He'd been at Stamford Bridge for five years after making his debut against Bolton. Although he was a member of the squad which had won the Championship the previous season, he hadn't played enough games to get a medal.

'When Spurs came in for me I didn't want to go at first,' says Smith. 'But [Chelsea manager] Ted Drake had a go at me. He said: "I don't think you'll make it". So I gritted my teeth and thought "I'll make you bite your tongue". I signed for Tottenham and never regretted it.' Smith travelled to Spurs by tube to sign for Jimmy Anderson.

Smith was overshadowed at Stamford Bridge by Roy Bentley and his tactical naïveté in the first few games at Tottenham seemed to explain why. Indeed, things were so bad at the start of his White Hart Lane career that the home fans jeered him as a carthorse – a label he had to fight hard to shake off over the years – and booed whenever he missed a shot. But he persevered and ended up with a respectable 13 goals, having helped Spurs to the FA Cup semi-final in his first season.

Smith was born in 1933 in the ironstone mining village of Lingdale near Middlesbrough, County Durham. It was the same north-east village that had produced the famous George Hardwick. Smith's father was a miner before he got a job at the chemical company ICI.

Smith started playing football for Redcar Boys' Club. They had a ground behind the stand at the Redcar racecourse but no changing-rooms. 'We used to get changed against a wall at the back of the stand,' he recalls. 'But we didn't have anywhere to put our clothes so we used to pile them up and put a mac over them in case it rained.'

Smith was a full-back at first. But one day the centre-forward didn't turn up and he took his place, scoring four goals. His break came when a Chelsea scout watched the Boys' Club play in a Cup final. Smith was originally picked to play at full-back because of an injury to one of the regular defenders. But the centre-forward turned up late and Smith was back in his favourite striking role. Redcar won, Smith grabbed a hat-trick and the scout asked him to go for a trial at Stamford Bridge.

Smith went to Chelsea at the age of 14 to join the ground staff. But he was homesick and caught a train from King's Cross back to his home in the north-east on the very first Saturday. Chelsea asked if his father wanted to come down to London for two weeks to help young Bobby settle down. He said he did and brought his boy back to Chelsea telling him: 'Son, you'll play football if it kills you'. He didn't think so at the time, but Smith now says it was the best thing his dad ever did for him.

At first he stayed with his aunt in Sloane Square, but later moved into digs with a couple of other apprentices. His parents never came to visit him in London. 'My mum didn't like travelling and it was a long way,' says Smith. But he went back to Yorkshire every Christmas. He was feeling more at home in London and was playing well for Chelsea.

Smith attracted a lot of attention in his early games, particularly in a Fifth Round FA Cup replay against Leeds at Villa Park in 1952. His opponent that day was the great John Charles. On a wet, slippery pitch the 19-year-old Smith scored a hat-trick, one goal resulting from a superb mazy dribble that left Charles stranded in the mud long after he'd gone past him.

Some said Smith was too bulky, a crude battering ram who lacked the necessary class. He was to prove his critics wrong time and time again. He was a big, powerful, old-fashioned centre-forward. Sometimes he got caught flat-footed and was flagged offside as the opposing defence moved upfield; he also lacked the ability to take on a centre-half and beat him. But he had skill and, at times, displayed an artistry that belied his bulky physique.

Smith was to make his debut for England in September 1960 against Northern Ireland and went on to establish himself as the country's centre-forward. His international performances helped to relieve him of the 'carthorse' tag.

One afternoon in November 1960 he stunned the Wembley crowd into silence with an inch-perfect chip over the head of the advancing Spanish goalkeeper Ramallets to clinch one of England's greatest post-war victories. Bobby Smith had graced the international stage.

He was only five feet ten inches, not particularly tall for a centre-forward, but Smith was deep-chested and thick-limbed, weighing 13 stone. With his thick jet-black hair and broad shoulders he could have passed for a heavyweight title contender or a husky film star.

Smith put the fear of God into defenders and could be awesomely aggressive. But he was no mere slugger. 'Battling', 'blockbuster', 'bustling' and 'bulldozer' were all labels used by the Press to describe Bobby Smith. Football was a tough profession and there were some hard players earning their living at the game in the early 1960s.

Among Smith's toughest opponents were men like Sheffield Wednesday captain Peter Swan, a good friend and one of his England colleagues, and John Higgins, the captain of Bolton Wanderers. 'One thing about them was that you got stuck in and then afterwards you were all the best of pals,' says Smith.

He played the game simply. When asked to give tips for younger players he said: 'Don't make the centre-half's job easy by standing next to him. If your team have possession in defence then be ready to move back towards your own goal to collect a pass. You'll take many a knock but it is often the build-up to a goal.'

Smith was used to taking knocks. He seemed immune to pain. 'I could take a lot of stick and I've played with a lot of injuries,' he says. Manager Bill Nicholson knew his centre-forward's pain threshold better than most. 'Smith was a tough performer. Often he was injured in matches but would insist on playing on. He didn't miss many games. Sometimes his ankles would be so swollen that he could hardly put his boots on, but he would still go out.'

Not that he allowed anyone to take liberties with him. Smith could definitely take stick, but he could also dish it out as well. 'A centre-forward always takes punishment, but some will take it and others will retaliate,' says Nicholson. 'Smith would give it back and defenders and goalkeepers were always wary of him. I don't think it's unfair that a centre forward should adopt this course, providing he is not deliberately fouling. I would remind Smith: "There will come a time when the bloke who has been giving you stick will be in possession and you can give it him back."'

Smith knew well enough the role he played in the Spurs team. Years later he reflected on his task. 'My job was to torment people so the others could pick up the pieces. I never retaliated [immediately] when anyone kicked me. I just bided my time to give them an elbow. Most people I ever played against accepted that if they kicked me I would kick them back and we got on very well that way.'

In the 1957–58 season Smith had equalled Ted Harper's scoring record of 36 League goals in a season. Now he'd broken George Hunt's record of 138 goals set in the years before the war. Smith's three goals against Blackpool had taken his tally to 141 in five years. Tottenham were hoping their main striker would continue to find the net.

They didn't have to wait long. When Manchester United came to White Hart Lane in early September, Spurs were at their peak. It was as if they had saved their best display for the most cherished and respected of post-war teams.

A crowd of more than 55,000 saw Tottenham take the lead after just five minutes. It was a shocking mistake by United which let them in. Maurice Setters foolishly attempted a pass across his own penalty area which was intercepted by White. He found Smith who couldn't fail to score.

Almost 20 minutes of dazzling brilliance from Spurs, which had the crowd shouting themselves hoarse in admiration, was followed by a second goal. Allen latched onto another White pass and, with rare impudence, dribbled around two United players before firing home.

Blanchflower, Mackay and White were running riot, plying their forwards with a series of cream passes. Their accuracy was faultless; their improvisation inspired. They dictated the pace of the game at will.

United keeper Harry Gregg gave an international performance. If he hadn't, Spurs would likely have been five goals in front by half-time.

Tottenham eased off somewhat after their second goal and Dennis Viollet took advantage of casual play by Norman to pull a goal back. But Spurs were never in danger of losing their grip.

After 65 minutes White brought the ball forward and crossed for Allen to head goal number three. And five minutes from time that man Smith popped up again to score the fourth after Medwin created the opening.

Cliff Jones was still injured and had to watch the match from the sidelines. But he was proud beyond words to see what he describes as 'an outstanding performance' in what was to be an outstanding year.

'John White gave an immaculate performance and I think it was during this game that I realised for the first time just how valuable this slim Scot was to Spurs,' said Jones.

'It was a pyrotechnic display that made the watchers' blood race in the heat and their hair stand on end with excitement,' wrote Julian Holland. 'If it was not clear what heady, revolutionary and inspiring new ideas were being expressed at White Hart Lane in those early matches, there was no doubt after the 4-1 defeat of Manchester United . . .'

CHAPTER 14
Saul Makes his Debut

BOBBY SMITH'S HEROICS came to an end for a while after the game against Manchester United. Opposing defences couldn't stop him but injury had. His replacement was a young red-haired forward called Frank Saul. He was to make his debut against Bolton at Burnden Park.

Most of the Spurs team dreaded playing Bolton, especially away from home. It was their defence that caused the most problems – something Saul would have to cope with if he was to make any impact.

Cliff Jones hated playing against full-backs Roy Hartle and Tommy Banks. 'Wingers always came back from Burnden Park with gravel rash,' says Jones, speaking from harsh experience. The pitch has a particularly high camber at Bolton and a strong tackle near the touchline could easily send a player flying onto the cinder track.

Bolton had finished sixth the season before and would be a tough proposition at home. They'd just signed Irish international Billy McAdams from Manchester City to replace Nat Lofthouse. The legendary 'Lion of Vienna' had 'retired' the previous season with a serious ankle injury. But he then changed his mind and was now trying to recover.

Tottenham, without Jones and Smith, got another scare when full-back Ron Henry went down with a heavy cold. 'Bill asked me how I felt,' recalls Henry. "Not bad," I said. He told me to try to keep warm.'

In the end, Henry played against Bolton, but he couldn't stop them taking a shock early lead when McAdams scored after just three minutes. It seemed that Spurs were heading for their first defeat.

Frank Taylor, reporting for the *News Chronicle*, lost count of the number of Bolton near misses. First, inside-left Ray Parry hit the bar. Then young Freddie Hill shot wide and McAdams blasted the rebound over the bar after Brown had brilliantly saved his first shot.

The 41,000 crowd roared their team on against the League leaders. Then disaster struck. Banks, Bolton's brilliant full-back, tore his right thigh. From that moment on Spurs were playing against 10 fit men. They seized their chance and gradually ground Bolton down.

Five minutes after Banks's injury, White floated the ball over, Bolton's England international keeper Eddie Hopkinson failed to cut out the cross and Allen equalised with a magnificent header. Ten minutes from the end White hooked the ball home from a cross by Blanchflower. It was a truly great goal.

Henry was glad he'd played. 'I sweated out my cold once the whistle went and I felt wonderful after the game.'

Saul hadn't scored in his first senior outing for Spurs, but he did show that he was a fast thinker and a fast mover. 'Frank had joined us from school and was indoctrinated in our habits,' says Nicholson. 'I hoped he might become an established first-team player.'

Saul grew up on Canvey Island in the Thames Estuary and began playing football seriously at the age of nine with the Canvey Boys' team. He started as a left-half but was so keen to move up with the attack that he was soon converted to centre-forward.

Saul was coached by former Tottenham player Sonny Hesketh who took him to Spurs for a trial on his 15th birthday. A year later he was playing for the reserves.

Saul travelled an hour and a half by train every day to get to White Hart Lane from Canvey Island. But the description of him as 'the most travelled youngster in football today' referred to his appearances for the England Youth team in Austria, Italy, Germany and Holland rather than his daily journey to London.

Saul signed as a professional for Spurs on his 17th birthday. A few weeks later he'd made his debut at Burnden Park. Now he had another chance to shine in the next match against Arsenal.

It was the day of the first-ever 'live' game on television featuring Blackpool against Bolton. But the cameras had gone to the wrong ground. They should have been at Highbury. 'This was the game that should have been on TV,' wrote Peter Lorenzo in the *Daily Herald*. 'It spotlighted Spurs at their one hundred per cent best, revealed the fighting heart of Arsenal – and could have served as Britain's finest soccer advertisement for years.'

A crowd of almost 61,000 turned out to see if the Gunners could halt their North London rivals' seemingly unstoppable run of victories. They couldn't. But it was a cracking game. 'Think of everything you desire from a football match and this one had it,' wrote Lorenzo. 'Chessboard moves, spectacular goals, tremendous atmosphere, a thrilling rally, then, to cap it all, a well-taken late winner to give deserved victory to the better team.' Not that the victory came easily.

Spurs were superb in the first-half. White shirts seemed to outnumber red by two to one. Arsenal had no answer to their opponents' silky skills. Tottenham were confident, composed. Whenever a forward became entangled among Arsenal defenders two or three team-mates appeared to give him options. Spurs always seemed to have a spare man.

This time Saul did get on the scoresheet. His first senior goal came after just 12 minutes when he got a lucky bounce and hit the ball first time with his right foot. It screamed into the net. Saul's red head popped up again 11 minutes later to flick on a long throw from Mackay which Dyson headed home.

Tottenham could, and should, have scored more. But they missed easy chances. Arsenal pulled a goal back when David Herd, until then marked out of the game by Norman, hit a hopeful shot which skidded into the net off a post. Four minutes later and a magnificent 35-yard drive from Gerry Ward brought Arsenal level. They were back in the match.

This was the moment for Spurs to show their resilience. In the past they'd often been knocked out of their stride by a setback. Now it was the cue for them to sit back and absorb the pressure until Arsenal ran out of steam. When the onslaught was over, Spurs came back with skilful, neat football. They regained the initiative.

Their third, and winning, goal followed an interchange of passes in midfield. A long, devastating free-kick from Blanchflower put Les Allen clear. He kidded centre-half Sneddon, who missed the ball, and lobbed the winner over Kelsey. Arsenal had been beaten by a sparkling Spurs display.

Tottenham had now won their first seven games to beat a record set by the Preston Invincibles in the League's first season.

CHAPTER 15
The Norman Conqueror

MAURICE NORMAN HAD been the outstanding player in Tottenham's defence during their seven-match unbeaten run. The big centre-half was a six foot one inch powerpack of muscle and athleticism. His shock of black hair heightened the impact of his dominance at the heart of the rearguard.

Norman had many qualities. His aerial ability was priceless. He was superb at intercepting the ball. And his sense of anticipation was helped by incredible speed over short distances which was remarkable for such a big man. 'I was one of the fastest over 25 yards,' says Norman. 'That was all the distance I needed really.'

Norman was slow when he first joined Spurs. 'I was big and thought I was awkward,' he says. Norman set about increasing his speed through intensive training. The big centre-half would sprint along the touchline at White Hart Lane, gauging the distance by the letters of the alphabet lined up along the low wall between the pitch and the Main Stand.

The match programmes included a list of the other games being played next to the corresponding letters of the alphabet: match A, for example, might have been Arsenal versus Manchester City. A club official updated the scores on match days by placing numbered boards next to the letters. Each letter was about a yard long.

Norman needed to be quick because he often had to fill gaps left by his more creative team-mates. But while the training did make him faster, his game was also lacking in other areas. Norman was weak in the tackle and often looked as if he couldn't decide which foot to use to control the ball. He compensated for these shortcomings by intercepting passes before they reached the centre-forward. In this way, Norman could avoid tackling.

His height and long legs enabled him to cut out balls that would have evaded most players. He could climb high to head away crosses, cut off the long sweeping through ball, and block any number of passes with surprising agility for such a big man. But he was slow on the turn and suspect before a centre-forward who brought the ball to him. He was exposed by quick, skilful players with the space to run at him.

Arsenal's David Herd had capitalised on Norman's main weakness at Highbury in 1958, scoring two goals. But in the latest encounter between the North London rivals Herd had been completely overshadowed by Norman. He scored a somewhat freakish goal, but otherwise had been completely dominated by the Tottenham centre-half. Norman had at last become a crucial part of Nicholson's developing team.

It was Arthur Rowe who first put a marker down for Norman. He was high on the list of players Rowe wanted to rebuild the 1950–51 Championship side. He knew Norman was an attacking centre-half, commanding in the air and careful and accurate in his distribution on the ground.

The negotiations with his club Norwich City dragged on until after Rowe had left Spurs. Jimmy Anderson eventually signed him in January 1955 for £18,000 plus winger Johnny Gavin. But just two days earlier, Anderson had bought John Ryden from Accrington Stanley to take over as centre-half from Harry Clarke.

Norman had to play out-of-position at right-back. He did so for three seasons and even won three Under-23 caps for England. It was amazing that a player whose major fault – being slow on the turn – was exposed at right-back for three years. He even honoured his country at Under-23 level in that position as well as winning a place on the England tour that included the 1958 World Cup in Sweden.

Norman was born in the Norfolk village of Mulbarton in May 1934. He began playing football as a centre-forward, turning out for Wymondham Secondary Modern School on Saturday mornings and at inside-left for Wymondham Minors in the afternoon. His father worked as a gardener for one of the Norwich directors and it was inevitable that he'd eventually join the club.

Norman worked on a farm during the day before training with Norwich in the evening. 'They used to gather swedes by hand then,' he recalls. 'I was up at five o'clock in the morning and I used to be dead by the time I went training. I played football two or three times a week. I was never interested in anything else.'

Norman had just come out of the Army when he joined Spurs. He was 21 years old. After failing to get into the Army team he guested for Portsmouth reserves. Now he was about to play with the stars. Not that Tottenham were having a good season. In fact, when Norman arrived they were bottom of the First Division. Amazingly, he didn't even know.

Norman's first match was against Cardiff at White Hart Lane. 'I remember going on the train and trying to find my way across London. I'd never been there before.' Norman was a country boy who'd found his way to the big city.

He was introduced to his new team-mates for the first time just before the match. 'It was like a daze. I went straight into the first team. Inside, I thought I wasn't good enough to play in that side. Alf Ramsey had just left and I'd taken his place.'

Norman lived in digs at Ponders End and missed home life. 'I used to slip off and go back to Mulbarton before I got married,' says Norman. 'I was severly punished.'

But Norman eventually settled down and helped save his new team from relegation in the 1955–56 season and they almost won the Championship in both the next two campaigns. The Spurs centre-half, nicknamed 'Swede' by his new team-mates because of his farming background, had to bide his time at right-back until he replaced the less-than-effective John Ryden at centre-half. It wasn't until the autumn of 1957 that he became the club's established centre-half; and even then he still lacked confidence.

When Tottenham toured Russia in the summer of 1959 Norman took his biggest step to success.

Norman had taken a lot of stick from the fans during the season as he battled vainly to shore up a poor defence. But the Russians loved him as they loved all giants. They gave him the sort of welcome they'd given to big Derek Kevan, West Brom's inside-forward. Like Norman, he'd also never found a place in the hearts of British fans.

After the Russian tour, Norman became the player Spurs always hoped he'd be. With experience had come authority. Ivan Ponting in *Tottenham Hotspur – Player-by-Player* describes Norman's game as 'infused with highly distinctive character, never more evident than when he sallied out of defence, cantering down the centre of the pitch with neck outstretched and long limbs extended in unexpected directions like some fantastic cross between runaway giraffe and quick-stepping spider.'

It was Norman and Harry Clarke, not Jack Charlton as is commonly believed, who were among the first, if not the first, defenders to go up for corners. Initially it was an emergency measure used only when Spurs were losing or desperate to win, but now he went up for corners nearly all the time. Blanchflower would drop back into the middle of the defence while Norman positioned himself at the far corner of the penalty area.

Surprisingly, given a man of his reach and his skill in timing his jumps and heading a ball, Norman hadn't scored that many goals. But his mere presence was enough to distract opponents and open up scoring opportunities for the Spurs forwards. He was to be a useful weapon.

CHAPTER 16
Records Start to Fall

BOBBY SMITH'S GOALS against Blackpool had made him Spurs' record goalscorer and the victory over Arsenal had beaten Preston's record of six wins in a row in the First Division (there was only one Division in the Football League at that time).

Tottenham's next target was Hull City's record for all Divisions of nine wins from the start of the season set under Raich Carter in 1948. Spurs would equal that if they beat Bolton at White Hart Lane and Leicester at Filbert Street.

Bolton scored first, as they had at Burnden Park the previous week. But that didn't stop Spurs, though they needed a disputed penalty to secure the points.

At first, their finely constructed attacks were repelled by the brilliant Eddie Hopkinson in the Bolton goal. But Smith equalised in the 24th minute and then Terry Dyson was supposedly pushed in the back. The referee awarded a penalty, but the decision was late and suspect. Blanchflower coolly stepped up to slot home the penalty and Spurs seized control of the match.

It was no surprise when Bolton's right-winger Brian Birch had his name taken twice in ten frantic, bad-tempered minutes following the penalty (though he was not sent off). Hopkinson was also enraged. He clenched his fists at the Spurs players and twice refused to take goal-kicks because of the relentless booing from the home fans.

Wet, depressed and down to ten men, Bolton conceded a third goal when Smith struck again five minutes from time. They'd been robbed of a match they really didn't deserve to lose. Spurs now needed one more win to equal Hull's record.

Next up were Leicester City. Smith scored first, Riley equalised and then Smith struck again. Spurs never looked in danger after that. The short passing of Blanchflower, Mackay and White supplied the artistry which Leicester couldn't match. They'd equalled Hull's record of nine wins from the beginning of the season.

Towards the end of September, Spurs reached even greater heights at home to Aston Villa. But they didn't just extend their winning streak, they positively rejoiced in the sheer pleasure of doing so. Villa were behind after just six minutes and were eventually slaughtered 6-2. Spurs turned the magic on and off at will. The work they'd done on the training ground at Cheshunt bore fruit as they found all the open space they needed.

It was 4-0 at half-time courtesy of two goals from White, one an exquisite volley, a soft tap-in from Smith and another from Dyson. In the second-half, after a fifth goal from Allen, they became a bit casual. Nicholson seemed annoyed that they appeared to have slackened off. Villa came back and scored twice.

But Spurs had saved the best for last. Henry played the ball to Mackay who knocked it to Allen. He passed to Dyson who feinted to unbalance the defenders. Then an ear-splitting Scottish voice screamed for the ball. It was Mackay again. Dyson, with a broad grin, lobbed it forward. Mackay volleyed home.

It was Tottenham's tenth straight win. At the end of the match a telegram arrived from Hull conceding the record of wins from the start of the season.

It was the quality of their play more than anything else which distinguished this Spurs team from all those that had come before.

By now, even the reporters couldn't find the words to describe their performances. 'Nothing I can write can remotely convey the majesty, rich theatre, and sheer entertainment of Spurs' enchanting brand of football,' wrote Alan Hoby in the *Sunday Express*.

The following Saturday they went to Molineux to face Wolves. Tottenham scored four times but might have won by ten or more. The goals came from Jones, Blanchflower, Allen and Dyson. Blanchflower's goal was a beauty. He picked up the ball 30 yards out, moved forward, and struck a firm drive into the far corner of the net.

After the match the Wolves captain Billy Wright came into the Spurs dressing-room. 'If a team ever beats you lot I'd be choked not to see it,' he told the players. 'You're the finest side I've seen.'

Tottenham's use of the long ball, the style of play favoured by Wolves, was devastating. Their display was described as 'soccer magic' by no less a legend than Tom Finney in the *News of the World*.

But the most telling comments came from Wolves manager Stan Cullis. 'Spurs are the finest club team I've ever seen in the Football League,' he said after the match. 'This present lot are better than the great side of ten years ago.'

CHAPTER 17
The Tension Mounts

AS SPUR'S LONG run of League wins continued the tension mounted. The thousands of fans turning up to watch Tottenham all over the country were there as much to see them beaten, or at least drop a point, as they were to see their entertaining brand of football.

But while the Spurs fans suffered the pressure, Bill Nicholson and his players were having a good time. There were fewer international matches in those days, which reduced the strain on the players. There was also less strain on the manager because his team didn't have to win to stay in business, as is the case at some clubs today.

After the 11th win reporters asked Nicholson if he felt the tension. '"What tension?" I asked. "It's just a job of work. If you keep losing you get the chop. If you keep winning you win a trophy. Even the players appreciate that."'

Dave Mackay remembers how relaxed they were. 'Nobody seemed to be worried about anything because we always thought we were going to win. We were super-confident. And if we really played well it was very hard for anybody to beat us.'

The team ran up the tunnel and out onto the pitch to the tune of 'MacNamara's Band'. And they always appeared in a particular order. Brown came behind Blanchflower; Norman was always last; and White didn't mind where he was as long as Jones was behind him. 'I don't suppose we'd ever play any worse if we were ordered to take the field in another order, but when superstitions like this cost nothing why ignore them?' says Jones.

Mackay always carried a ball when he came out onto the pitch. And he oozed confidence. As he ran out he'd throw the ball high into the air shouting across to the other team: 'Have a kick now because you won't get one when the game starts.' When it came down he'd kill the ball stone dead. His control was frightening. It was meant to be.

Every goal provided the players with a moment to relish. They expressed their joy by embracing each other after they'd scored. The Press criticised them for what they called 'a-huggin' and a-kissin'. The behaviour was called 'un-British', 'effeminate' and 'childish'.

But it was a release. The mutual admiration reflected their joy and exhilaration, excitement and sheer pleasure at scoring. Blanchflower knew it was good for his team-mates to show their enthusiasm in this way. It was never brought up in the dressing-room. Bill Nicholson just said: 'I wish I could see it every five minutes.'

The celebrations were good therapy and eased the tension. The players may have looked relaxed in the heat of battle, but some of them were uptight before games. Goalkeeper Bill Brown was as cool as a cucumber on the pitch, but he was very nervous before matches. 'I had butterflies before a game and was sick to my stomach,' he remembers.

Brown's antidote was cigarettes. 'I smoked before the game because of my nervous disposition. In fact, I smoked a pack a day all through my career. But once I got on that pitch it was just a job of work. I switched off the crowd. The bigger games didn't worry me. They were just the same to me whether it was Wembley or the training ground.'

His smoking habit followed in the footsteps of Tottenham's great inside forward Tommy Harmer. Nicholson didn't allow the players to smoke in the dressing-room before a match so they'd go to the washroom. 'There were only two toilets,' recalls Maurice Norman. 'They were the old-fashioned ones and Tommy Harmer was always in there smoking. The only way to get him out was to light a piece of paper and shove it under the door.'

Harmer was so addicted he'd even slip away for a cigarette at half-time. Some of the other players also smoked, but more out of habit than to cure their nerves. 'I used to smoke back then,' says Ron Henry. 'It did me no harm. We'd smoke in the dressing-room after a game. And we'd even get into the bath with a fag.'

As the season progressed, the players came closer together off the pitch as well as on it. There had always been a good atmosphere in the squad, but with success came a tighter bonding. They closed ranks to cope with the demands of the fans, the Press and opponents who had an extra bite to their game when they played the runaway League leaders.

'The camaraderie was brilliant,' remembers Tony Marchi. 'Everyone used to have a go at each other. We laughed a lot. I was a reserve for most of the season, but I felt a part of all that.'

'To have a successful club you've got to have nice guys, although they've not got to be so nice that they're frightened to have a go if you do something wrong,' says Dave Mackay. 'But it was a happy atmosphere. I enjoyed it. We played some wonderful football.'

The players may have been nice guys, but they also had an edge to their game. With Mackay, Norman and Smith in the team they were never going to be pushovers. Even in training they had a 'do or die' attitude. A lot of that was down to Mackay. When he joined Spurs the atmosphere changed.

Nicholson noticed the difference at once. 'Suddenly our training routines became just as important as the matches,' he recalls. 'Six-a-side games and full-scale practice matches assumed a greater importance. Mackay had to be a winner. His barrel chest would be thrust out and he would emerge on the winning side, no matter what the odds against him. If he had served in a war, he would have been the first man into action. He would have won the Victoria Cross.'

Mackay epitomised the determination that could be found at all levels throughout the club. He hated losing whether he was playing snooker, cards or football; whether he was at Old Trafford or in the Spurs gym; whether he was playing a one-on-one against John White, a five-a-side or a crucial League match. He thrived on competition.

But Mackay was also well liked at Tottenham. He got on with everybody except in the mornings in the gymnasium when he was 'nobody's friend'. When former England manager Terry Venables joined the club in the mid-'60s he got first-hand experience of Mackay's resolute attitude. 'I remember the first day Terry had at the club,' says former Spurs captain Alan Mullery. 'In the very first minute of the five-a-side he stuck his backside out and knocked Dave Mackay over. Dave got up and kicked him and it led to a right old scrap.'

The training routine during the season was designed to keep the players in top condition. They reported to either White Hart Lane or

Cheshunt just before 10 o'clock every morning to pull on their numbered kit.

On Mondays, trainer Cecil Poynton took the first team training. Poynton was devoted to Tottenham Hotspur Football Club. He'd played for Spurs in the 1920s and was the last player to be sent off, way back in 1928. He had a dry sense of humour and a deep love of the game.

The odd man out in training was goalkeeper Bill Brown. 'They didn't know what to do with goalkeepers back then,' says Brown. 'Bill [Nicholson] used to say to me, "What do you want to do?" and I'd say, "Just give me a couple of players" and I'd get them to take free-kicks against me. I'd also take part in the ghost football and stuff like that which kept me occupied.'

After training at White Hart Lane the players usually went to one of the two local pubs, the Bell & Hare or the White Hart, next to the ground on Tottenham High Road for a half-pint of beer, or a shandy, and some lunch. 'About half a dozen of us would have a meal and a chat,' recalls Mackay. 'It was good for team spirit.'

The players also went to the pub on Saturdays after home matches. Their favourite spot was the Bell & Hare though they also went to the Corner Pin. They were rarely seen in the main bar but could usually be found in a private room at the back called the Buttery Bar where they'd meet their wives, friends and invited guests.

'The owner usually kept that room for us,' remembers Bill Brown. 'We were the attraction for the rest of his customers. The fans used to give papers to the barman so he could pass them across for us to autograph.'

Dave Mackay could usually be found chatting at the bar to his mate 'wee Dyson' as he affectionately called him.

A pint in one of the pubs near the ground is a pastime that goes back a long way with the players at Spurs. Even today some of the 'push and run' side, like Len Duquemin and Les Bennett, drink in the Corner Pin. The 1960–61 team were carrying on a long-standing tradition.

On matchdays the players' wives – eight of the first team were married – would meet at the club in their own Ladies' room where they could bring guests to chat over tea and sandwiches before watching their husbands from the stands. 'They used to serve dainty little cakes, and a lady made the tea and chatted to you,' remembers Sandra Evans, the daughter of assistant manager Harry Evans and John White's future wife.

'It was wonderful. You used to see a lot of people you didn't know but because you saw them each time you went you just used to say hello,' says Maurice Norman's wife Jacqueline. 'We were on a high and the high lasted a long time.'

There was a bar but the alcohol was strictly limited. It was also very unusual for a women to cross the threshold into the man's world of whisky and cigars in the boardroom. The first lady allowed into the inner sanctum was actress Jayne Mansfield. If there was a celebrity like her at a match then the players were also invited along for a drink. It was all part of the special treatment laid on by the Tottenham board.

Mansfield caused quite a stir when she watched Spurs beat Wolves 5-1 (on 10 October 1959) at White Hart Lane with her second husband, muscle-man Mickey Hargitay. Bobby Smith vividly remembers her visit. 'I met her and she put her arms around me. She said, "You've got lovely legs" and someone at the back shouted out to her, "And you've got a lovely bust".'

Mansfield was later described as the 'bosomy sexpot of Hollywood films' so the comment was perhaps appropriate even if it did cause a ripple of embarrassment among the directors. (Mansfield was to die tragically in 1967 when she was decapitated in a car accident near New Orleans as she made her way to a television engagement.)

But while the club occasionally catered for a special female visitor like Mansfield, the players' wives were generally kept at arm's-length. And not all of them, for different reasons, could come along to the matches.

Bill Nicholson's wife Darkie didn't come. 'In the first place there were our two little girls who needed looking after,' says Nicholson, 'and then our friends would come home after the match so Darkie had to get a meal for us when we arrived at about six or seven o'clock.'

Betty Blanchflower was another wife who didn't go to that many games, particularly the Saturday matches. She also had children to look after. 'I was in London without any family and very much the housewife and mother. I sometimes took pot luck with baby-sitters, but I didn't have a social life. I missed out really.'

Betty Blanchflower generally got on quite well with the other wives and girlfriends. 'There was always that bit of jealousy because Danny was a transferred player and got a better house, but that was all.'

At first Sandra Evans didn't mix with the players' wives very much. She thought there was some resentment towards her because her dad was the assistant manager. There were also more practical reasons. 'A lot of them were married with kids and I had only just left school,' Sandra remembers. 'But they were a nice bunch.'

Of course, not all the players were married. Peter Baker, John White and Terry Dyson were all bachelors and enjoyed their freedom. Dyson could often be found at a dance hall called the Royal Tottenham. Sandra frequently saw Baker, Dyson and even some of the married players, like Mackay, at the Royal.

'A crowd of them used to go. The married ones didn't bring their wives, but it was harmless fun,' says Sandra. 'We'd dance the twist and rock & roll. A Spurs fan called Dave Greenaway, a sort of male groupie about my dad's age, used to come and pick up myself, Lynn, who became Peter Baker's wife, and a few others. He'd take us to the Royal and bring us home afterwards. The supporters do a lot when they like a team.'

In 1960 they had one hell of a team to like.

CHAPTER 18
The Ghost

SPURS HAD CHANGED from a fine team to one of genius. They were flexible and inventive. They could change the pattern of play with one pass. They probed and prodded patiently, waiting for the right opportunity to open up a defence. When it came they struck without mercy.

Much of the transformation was down to Scottish international John White. He'd taken over from Dunmore at inside-left when he first played for Spurs but was too similar to the club's other great inside-forward Tommy Harmer. Nicholson was reluctant to break up the Blanchflower-Harmer link so he moved White to the right-wing. It was a waste of his talent.

When the 1960–61 season began, White took over from Harmer at inside-right and became the general of the forward line. White had a mobility Harmer never possessed. He could lose his marker seemingly at will. White was also more of a team player. He could improvise an attack instantly or contribute to a move fashioned by another player.

'He is always looking for the open space and the alternative position that can mean so much to the man in possession,' said his pal and room-mate Cliff Jones. 'I always seem to do more running when John isn't playing. When he's there I always know there will be an "extra man" waiting for my pass.'

White's play was masterful and his genius dazzled most teams. 'He does so much intelligent running that he seems to cover the whole width of the field,' said Jones. White had a slender, almost fragile physique. But it was filled with untold stamina and amazing energy. His wiry frame seemed to cover every inch of the pitch during a match. White just never stopped moving.

He was known as 'the Ghost' because he would float into positions and catch opponents by surprise. He was a play-maker in every sense of the word, a subtle schemer who could dominate a match without the crowd even noticing. You had to play alongside him to really appreciate his contribution. He often pulled all the strings in midfield.

White had an almost perfect understanding of the importance of space. He would move stealthily into position unnoticed by defenders. His tip for young players was to never be still. 'People talk about open spaces in soccer,' said White. 'They are not there to be seen. You have to create them by your own hard work and positional play. Inside-forwards who stand about are easy meat for the opposing wing-half. Always be looking for the sudden diagonal burst behind the defence.' It was good advice.

White's control was superb. His passes were almost always perfectly weighted. 'He could control the ball from any angle and in such a way that a defender couldn't take it off him,' says Nicholson. 'He was such a good passer, either short or long, left foot or right foot, and his vision was unsurpassed. He was a very positive player who was always looking to get round the back of defenders.'

The one criticism levelled at him by some of his team-mates was that he didn't use his speed enough. He was fast, there was no doubt about that, but often he'd get past a player only to check his run too soon, thereby giving his opponent a second chance.

As a teenager, White had been rejected by Rangers and Middlesbrough because they said he was too slight. Bill Nicholson was a shrewder judge of character and refused to be put off by White's deceptive build. He knew that as a cross-country runner he could go the distance. White was born at Musselburgh, Dave Mackay's home town. When his father died his mother was left to bring up four children on her own.

White played on the wing as a boy for teams like Prestonpans YMCA, Musselburgh Union Juveniles, and Bonnyrigg Rose. He became an apprentice joiner and was signed by Alloa. They once offered him to Charlton for £3,000. But the South London team turned him down.

Falkirk bought White for £3,500 in August 1958 and turned a 500 per cent profit 22 months later when they sold him to Spurs for £22,000. Falkirk's manager, former England winger Reg Smith, had called White 'the most complete footballer I have ever seen'.

When John White joined Tottenham in October 1959 he was still in the Army doing his National Service. Stationed at Berwick, he had to make a 700-mile round trip to London to play for Spurs. The strain showed in his early games when he faded towards the end of matches. But he worked hard on his fitness and gradually improved his self-confidence.

White wasn't from a cosmopolitan background. When he first came to London he took a taxi from King's Cross Station. He couldn't believe there were shops and houses all the way to Tottenham. 'In those days things were a lot different between the north and the south,' recalls Sandra Hart, who was to become White's wife. 'They thought you were really trendy if you were from London.'

When White was demobbed, Spurs couldn't arrange digs for him because it was the August Bank Holiday weekend. Sandra, the daughter of assistant manager Harry Evans, had only just left school when White came to London. 'They wouldn't sort out anything posh like going to a hotel in those days so my dad said: "We have a spare room. He can come and stay with us for the weekend and we'll sort something out afterwards."'

Sandra's family had moved up to London from their home in Farnborough, Hampshire in January 1960. She remembered seeing John when she was still at school. 'I had seen him a couple of times and I thought he was quite nice. But he was very shy and I was very shy too.'

Sandra was going to the pictures one night in London near where she worked for the Canadian Civil Service when John asked her what she was going to see. 'I can't remember the film, but he asked if he could come with me. I said, "OK" and then we started going out together.' Sandra was 18 years old and had just finished her 'A' levels. John was 24.

'It wasn't difficult living in the same house. It seemed natural. He used to come home for lunch. My mum always cooked a lunch for him and my dad. Then he'd often go back training. He was very conscientious. Or he played golf. He used to do things around the house, building and making things.'

White, with his shock of untamed hair and ready smile, looked like the entertainer Tommy Steele. But he was very shy away from the adoring crowds who applauded his skills. 'I remember going to a dance at the Trocadero in London,' says Sandra. 'When we walked in the band started playing the Spurs song "MacNamara's Band". John came out in a sweat he was so embarrassed, yet he'd play football in front of all those crowds.'

But White wasn't lacking in personality and when he became more settled at Tottenham he developed a reputation as a practical joker. He was one of a quartet, including Dave Mackay, Cliff Jones and Terry Dyson, who spent hours playing games with a coin. One of them would think up a stunt and challenge the rest to repeat the feat.

They might flip a penny up from foot to forehead, catch it on their foot and flip it up again so it landed in their pocket. Or they'd start with the coin on their instep, flip it up and catch it on their forehead and then slide it down the lower part of their leg onto their instep again. They'd compete with each other to see who could do it the most times.

White could have been in the circus he was so good at juggling. He was always performing with a ball. He'd flick it onto his thigh, chest, thigh, instep and then the back of his neck before rolling it down his arm and back onto his instep. Give him a car key, an orange or a penny and he'd juggle any of them as easily as a football. The ball seemed to obey his every command and some of the Spurs players thought he could go on forever.

White and Jones were always up to something. Their repertoire included pulling chairs away as their team-mates sat down and hiding their clothes when they got changed. It was schoolboy humour, but it helped to lighten the atmosphere. On one occasion, the team was staying in a hotel in Sheffield where they were playing a First Division game. The players had been to see the film *Spartacus*. When they got back to the hotel most of the players went to the dance hall for a cup of coffee. Suddenly, White and Jones appeared at the top of the stairs with their trousers rolled up. 'They had half a table-tennis table each and one of those long ash trays,' recalls Ron Henry. 'They came down the long staircase pretending they were Spartacus. They used to get up to all sorts of things.'

Another time the Tottenham players were in a private compartment on a train travelling to an away game. The window was open just slightly. 'I bet you can't chuck your shoe through that small opening in the window,' Cliff dared Whitey. John thought it couldn't go through but when he threw it the shoe flew out of the window. Sensibly, he'd thrown Cliffie's shoe instead of his own. 'Jonesy had to ask the trainer for his football boots because he didn't have another pair of shoes,' remembers Ron Henry. 'That's the sort of thing they used to get up to.'

On the pitch White was more characteristic of Nicholson's concept of the game than any other player. If Spurs were to lift the title then John White was the man who held the key to their hopes.

CHAPTER 19
The Winning Streak Ends

IT HAD TO happen sometime. Spurs had played 11 matches and won them all. The run couldn't go on for ever. And it didn't.

Manchester City were the team that brought it to an end in a Monday night game under floodlights at White Hart Lane. It had been moved from the Saturday because of an Ireland v England international in Belfast.

Smith and Blanchflower were representing their respective countries so Spurs took advantage of the League rule that if a team had two or more players involved in an international they could postpone a League match taking place on the same day.

City had dented Spurs' hopes of winning the Championship the previous season, and if anything, they had a more skilful team this time around. The cultured football served up by both teams was such a joy to watch that the result seemed almost irrelevant. Except that it wasn't.

Spurs started off well enough. After 27 minutes Smith headed home what looked to be the first of a host of goals. At half-time the near 60,000 crowd gave Tottenham the loudest ovation many of the journalists present could remember hearing at any ground in the country.

Spurs had fired in 25 shots to just five from City. They could have been at least five goals ahead. In the first few minutes of the second-half White and Smith might both have scored. They were at their best and the 12th win looked secure.

Then former Crewe winger Clive Colbridge cut in from the left and rifled the ball into the far corner of the Spurs net past Brown. The Tottenham players protested that Colbridge had handled the ball but the referee pointed firmly to the centre spot.

Spurs pulled out all the stops to try to restore their lead but they were a little impatient, a touch over-keen. Too often, they resorted to hopeful crosses from the wings. It wasn't their trademark and didn't sit easily with their usual precise build-up play. When they did break through, City's keeper Bert Trautmann was equal to the task.

In the 80th minute City almost snatched the winner. Fortunately for Spurs, right-winger Colin Barlow blasted the ball over after being left with an open goal following a sparkling run from that man Colbridge.

The winning streak had ended because the Spurs forwards didn't take their chances. There were enough of them: 39 shots against 9, 14 corners against 2. But they were all wasted with the exception of Smith's solitary headed goal. It was the highlight of City's season. They slipped down the table and struggled against relegation for most of the campaign after their superb battling display against Tottenham.

The winning run may have ended, but defeat was still a long way off. The next victims were Nottingham Forest. Bill Nicholson was ill and couldn't travel with the team, but he would have been delighted with their display. The hopeful cross was replaced by measured passes.

Spurs scored four times, through White, Mackay and a couple from Jones. They were three up inside 25 minutes and eased up in the second-half.

One of the Forest players told Peter Baker: 'The League should come up with a reason for just giving games away. We have no chance against you.' *The People* gave the whole team a mark of ten in their Form Report – the first time it had ever happened. 'Every Spurs player was 100 per cent . . . you just can't single out one man,' wrote *The People*'s Ralph Finn. 'They were all wonderful, and for the first time in my soccer history I've scored full marks to every member of the team. Believe me, Spurs are worth it.'

CHAPTER 20
Baker and Henry

SPURS KEEPER BILL BROWN had only one save to make against Forest. That was because the defence in front of him was superb. There were no finer full-backs, as a pair, in the country than Ron Henry and Peter Baker.

They hadn't been capped by England. And there were others who, individually, were better players in that position. But some of the shrewdest commentators in the game rated Henry and Baker as the best combination of backs in the Football League.

Henry was one of twin brothers born in Shoreditch, London on 17 August 1934. The addition of the two boys brought the family to a grand total of five brothers and a sister. When the war came the Henry's got bombed out and young Ron was evacuated with his family to Redbourn, near St Albans in Hertfordshire.

Henry's father was a furrier by trade. During the war he had to travel all the way from Redbourn to Bermondsey in South East London.

Henry played regularly for the Manland Secondary Modern School at Harpenden and also for the Harpenden District team at county and national schoolboy level.

When he left school, Henry worked at the Empire Rubber Company in Dunstable. He was paid £8 a week. He also joined Redbourn and Harpenden Town in the Mid Herts Premier League and Herts County League. Henry played outside-left and never thought of himself as a defender.

He had a trial for Wolves at outside-left and then played as an amateur for Luton's 'A' team in the Metropolitan League.

Henry was called up for National Service in December 1952 and was paid 25 shillings a week. He did his basic training at Oswestry and was sent to join the Royal Artillery at Woolwich. He then volunteered to go to Korea after the war there had started.

'I was waiting on the square at Harwich at 5.30 in the morning to catch the boat to Korea when I was suddenly marched off and told to see the Sergeant-Major,' says Henry. 'In his office at 8.30 the next morning he said, "I hear you play football." I said, "Yes, a little bit," and he said, "OK. Would you like to be permanent staff here?" I said yes, and so they sent me back to Woolwich. I stayed at the guards depot.'

Henry spent the rest of his two years with the Royal Artillery at Woolwich where he met another left-winger by the name of Terry Dyson.

They both played for the Army XI. 'I basically went through the Army with Terry,' recalls Henry.

Since Henry was based so near home he also played plenty of games for the Luton 'A' team. It was at Woolwich that Spurs manager Jimmy Anderson first saw him play. He was suitably impressed by the reports he'd heard and sent one of the Tottenham scouts to sign Henry.

'We used to get a coach to football and this particular day it was pouring with rain,' remembers Henry. 'I was under the boot with Terry Dyson when this little old man came to the back of the coach and said to me, "Who do you play for son?" I said, "No one. I play for the Army." He said, "I've been watching you. Would you like to play for Spurs?" I said yes. "Sign this paper." he told me.'

Henry signed amateur forms since he couldn't be a professional while he was still in the Army. 'He asked me when I got demobbed and I told him 2 December,' recalls Henry. As soon as he was demobbed Henry signed professional forms for Spurs, not that he knew what he'd placed his signature on.

Henry returned home three weeks after being demobbed. He had little time to enjoy his new-found freedom before his mother was on at him. 'When are you going to get a job?' she asked. 'Leave me alone, Mum,' protested Henry, 'I've just come out of the Army.'

Shortly afterwards Henry received a telegram from Tottenham asking him to phone the club. When he got through he was connected to Arthur Rowe. 'Where have you been?' said Rowe. 'There are three weeks' wages waiting for you here.' Henry got the next train to White Hart Lane.

He was paid £5 a week by Spurs, a sum that didn't exactly fill his father with enthusiasm about his new career. 'My father said, "What? You're getting £5 a week? That's not very good when you were earning £8 a week at the Empire Rubber Company."'

'I knew it wasn't well paid, football, but it was the joy of playing for Spurs. We didn't do it for the money, although we'd have never said no to a bonus. You signed your contract, got your money, and there was nothing more you could do about it.'

Henry signed as a professional on 13 January 1955. He worked his way through the 'A' team and the Combination side and three months later made his first-team debut at home to Huddersfield. In May 1955 Henry married a Redbourn girl called Edna. She worked at Brock's, the famous fireworks manufacturers, in Hemel Hempstead. Edna watched all her husband's matches until their son Stephen arrived in May 1957. She missed the football a lot when she couldn't get to games any more.

But at least she found herself closer to White Hart Lane when they moved into a club house at Ponders End, Enfield the following November.

Meanwhile, on the pitch Henry had been switched from centre-half to left-half and then left-back. His problem was the form of Welsh international Mel Hopkins who'd made the left-back position his own.

Henry was Hopkins' understudy until November 1959 when the Welshman was badly injured in an international match at Hampden Park. It was a cruel blow for Hopkins, but it opened the door for Henry.

Henry had been on Spurs' books for four years, but was still an unknown when he got his chance. Even then he was never viewed as anything more than a second choice. It was assumed that as soon as Hopkins had recovered Henry would stand aside for the Welsh international.

But Henry wasn't going to waste his opportunity. He wouldn't give up his place in the first team without a fight. Gradually, as the weeks and months passed, something happened to him. Like some of the other supposedly less talented players in the Spurs side he flourished.

Suddenly it became clear that this modest, unassuming defender had two invaluable qualities: a natural positional sense and speed. Six months after he'd stepped out from Hopkins' shadow Henry had cemented his position in the first team. It was Hopkins who was now forced to play Combination football. Henry knew better than anyone else how that felt.

'Ron was stronger in the tackle than Mel, good in the air and possibly more composed on the ball,' says Nicholson. 'Mel was long-legged and, like most players of that build, he found tackling more difficult than a shorter man with stockier legs. Mel was unlucky because he broke his nose and lost his place to Ron and was unable to regain it.'

Henry's elevation into the first team helped to strengthen the Spurs defence. This steady, cultured, accomplished full-back brought consistency to a rearguard which lacked confidence and was often caught out of position when under sustained pressure.

Henry's presence seemed to be a calming influence on Norman and Baker, while Brown now had a solid, unflustered defence in front of him. Henry was transformed and seemed to be playing above himself almost every week. The fact that he was keeping good company helped.

Henry responded to the promptings of Blanchflower and Mackay. He was like a worker ant, always busy fetching and carrying for his masters. He also devised ways of helping his team-mates build attacks by making himself available for a reverse-pass and even taking the odd corner.

Once Henry had possession he would slip a pass inside to Mackay and then race up the wing to give the 'craggy' Scot an option. He always remembered Bill Nick's sayings: 'The man without the ball makes the play'. Henry knew the importance of space and did his best to find it.

'We were defenders,' says Henry, 'but we could attack from the back too. The one thing Bill insisted on was that we always had the ball in front of us. We were never allowed to have the ball knocked over the top of us and then scramble back.'

'Henry learned to enjoy his football till he was joining in the touchline jokes of Mackay after playing a part in some particularly dexterous close-passing triangle that had subtly taken the ball away from danger,' wrote Julian Holland in *Spurs – The Double*.

But as much as he enjoyed joining in when Spurs attacked, he was always aware of his defensive duties. He had to be with Mackay in front of him. 'Many times I thought, "Where's bloody Mackay?" He's been in the outside-right position and I've got his inside-forward and my outside-right and I've got to jockey the pair of them. But I always got back and when I knew Mackay was back in position and I'd got cover then I could have a bite at one of them.'

Henry was a consistent all-rounder with a reputation for perfectly timed sliding tackles. He performed sterling work in the Tottenham cause by ushering players away from the goal until help arrived. When it did he made one of his crisp, but always fair, challenges. Rare indeed was a missed or bungled tackle by Ron Henry. It just wasn't his style.

If there were criticisms of him it was that he could be slow on the turn and was too left footed. But his slowness in turning was deceptive. It was rare indeed for a winger to get past him and, if he did, Henry would chase back to make his tackle.

And while he preferred his left foot, he was also happy to use the right when necessary to take part in Spurs' many attacks. Besides, his predecessor, Alf Ramsey, was criticised for being ponderous on the turn and yet he was the best full-back of his era.

Henry's accomplice was Peter Baker. He was Ramsey's understudy before he broke into the first team. Baker made his debut against Sunderland in April 1953 alongside Bill Nicholson. He was one of the few members of the 1960–61 squad to play with Nicholson along with Mel Hopkins.

Baker was born in Hampstead. As a schoolboy he excelled in most sports, winning trophies as a quarter miler, a javelin thrower and a cross-country runner. He was also a talented footballer.

Baker joined Enfield before signing for Spurs in 1952. He looked to be the natural successor to Ramsey both at Spurs and for England. Tottenham manager Arthur Rowe even told England boss Walter Winterbottom that Baker would be an ideal replacement for Ramsey.

He would have secured a first-team place with most other clubs in the country much sooner than he did but Ramsey was still the obvious choice. Baker had to be content with being his understudy. But he learned a lot from Ramsey and could be thankful for that.

Then suddenly something happened to Peter Baker. He failed to fulfil his early promise. When Ramsey left in 1955 Baker suffered from the weight of expectation and the challenge of replacing an England international. When the responsibility was thrust upon him he was found wanting.

'In my earlier games I tried to follow the high standards set by Ramsey, but my anxiety to do this resulted in several mistakes,' said Baker. 'Arthur Rowe helped me smooth matters out. He stressed that Alf's style took him several years to perfect and that his standard could not be achieved by a youngster with only a few years' experience. "Play your own style and, above all, be fast and direct," was his advice.'

Baker found there was nothing 'natural' about succeeding Ramsey. He found thc right-back position filled, not by himself, but by Charlie Withers. Then manager Jimmy Anderson bought Maurice Norman from Norwich to fill the right-back slot.

Baker, though disappointed, was not giving up without a fight. He may have been consigned to reserve-team football, but he'd listened to Rowe's advice and his game gradually improved in the less rarefied atmosphere of the Football Combination.

Meanwhile, Norman was struggling at right-back. 'He told Anderson, "I can't play at right-back, not with Danny",' recalls Baker. 'Danny was a pure attacker and Maurice was exposed.' Norman wanted to play at centre-half where he had players around him. 'He felt good there,' says Baker. 'He had players to gee him up. At full-back you're so exposed. Maurice didn't like that. He hated it if a winger ran past him.'

Baker regained the right-back spot in 1956–57 and survived a challenge from Johnny Hills the following season.

He was fast, intelligent, composed and reliable. It was just as well for Spurs that he was. Like Henry, Baker often had two players to mark, courtesy of the privilege of playing behind Blanchflower.

'Danny was always half-way up the field creating havoc and I had to plug the holes behind him,' says Baker. 'But it worked out very well. We had a 2-3-5 formation then, the old-fashioned way. The full-backs had to cover the centre-half and when Danny was attacking I'd push up on my side and Maurice Norman would come across.'

Nicholson had faith in Baker and knew his worth even if the fans didn't. 'The crowd sometimes criticised him for not marking his winger more tightly, but I never worried. The fans overlooked that he was playing behind Blanchflower and often Danny would be caught out of position. By holding off, Baker gave the rest of the defence more time to cover and by leaving his winger free he persuaded the opposition to play the easy-option ball out to the wing and away from danger.'

Blanchflower also realised the importance of Baker's contribution. 'Would Ramsey have been as successful behind a player like me as Baker was?' he said in comparing the 1950–51 side with the 1960–61 team.

Baker's play had been lifted by his team-mates. He probably couldn't have reached such heights in any other team. The promptings of White, Mackay, Blanchflower and Jones had given him the confidence to improve his game and play an important role in the Tottenham team.

Baker had been a professional with Spurs for ten years and in that time had become a cool, dependable defender. Like Henry, he eschewed the rash challenge, preferring instead to shepherd attackers away from danger until cover arrived. He was brave and feisty; his tackling was fearsome; and he liked nothing better than urging on his team-mates.

Baker always did the simple thing. He followed the Tottenham rule: never waste a ball. Baker avoided fancy footwork that could get his team into trouble, preferring instead to play a simple ball to Mackay or Blanchflower, or square it across the pitch to Henry or Norman. Occasionally, though, he'd produce an unexpected long through ball to his forwards which could open up an opposing defence in an instant.

Baker's distribution was nearly always accurate and his positional play was improving fast. He was an unfussy, unspectacular player. But Tottenham needed him, and Henry, as much as any of their 'star' players. They may not have cost a large fee, but they were invaluable.

'There isn't a member of the Spurs side who doesn't realise the big role played by the full-backs Baker and Henry,' said Cliff Jones. 'In fact, I regard them as the best pair of backs in the country. Speaking as a winger I would say the strength of their game is their positioning and distribution – but you can take it from me they are faster than average and can tackle with power and a crisp sense of timing.'

CHAPTER 21
The Unbeaten Run Goes On

NEWCASTLE WAS THE venue for Tottenham's next match. In those days Britain's motorways weren't as extensive as they are now so the players travelled mostly by train instead of coach. The club booked a private compartment to take them to away matches.

The trek to Newcastle was long and the players filled the hours playing cards, reading or talking football. 'We enjoyed going away on the train,' says Tony Marchi. 'We'd get a table and start a card school. Sometimes we travelled overnight which was very tiring.' The card school nearly always included Bobby Smith, Terry Dyson and Dave Mackay.

Smith and Dyson were good mates and liked to gamble. Dyson was more successful than Smith but they could always be found together at the dog track or in the betting shop. They didn't mind if it was the dogs, horses or cards as long as there was a wager.

Smith used to bet a week's wages on a horse. 'It doesn't sound a lot now, 20 quid, does it?' he says. 'He was a fearless gambler,' says Dyson. 'If you loaned Bobby money he could only pay you back if he won a few bob!'

On one occasion the squad went to a hotel for a mid-season break. When Nicholson settled the account he questioned the size of the phone bill, claiming it was exhorbitant. It turned out to be the cost of calls made by Smith to his bookmaker in London. 'I had a local bookie hammering at my door once for £500, and Billy Nicholson got to hear of it,' remembers Smith. 'That was a lot of money in those days. They were phoned bets and most of it was down to a couple of my team-mates. The bookie came after me because I was the name who played for England. The publicity got a bit nasty but my mates finally settled.'

The Newcastle match was one of the games of the season. More than 51,000 crowded into the stadium – 17,000 more than Newcastle's biggest gate so far. Spurs were a big draw. Of course, those on Tyneside were hoping the men in black-and-white stripes could end Tottenham's unbeaten run. After 33 minutes Len White took a square pass from Ivor Allchurch, rounded three players and hammered the ball home. A goal down, this was not the Tottenham of old who crumbled at the first setback. They'd learned from harsh experience and knew there was a long way to go before the final whistle. Patience was the virtue which they carried with them into battle.

On this occasion their patience was hardly tested. It took only two minutes for a floated cross from Dyson to deceive Newcastle keeper Brian Harvey, and Maurice Norman stretched out his long neck to equalise with a firm header. Then disaster struck – and it was Norman who undid all his good work as, a minute after scoring, he miskicked to White who drew Brown and then watched in delight as Henry helped the ball over the line.

At the interval the Spurs players trooped dejectedly into the dressing-rooms. It was the first time they'd trailed at half-time all season. They thought Nicholson would have a few choice words to say about their performance. But they were wrong. 'Well played, lads,' he said, 'and go on playing as you are playing and you'll win.' It was a great example of Nicholson's human approach to his players. He knew they needed encouragement and was perceptive enough to give them a boost instead of a rollicking.

In the second-half, Newcastle slipped up again when Harvey pushed a back pass out to John White who fired home. Just before the hour, Cliff Jones put Spurs ahead for the first time, though he looked offside. Then, after 62 minutes, it was Brown's turn to misjudge a cross, this time from Hughes. He could only watch in horror as the ball floated into the net. With four minutes to go and the crowd all but settling for a draw, Smith met Allen's cross to score the winner.

The Spurs players had little time to celebrate at the final whistle. They had to rush from St James's Park to the station to catch the last train back to London. The train always waited a little longer than usual for the away team to arrive, but it still departed at five o'clock sharp. Most of the players were only half-changed when they breathlessly climbed on board.

When Cardiff arrived in London from Wales on the first Saturday of November, Tottenham had gone 14 games without defeat and were four points clear of Sheffield Wednesday. But the mounting tension was beginning to affect the way they played.

In the first-half against Cardiff they looked nervous and vulnerable to attack. After 20 minutes inside-forward Peter Donnelly ran through the middle unmarked and beat the advancing Brown to put Cardiff in front.

Tottenham's play was as overelaborate as Cardiff's was straightforward. The Welsh side played a quick, open game which had the Spurs players chasing shadows. Then suddenly, when the match could have got away from them, Tottenham woke up.

The inevitable equaliser came in the 35th minute after a series of passes that had class written all over them. A Medwin throw found Mackay who crossed for Dyson to nod home. He celebrated with his solo war dance. Of all the Tottenham players, Dyson was the most animated when he scored.

Dyson was the son of the famous jockey 'Ginger' Dyson and with the same red hair as his father. He used to ride horses out during his school holidays for a fellow called Bill Dunn. 'The first horse I rode out ran away with me, but he used to do that with everyone,' recalls Terry.

At five feet three inches Dyson was the ideal height to take up the silk himself. 'I thought of becoming a jockey but you have to weigh about seven stone and I was too heavy.' Instead, he played non-League football for Scarborough before joining the Army.

He was spotted by a Tottenham scout while playing in the same team as Ron Henry for the Royal Artillery against a Guards team. 'Courage?' Arthur Rowe used to say. 'You should have seen him play against the Guards at Windsor.'

Dyson scored five goals on the same afternoon that brought Henry to Spurs. They were asked to go to Tottenham for a trial from their base at Woolwich. 'I'd never been there in my life,' says Terry. 'I remember I got on a bus at Manor House and the conductor put me off at Spurs.'

When he arrived, Dyson was told he was playing away against Crystal Palace reserves. Jimmy Anderson was in charge and Spurs drew 1-1. Terry scored the goal. 'I didn't think I'd played that well, but then I played against Oxford and scored again.'

He signed for Spurs as an amateur in December 1954 while he was still in the Army. When he was demobbed in April 1955 Terry became a professional. He signed the forms in a little cafe outside the Woolwich barracks.

Terry played well for the reserve side and after just seven weeks he got into the first team. 'I was supposed to be playing against Luton reserves but when I got to White Hart Lane to meet the team coach I was told, "You're not playing away at Luton, you're playing here."'

Johnny Gavin scored five goals that day for Spurs and 'never hit the back of the net once' remembers Terry. He was in and out of the team as understudy to England winger George Robb, a school teacher who played for Tottenham as an amateur. 'When he was injured I played,' says Terry.

Dyson was a regular in the Football Combination team for some five years, making only occasional appearances in the first team. But he always expected that some day he'd establish himself in the senior side. His hopes seemed to have been dashed when Spurs splashed out £35,000 for Cliff Jones from Swansea Town in February 1958.

Terry saw the transfer as a shattering blow to his pride and his future at Spurs. He knew Cliff was a great player but he was fed up with always being the stand-in and never the star. He made it clear that he wouldn't mind leaving White Hart Lane.

There was a long queue of managers waiting to sign up the man known as the 'Tearaway Tyke'. But he decided to stay and fight for a first-team place. Terry's big break came towards the end of the 1959–60 season when he replaced out-of-form Terry Medwin on the left-wing, with Cliff Jones switching to the right. Nicholson was looking for the right formula among his out-of-sorts strike force. The missing ingredient seemed to be Dyson.

A series of impressive displays at the start of the 1960–61 season, when Cliff Jones was injured, secured Terry a permanent place in the team. He had taken his chance with both hands and played his heart out. He made it impossible for Nicholson to leave him out.

'I was in and out of the side every year, but in 1960 I got in. Until then Terry Medwin and Cliffy were the regular wingers. Bill sometimes dropped Terry and played me, then dropped me and played Terry. But there was no ill-feeling. We were friends. Besides you couldn't get annoyed with the other player because it was the manager who picked the team.'

Dyson was perhaps less skilful than Medwin but he always gave 110 per cent and was willing to run for 90 minutes. 'He was tremendously enthusiastic and never let himself be bullied out of a game,' says Nicholson. 'If I had to nominate a player who had the attitude I wanted, it was Terry. He needed no motivation.'

Dyson thrived on the left-wing in front of his best mate Dave Mackay. He roomed with Les Allen when the team stayed away overnight, but him and Dave were muckers. They socialised together and their closeness off the field was reflected in some fine performances on the pitch.

Dyson linked effectively with Mackay, but he had a roaming role in the side. One minute he'd appear alongside Bobby Smith, looking to get on the end of a cross or a through ball, and the next he'd be back in his own box snapping at the heels of opposing forwards.

Dyson might drift to the right-wing to free Jones or drop deep to support Henry by giving him an option for playing a one-two out of defence. The one place you wouldn't find him was on the left touchline waiting for the ball.

He knew the advantages of his flexible role in the team. Asked to give his tips for young players he had this to say: 'If you get a roving commission, use it. Be ready to link up with a team-mate anywhere along the line. And don't run into trouble if a pass can be made to carry a movement on. Matches are won with goals. And it's a winger's job to get them, so don't be frightened of having a go.'

Dyson was beginning to score regularly for Spurs and his goal against Cardiff was vital. No one took more delight in scoring than the Tottenham left-winger. After grabbing a goal he was the first past the nearest goalpost and onto the track with his arms spread wide to the heavens; then he'd run back to his team-mates and sink himself in their welcoming arms. 'There isn't a man in the team who takes greater relish in scoring a goal than our Mr Dyson,' said Jones.

Dyson was joined on the scoresheet against Cardiff by the man with whom he'd so often competed for the coveted left-wing position: Terry Medwin. The fast-improving Les Allen went on a dazzling run down the right before slipping a precise pass inside to Medwin in the inside-right position. The Welsh winger crashed the ball into the back of the net to put Spurs ahead before half-time.

The ever-smiling Medwin had joined Spurs before his Welsh compatriot Cliff Jones. They'd grown up together and were good friends. But it was Medwin's misfortune that he was always being compared with Jones on both the international and domestic stage. Jones was one of the finest wingers in world football so it was natural Medwin would suffer by comparison. He was nonetheless a skilful player.

When asked for his birthplace Medwin often replied: 'I was born in prison'. In fact, his father was a warder at the Swansea jail and Terry was born in a prison officer's house. The prison overlooks Swansea Vetch Field ground and if they played badly the fans would shout: 'Send the prisoners down to watch this as extra punishment.'

Medwin was one of seven children, the other six were all girls! He was a good footballer and was soon playing for Swansea Schoolboys and the Welsh Schoolboys team. He spent a lot of his boyhood around the seaside resort of Mumbles Bay – and would return there with Spurs for training and relaxation during their 1961 FA Cup campaign.

Terry lived outside the entrance to Swansea, while Cliff Jones' house was behind the main stand. Medwin was three years older than Jones but it was quite remarkable how closely their careers developed. They went to the same school, St Helen's, met their wives while still at school, both played on the wing and were in the same Welsh Schoolboys team.

When Medwin left school he worked as a mechanic in a local garage and signed as an amateur for Swansea. On his 17th birthday he signed as a professional but still worked part time in the garage. He played with Jones in the Swansea third, reserve and senior teams.

Medwin was a traditional speedy winger with skill and flair; a gifted player and an opportunist. He was first picked for Wales in the 1952–53 season when he was just 21. But Swansea switched the young Medwin to centre-forward and with the change of position his opportunities to play for his country became more limited. 'I didn't get any caps for a few years because I was playing centre-forward so I made that an excuse to get away from Swansea,' says Terry. 'I wanted to play outside-right to get back in the Welsh team.'

Spurs, Manchester City and Leicester were interested in signing him. 'Roy Paul, the former Wales captain, was at Manchester City at that time and he was after me. But London appealed to me. It took six hours by car and five hours by train from Swansea and didn't seem too far.'

There was also a strong connection between Tottenham and Swansea: Ron Burgess, the Swansea manager, and his assistant, Arthur Willis, had both been members of the famous 'push and run' team of the early '50s. Swansea wanted Medwin to join Tottenham.

'I wouldn't say I was pushed into it but they wanted me to go to White Hart Lane,' says Medwin. The newspapers were full of speculation that he'd soon be joining Tottenham. But Medwin had never been to London and that worried him a little. He decided to skip the last game of the 1955–56 season at Swansea and instead travel down to watch Spurs. 'I did it off my own back and caught the 6.15 train. If they wanted me to go to Spurs then I wanted to see the place.'

When he arrived in London, Medwin called a friend in the entertainment business who had a season ticket at Tottenham. 'I made for his house and he took me to the ground,' says Medwin. 'I sat in the stand and thought it was magnificent. It was like going from the local cinema to the Palladium.' Spurs manager Jimmy Anderson didn't know what to do and asked Medwin why he was there. The Swansea winger told him: 'If you want to sign me I want to come here and see the place.'

Tottenham were playing Sheffield United on that final Saturday of the season and Bobby Smith scored a hat-trick watched from the stands by Medwin. The Welshman signed three days later for £18,000 and a £10 signing-on fee.

Medwin was a young man with a wise head on his shoulders and he was determined to continue working part time as well as playing football. After joining Spurs he took a job at an engineering works at Waltham Cross run by one of the Supporters Club vice-presidents. He was settled in London with his wife Joyce, whom he married in 1953.

The family lived in a club house in Palmers Green a few minutes' walk from Bobby Smith, Cliff Jones and Mel Hopkins.

The slight, smiling, eager Welshman was well liked at Tottenham, not least by Nicholson. 'Terry Medwin was one of the most pleasant people I ever came across in football,' said the Spurs manager some years later. 'He was always happy and cheerful and would talk to anyone.'

But Medwin never achieved the level of performance Spurs had hoped for and was eclipsed not long after his arrival by the brilliant Cliff Jones. He lacked the killer instinct that both Dyson and Jones had. Medwin filled in for the injured Jones in the early part of the season, but he'd struggle to get a regular first-team place despite his goals.

Tottenham had taken control against Cardiff after half-time and began to play some superb football. White was at his best, teasing and tormenting the defence and creating a hatful of chances. But the forwards were still not firing on all cylinders. Allen and Smith, who, until now, had been joyfully scoring with ruthless confidence, missed easy chances.

In the end it was a harsh penalty decision which clinched the match for Spurs. A Dyson cross was handled by right-half Steve Gammon and the referee pointed to the penalty spot. The Cardiff players protested that it was an accident. Blanchflower ignored the furore and slammed the ball high into the net.

CHAPTER 22
Cliff Jones Returns

TOTTENHAM WERE STRUGGLING more than at any time since the season began. The missing piece in the jigsaw was Cliff Jones. His darting runs and ability to keep possession when Spurs were under pressure were sorely missed. As his team-mates said, if they ever needed a rest they'd simply give the ball to Jonesy.

He was the one player Bill Nicholson would allow to hold the ball. But even Jonesy was only expected to run with it occasionally. He played more within the framework of the team at Tottenham than he did for Wales. But out of all the players at White Hart Lane he was unique.

'He always looked as if he'd be something special,' says Ken Jones, Cliff's cousin and later a renowned sports writer.

Mackay once said of Jones: 'Spurs won't have any trouble when they want to get rid of you. They'll just have to give you a ball, set you running, open up all the gates and you'll disappear up the Tottenham High Street.'

But Jones had suffered his share of injuries in the early part of the 1960–61 season and after missing a string of matches with an ankle injury sustained in the first game against Everton he was again sidelined after injuring his knee in a mid-week inter-League match versus Italy. That game had kept him out of the previous fixture with Cardiff.

There was little doubt he was sorely missed and Nicholson decided to take a chance on Jones' fitness for the next League encounter at home to Fulham. Although his knee restricted his speed, Jonesy headed two great goals. All that heading practice as a teenager at Swansea on the advice of his father was clearly reaping dividends. Nicholson's gamble on Jones' fitness had paid off.

Cliff was a very brave player who was always willing to risk life and limb in the Tottenham cause. Dave Mackay described him as the most fearless player he knew. The fans came to appreciate his unrivalled courage and his willingness to get among the boots and limbs if there was the slightest chance of scoring.

'There was no braver player in the game than Cliff,' said Nicholson, 'and for a small, slight man he scored some memorable goals with his head.' He told him: 'The defender cannot afford to make a mistake with his timing of the cross, while you can. Take a chance.' Nicholson wanted Cliff to make the best of every chance he had to meet the ball ahead of his marker. The price the Spurs winger paid was a few cuts around the eyes and the head, but it never put him off his game.

Against Fulham he showed all his remarkable courage to ensure another victory. His first goal, and Tottenham's second, was a brave effort considering the attempts made by Fulham's left-back Jimmy Langley to reach a low cross from Dyson with his boot.

Tottenham had a real fight on their hands for the first hour of this match with Mackay struggling to contain England inside-left Johnny Haynes after switching to right-half to mark him. But all Haynes' good work was undone by the profligacy of his forwards who failed to take advantage of his accurate passes.

'Fulham inside-right Jimmy Hill, who should have had at least two goals, rarely put a foot right all through,' wrote Jack Peart in the *Sunday Pictorial*.

Jones scored a second, 15 minutes from the end, to put Spurs 3-1 up just when Fulham were gaining control. Tottenham won 5-1. Jones had returned in the nick of time.

The win over Fulham was Tottenham's 15th in 16 matches. They had 31 points, seven more than their nearest rivals Sheffield Wednesday who'd lost ground in a goalless draw at Old Trafford on the same day. Even Nicholson had the feeling they could win the Championship. 'Looking back it was almost won after those first 11 matches. You draw the 12th and then win the next four and you're in with a great chance. At the time there was a great feeling amongst the players. They did their work, got stuck in and enjoyed it. It was hard work but they were keen and conscientious.'

Cliff Jones was also aware of how important Tottenham's incredible early-season form had been for the club's title ambitions. 'During that early part of the season the months of March and April, with their needle League matches and thoughts of Wembley, seemed a hundred years away. Yet, although we didn't realise it then, we were already laying a solid foundation . . . Even as we were sweeping all before us in those early stages, we were building up a bank of confidence, a reservoir of team spirit, on which we were able to draw for the rest of the season.'

They would need all their confidence and spirit as the title race began to heat up. There could have been no finer showdown than the match arranged for the following Saturday; Spurs were due to visit Hillsborough.

CHAPTER 23
The First Defeat

'HERE THEY COME! Tottenham Hotspur, proud leaders of the League and, undoubtedly, *the* team of the moment. Hats off to them. Unbeaten in their first 16 League matches they have dropped only one point . . . They have scored 53 goals against 18 conceded. Truly, a magnificent achievement.' That was how the Sheffield Wednesday match programme welcomed the arrival of the Spurs on Saturday 12 November 1960.

The match had been eagerly awaited by the Wednesday fans for weeks and the club expected a crowd of 50,000 for the first time that season. As it turned out, almost 54,000 came through the Hillsborough turnstiles to see if their heroes could become the first side to beat the runaway League leaders.

Spurs had been up to Sheffield as the League's top team in three out of four years. The previous season Wednesday had ended Tottenham's 12-game unbeaten start to the campaign by beating them 2-1. Of the 24 League matches between Wednesday and Spurs at Hillsborough since 1909 Tottenham had won only once – in the 1937–38 season.

And it wasn't only history that supported the Owls' hopes of stopping Tottenham. They also had an impressive home record and were almost unbeatable at Hillsborough. The eight previous clubs that had travelled to play Wednesday had all been beaten. They had a 100 per cent home record; Spurs were unbeaten. Something had to give.

In some ways, defeat was now seen by many commentators as essential to Tottenham's Championship hopes. The constant pressure of being top of the First Division was enough without carrying the burden of being the League's only unbeaten team.

The players themselves insist to this day that they didn't feel any pressure when they were winning, but their performances on the pitch told another story. In their last few matches they'd struggled to play the open, fluent, attacking football that had graced League grounds across the country. Their play needed to be loosened up.

There was little chance of that happening inside a packed Hillsborough. It was a huge game for both sides. Wednesday would adopt their usual defensive posture and try to grind out a result. Spurs were bound to attack. They couldn't play any other way. The contrast in styles was one of the attractions of the game that everybody in the country wanted to see or at the very least hear about.

Could Wednesday close the seven-point gap at the top of the table? The neutrals hoped they would at least open up a chink of light in the title race. Wednesday, a side which cost just over £17,000 to assemble compared to the £250,000 it took to put the Spurs together, were determined to battle it out all the way.

The strapping England defender Peter Swan was told to snuff out Bobby Smith. Alongside him was the red-headed Tony Kay and the burly Don Megson. All three were rugged defenders; tough, mean, abrasive players who set the tone for the match itself.

Swan and Kay were soon to be banned from football after being caught up in a bribery scandal. But no amount of money would have swayed them from their task against Spurs. They'd decided to block Tottenham's charge for the title as if their lives depended on it. The match was the most physical encounter Spurs had experienced all season.

Bill Nicholson knew Wednesday were always a hard side to play against and would be difficult to beat. His worst fears were confirmed. 'I always expect a tougher game the further North I go,' said Nicholson. 'This is an accepted part of football. It's not that the players in the South are soft; merely that those in the North are hardier.'

The game was described as 'a rip-roaring tussle of temper, tantrums and tremendous excitement' by Gerry Loftus in *Reynolds News*. Wednesday had the upper hand in front of their roaring fans during the first-half. Their defence was superb and was never really troubled by the Spurs forwards.

But, ironically, it was a bad back pass by Swan which gave Allen the first clear chance. He had all the goal to aim at but reserve keeper Roy McLaren made the save of his life. From his clearance the diminutive Bobby Craig whipped in a cross from the right. Little-known winger Billy Griffin, who'd only just changed wings, fired the ball past Brown. The Owls fans were elated; the roars of the Spurs fans silenced.

Just three minutes later Allen tore down the left and a linesman flagged for a goal kick. The ball did cross the line but the referee had already blown for a free kick to Spurs. Mackay centred and Norman charged forward to head home the equaliser. The noise from the Tottenham fans was revived. The Wednesday supporters were left in a state of despair.

That psychological blow by Spurs came at a vital stage of the game and seemed to have altered the balance of the match. In the early stages of the second-half Tottenham began to knock the ball about comfortably as they'd been doing for most of the season.

Then Megson ran down the wing and put in a beautiful cross which Keith Ellis first headed over Norman and then fired against a Spurs defender. Wednesday's England Under-23 international and inside-left John Fantham gleefully crashed the loose ball home. It was not a memorable goal, coming as it did from a mix-up. But the Wednesday fans didn't care. They erupted in a roar of delight, sensing a famous victory.

Blanchflower, of course, was having none of it. He clapped his hands and tried to rally his troops. Mackay joined him and tore all over the pitch. Norman began to take chances by running at the Wednesday defence from inside his own half. But the home side had an iron grip on the match and wouldn't let go.

It started to get rough after Wednesday had taken the lead and the referee had to talk to two players from each team. The one real attack by Spurs almost ended in a bitter brawl when Wednesday keeper Roy McLaren was nearly knocked out. Unusually, Tottenham were giving away far too many fouls. They only just held onto their dignity.

When the final whistle went, Blanchflower ran to congratulate Owls captain Alan Finney and the teams walked off the pitch arm in arm. But a linesman still had to report Peter Baker to the referee after the game was over. The Tottenham full-back was given a stern lecture. It had been that sort of match.

Nicholson and Wednesday manager Harry Catterick were old rivals. As the Spurs boss left Hillsborough he shook his fist, only half in jest, at the Owls manager. 'When you come to us, we'll give you more of this!' he told him. Years later, when Catterick had moved on to Everton, the club's chairman John Moores would hold Spurs up as the example he wanted to see copied at Goodison Park.

So Tottenham had failed to equal Liverpool's League record of 19 matches without defeat at the start of a season set in 1949. Spurs' run of ten straight wins away from home, including two from the previous campaign, was also ended. The critics said they were about to crack. The players knew otherwise.

In fact, far from being dejected, the Tottenham party sang and cheered in the coach all the way back to Sheffield Midland station. 'We were saying on the coach back that we were relieved to be beaten,' says Ron Henry. 'It was a load off our backs. It relieved the tension. We didn't worry about how many games we were going to lose, but how many we were going to win.' The tension had been dissolved. They could relax at last.

CHAPTER 24
Allen Comes of Age

SPUR'S FIRST LEAGUE game after their setback at Hillsborough was at home to Birmingham City. In the past it had taken Tottenham teams quite a few matches to recover their form after a defeat. They'd traditionally been a temperamental side which couldn't bounce back quickly.

But this Spurs side was different. They had the ability to play each game on its own merits and not let defeat get them down. Against Birmingham City they were back at their best in the sunshine at White Hart Lane and seemed able to turn the heat on their opponents at will.

They scored three goals in 17 minutes and another three in the last 19 minutes. The victory was inspired by Les Allen. The ex-Chelsea forward didn't score, but he made three goals and matched his more expensive colleagues in the art of being in the right place at the right time.

Allen was born in Dagenham, Essex – a town known for its Ford car factory and its footballers. Spurs and England full-back Alf Ramsey, West Ham captain Bobby Moore and the Chelsea duo of Terry Venables and Jimmy Greaves all hailed from Dagenham.

Allen worked for Ford's and he almost pursued an engineering career instead of a footballing one. But he'd already been recognised as a young player of exceptional talent and, at 16, helped his club Briggs Sports reach the semi-final of the Amateur Cup. Ironically, Allen played for Spurs as an amateur, but he was spotted by Chelsea and signed professional for the Stamford Bridge club after joining them at the start of the 1954–55 season.

Allen was seen by many as another of Chelsea manager Ted Drake's youth prodigies who never quite lived up to his early promise. But others said he was the best number nine at the club since Roy Bentley. Drake himself described Allen as 'the best young football-playing centre forward in the First Division' during the 1956–57 season. But Allen was too often the scapegoat among the Stamford Bridge faithful and Drake decided to sacrifice him to Tottenham in exchange for Johnny Brooks in December 1959.

Drake thought Brooks could help Chelsea escape from the relegation zone, while Nicholson needed a fast, capable forward with skill, pace and power. Neither Brooks nor Dave Dunmore seemed quite up to the job at White Hart Lane. The Spurs boss was ready to spend big again until he remembered the promise Allen had shown in his teenage years at Chelsea.

Many people thought it was ridiculous to exchange the curly-haired inside-forward Brooks, who'd played for England, for a typical Chelsea product who promised so much but had failed to develop. It seemed Spurs were swapping a player of great potential for one who was mediocre.

At first the critics seemed to be right. Allen was lost in the fast-paced, quick-thinking Spurs team. For a long time, especially in the early months of 1960 when the winter mud clogged the efforts of all the players, Allen was nervous and lacked self-confidence. His inferiority complex got the better of him. It had become his biggest problem.

Allen's baptism of fire and his failure to respond immediately to the task was hardly surprising. After being in and out of Chelsea's first team for so many seasons he suddenly found himself playing alongside established internationals in one of the finest club sides in Britain. Allen patently lacked the skills of a Jones, White or Harmer.

He was frequently criticised by the home supporters in the early days for not taking the many chances carved out by his illustrious team-mates. Allen was very sensitive to the impatient White Hart Lane crowd. His job, like Smith's, was to score goals. But that responsibility seemed part of the problem. The fact he wasn't involved in the skilful build-up play that was Spurs' trademark left him feeling excluded. He was on the fringes.

But Allen wasn't expected to defend like Henry, Norman and Baker, or to set up chances like Mackay and Blanchflower. His job was to concentrate on being in the right forward position to get on the end of an attack created by the wing-halves. Spurs didn't need another defender or midfield player. They wanted an attacker to support Smith.

It took a while, but gradually Allen got used to the team's style. His performances improved and so did his confidence. In January 1960 he suddenly became a firm favourite with the Tottenham faithful when he scored twice against rivals Arsenal on a frozen White Hart Lane pitch. But he really put himself on the map with an amazing performance against Crewe in a Cup replay at the Lane in February, scoring five of Tottenham's 13 goals. It suddenly dawned on him that perhaps he wasn't such a bad player after all.

Allen started beating his marker more easily, especially on the flanks where he could cut inside and make diagonal runs towards goal. Allen let Smith chase the keeper around the penalty area, while he moved away to stray free of his marker. But he also helped take the pressure off the England forward and began to match him goal for goal.

Allen soon developed a perfect understanding with his team-mates and worked unselfishly to keep Spurs on the attack. He was fast for a bulky forward and an expert at finding space, especially around the goalmouth where he was at his most dangerous. The advice he gave younger players was based on his own role in the Spurs team. 'Always be looking to join as the third man in a movement,' he'd tell them. 'Inter-passing by your colleagues could be the start of a goal if you are running at the right time and into the right place. Look for the break through to the near post and if you get there cut the ball back low across the goalmouth.'

Allen settled into the Spurs set-up and was now playing above himself. But despite his improvement he lacked confidence. He'd never been self-assured as a young man, but now his shyness was exposed. His expression was always so tense on the pitch, but he had no reason to feel inferior. His strength on the ball, high work-rate and team-play combined well with his fine ball control and fierce shot. But it was his intelligence that wedded all these elements together.

Allen was the most improved player in the Tottenham team. His progress was rewarded when he was selected for 'trial' internationals. And he had youth on his side. 'It was only when he was picked for the

England Under-23 side [for a match against Wales at Goodison Park] that we realised how young he was,' said Blanchflower.

Brooks, meanwhile, was struggling to keep his place in what most people regarded as a poor Chelsea side. Allen had not only secured his position, he'd made it his own and in a much better team. Critics of the Brooks–Allen swap deal had to eat their words. Nicholson's hunch had paid off. Allen was the last link in his attacking chain.

CHAPTER 25
Just Champion

BY THE TIME the reigning Champions Burnley came to White Hart Lane on the first Saturday of December, Spurs had opened up a nine-point lead over Sheffield Wednesday at the top of the table. Burnley were 5th, 11 points behind Tottenham having won 12 and lost 6 of their 18 matches.

Irish international Jimmy McIlroy was Burnley's outstanding player and a good friend of Danny Blanchflower's. When asked why he didn't play as well for Ireland as he did for Burnley McIlroy replied: 'It's because Danny keeps me up half the night before a game talking about football.'

The clogging, muddy pitch offered little hope of a classic between the Champions and the team which had made it clear they intended to steal the crown. But Tottenham and Burnley produced majestic football of such quality, drama and thrilling excitement that many regulars at White Hart Lane rated it as the finest match they'd seen since a classic encounter with Middlesbrough ten years before ended in a 3-3 draw.

Ian Wooldridge of the *Sunday Dispatch* called it 'the most thrilling match I've seen since Stanley Matthews turned a Cup Final into a one-man mutiny against fate'.

The game was played against a backdrop of troubled times within football as arguments raged between the Football League and the Professional Footballers' Association over players' wages and the terms of their contracts. There was even talk of a players' strike.

The dispute had dragged on for years but it was now coming to a head. Professional footballers were restricted to earning £20 pounds during the season and £17 a week in the summer.

Spurs and Burnley sent football into its crisis week with a game to savour. They were to prove wrong all those critics who said the players didn't care about the game and were only interested in money. The passion and commitment at White Hart Lane was all about glory.

Over 58,000 fans showed up – more than attended all the Third Division games – on what was a miserable, cold and very wet December afternoon. Their dedication was amply rewarded and in retrospect they were privileged to be there. It was a match that lived up to the wildest expectations and was worthy of all the time-worn clichés. It had everything.

Burnley dominated the opening exchanges leaving the home fans watching in near silence as the visitors fired in three shots and forced four corners before Spurs attacked once. But, despite the pressure, Burnley just couldn't score. Their failure to find the net was something they'd soon regret. Tottenham blunted Burnley's early aggression and then struck three times between the 18th and 21st minutes. The sensational Tottenham scoring spree sent a wave of relief sweeping across White Hart Lane.

Maurice Norman started the flurry when he took the Burnley defence by surprise with one of his impromptu sorties upfield. His head did the rest. The Tottenham fans hardly had time to celebrate before Cliff Jones stamped his authority on the match. A minute after Norman had put Spurs ahead, the Welsh winger emerged as a deadly opportunist. He was much too quick for Burnley's reserve centre-half Tommy Cummings as he flew across the muddy White Hart Lane pitch at amazing speed to fire home two goals in two minutes.

When Mackay made it 4-0 after 36 minutes the game seemed dead and buried. He even had the audacity to bow to the crowd after that fourth goal. The game seemed as good as over and the fans thought Tottenham had done it again – in style and against the reigning Champions. Such a display demanded respect. It was as certain as anything could be that Burnley would be added to the list of Tottenham scalps.

Even when Burnley winger John Connelly strode through the home defence to score what seemed to be merely a consolation goal before half-time the Tottenham faithful had little reason to be concerned.

After all, few sides would fight back from 4-0, and not many would contemplate pulling a game round from 4-1 down.

But Burnley were no ordinary team. They seemed to know that the score didn't reflect the balance of power in the match. Burnley believed they had the right to be 4-0 ahead, not Tottenham. They were also fighting to show the South that British football extended further than White Hart Lane.

They came out after half-time with probably more determination than had ever been seen from a football team. Their play more than matched Spurs. They drew on pride and pedigree to push Tottenham completely out of their stride. Even when Mackay broke down attack after attack the Burnley players were not disheartened. It merely strengthened their resolve to come again.

A little help from the smallest of defensive errors let them back into the match. First Henry failed to trap the ball precisely in the mud and, before he could move, Burnley's inside-forward Jimmy Robson had whipped it into the net. Then Norman struggled to gain control on the slippery surface and blonde-haired centre-forward Ray Pointer fired home with half an hour left.

The noise was truly deafening when, with only 12 minutes left, Burnley withstood a siege in their own penalty area. When Connelly broke away with the ball, hearts were in mouths among the Tottenham faithful. As the Burnley winger, a match for even Jones' penetration, hared towards the middle of a threadbare Spurs defence, hush descended over White Hart Lane. The elusive Connelly swept the ball out to Robson, collected the return pass and rifled home the equaliser. Burnley had 'turned a massacre into an epic' in the words of Ian Wooldridge.

Their attacking effort spent, Burnley relied on their defence to hold out against the final onslaught from the Tottenham forwards. The away side gritted their teeth and hung on for one of the most memorable draws in the history of both clubs.

Few could quite remember the like of this remarkable match, or such a topsy-turvy result. At the end, the gleaming faces in the packed directors' box told their own story. They seemed to be saying: 'What's wrong with British football when you get a game like this in the pouring rain?' The fans stood side by side to applaud the 22 players off the pitch.

Wooldridge summed it up in his report for the following day's *Sunday Dispatch*. 'The flat accents of Burnley's few followers and the Cockney cheers of Spurs' thousands soared in one chorus of adulation which told the whole story . . . it would have been tragedy had either team lost.'

Burnley were the heroes. They were calm under pressure and kept trying to play controlled, direct, attacking football. Spurs didn't lose; but they'd made more defensive mistakes and were punished for them. Burnley showed Tottenham how to come from behind and play well under pressure. It was more a lesson for the prospective champions than the resilient titleholders.

There weren't many occasions in the 1960–61 season when Bill Nicholson was angry with his players, but this was one of them. It was a brave man who would have voluntarily entered the home dressing-room. 'I sometimes went into the dressing-room after a match if they'd won,' says assistant secretary Alan Leather. 'If they hadn't won, you avoided it like the plague.'

The reporters waited around in the Tottenham car park for a long time to get Bill Nicholson's reaction. 'We scored all eight and only drew,' he told the reporters when he finally emerged. Nicholson hadn't said much, but he never did. Just a few words from Bill were worth more than a whole sermon from some other managers.

CHAPTER 26
Victory in the Fog

SPURS HAD DROPPED four points out of a possible 42 and were soon back on the winning trail. They travelled to Goodison Park on 17 December to play second-placed Everton in thick fog.

The programme teed the game up nicely. 'Probably the greatest galaxy of talent to appear in a League match since the war will step out on the field about 2.55 p.m.' They were a bit out on the timing though. The kick-off was delayed until 3.15 so everyone could get out of the pubs and still get in to see the match from the start.

Everton were a brilliant ball-playing side shaped by manager Johnny Carey, former captain of Manchester United and an Irish international. They had five Scots, four of them internationals, plus Irish international Billy Bingham, signed in October. Centre-forward Alex Young had only recently joined the club for £42,000 from Hearts.

The game was played under a stone-coloured sky in the floodlit yellow murk of Goodison Park. And for 35 minutes the crowd of more than 61,000 screamed and roared as Everton, inspired by their half-pint Scot Bobby Collins at inside-left, swarmed all over the Tottenham goal.

Spurs could have been two goals down in that early period of the match. But once Mackay crossed over to the right to shackle little Collins the result was a foregone conclusion. 'Suddenly, with the venom of uncoiling cobras, Spurs struck,' was the way Alan Hoby was to describe the transformation in the *Sunday Express*. It was Blanchflower, until then a pale imitation of his usual self, who inspired the turnaround.

Tottenham scored twice in four minutes. First, Blanchflower sent

Jones streaking away through Everton's defence with a dazzling flighted ball. Jones' curved cross was pulled down by White who steadied himself and fired the ball past the advancing Albert Dunlop in the Everton goal.

Then Blanchflower again moved menacingly up the right wing, his white shirt ghostly in the fog, before turning the ball to Dyson. The diminutive winger pushed it back inside to his captain who took it to the goal-line and crossed. The ball brushed White's head and dropped to Dyson's foot. He pushed a short square pass to Allen who hooked the ball home from close range.

Everton pulled a goal back through Frank Wignall early in the second-half, but Spurs, as they so often did, had saved the best till last. Jones sprinted across the pitch before pushing the ball to Mackay. As the 'craggy' Scot pulled back his left boot, a hush descended over Goodison. Mackay's fierce drive flew into the top corner from all of 35 yards. As he was mobbed by team-mates Blanchflower, the architect of this famous victory, clapped his hands.

Blanchflower had put behind him all the trials and tribulations he'd experienced at Tottenham in the early years under Jimmy Anderson. He'd matured and had benefitted greatly from the experience. Geoffrey Green of *The Times* said Blanchflower played as he talked, 'fluently and without drawing breath. Delicately balanced and cool as a cucumber, accurate as a slide-rule with his passes, he was always available to his colleagues in an open space, a magnet for the ball.'

Arthur Rowe once said of him: 'In nine matches out of ten Blanchflower had the ball more than any other two players on the field. It's an expression of his tremendous ego, which is just what a captain needs.'

Blanchflower's idol was Northern Ireland manager Peter Doherty, a wonderful, non-stop inside-forward who'd taken his country to the quarter-finals of the World Cup in Sweden in 1958. Blanchflower, of course, was his inspirational captain. 'We wouldn't even have reached the World Cup finals without him,' said Doherty.

Northern Ireland had beaten Italy and Czechoslovakia on their way to a 4-0 drubbing by France in the quarter-finals by which time the players were exhausted. 'We didn't win anything,' Blanchflower said at the time, 'but as the Cinderella of the Soccer world we made quite a stir at the ball.'

Like so many Irish players, Blanchflower sat at Doherty's feet emotionally. 'He was the great North Star that twinkled brightly in the heavens, promising untold glory, beckoning me to follow, and always showing the way,' Blanchflower once wrote. Blanchflower was often critical of the English temperament and was happiest among his own free and easy Irish team-mates – and, of course, his idol.

Doherty had clearly had a great influence on Blanchflower's development as a man and as a player. 'Always remembering Doherty, I aim at precision soccer. Constructiveness, no matter what the circumstances, ball control, precise and accurate distribution, up in support at all times possible, back in defence to blot out the inside-forward when necessary. I am described as an attacking wing-half, and I suppose that is correct. Sometimes I even score goals.'

But Blanchflower knew his limitations. He rated himself less highly than what he called a 'natural' player like John Charles of Leeds. 'Everything John does is automatic. When he moves into position for a goal chance it is instinctive. Watch me and you will see I am seconds late. I do not possess this intuitiveness – I have to work it all out up here [in his head]. I work at the skills as hard as I can. But all my thinking has to be done in my head. My feet do not do my thinking for me as they do for a player like John Charles. That is why I can never be as great a footballer as he.'

Blanchflower was also, in football parlance, a 'one-pace' player. Speed was never his forte. 'Danny had a very good ordinary pace, but what made him better was his ability and his anticipation in reading the game,' says Bill Nicholson. As Danny himself said many times, it was his footballing brain that was the key to the workings of the tempo-changing gears that dictated his play. His hunger for the ball enabled him to create a rich variety of pace in the play around him. He seemed able to change the rhythm of a match at will.

Julian Holland in *Spurs – The Double* described this unique aspect of Blanchflower's game. 'Time and time again when Spurs' goal has been threatened by a sustained spell of attack, it is Blanchflower who has quietly and steadily lowered the temperature; slowed down the game's pace; infused order into a defence momentarily in panic; called for the ball and held it excitingly long in an area of danger; stroked it with an inch-accurate short pass to a nearby colleague; immediately moved into a freed space for the return; deliberately, self-consciously, demonstratively, reset the pattern of Spurs' play and dictated his stamp once again onto a game that momentarily had been in danger of going over to the enemy.'

Blanchflower's relationship with his manager was often portrayed as a match made in heaven. It was never that. Nicholson was a dour Yorkshireman who didn't always understand his loquacious captain. He certainly never shared Blanchflower's romantic vision. But Nicholson was a good enough judge of football to know what Blanchflower could give to turn a very good team into a great one. 'He thought a lot of himself,' Nicholson said years later, 'and I thought a lot of him. He had imagination. He perceived what was happening and provided answers – an extremely able captain because he communicated so well.'

But Blanchflower's view of the role of a captain was somewhat cynical. Having been stripped of the captaincy early in his Spurs career he had a healthy scepticism about the way the captain was viewed by others. 'Good captains, like dinosaurs, are threatened with extinction. They are hounded into a state of nervous nonentity by a huge pack of masterminds who inhabit the higher, drier lands of the grandstands.'

Blanchflower had developed his approach to captaincy along the same lines as he'd progressed with his abilities on the field: through experience. 'Usually I let things take their course, content with urging the players to keep alert to the drills and habits of teamwork that we expect of them,' he said. 'I try to value their moods and to react to them in the most effective way. Some players will respond immediately to my advice; others may be suspicious that I am laying the blame for something on their doorstep and I have learned to relate advice to them through some other member of the team. A captain cannot wave a magic wand and make a bad team into a good one; but a good captain can help a team along by making good decisions. You cannot define captaincy or reduce it to fixed conceptions: it is a complex business, an art, an eternal improvisation. It is a battle of wits and you can never be sure.'

Blanchflower brought thought and vision to his captaincy as much as he injected belief and expectation through his play. Most footballers played from habit, but Blanchflower was above that. He could read a situation, analyse it and try to change the habit or tactic straight away. He knew what to do and when to do it and he had the authority to carry it through. The players respected him. He demanded it and they gave it. He led by example, and rarely made the wrong decision.

'Like Cliff Jones, and other outstanding soccer men, you cannot ruffle Danny,' said Dave Mackay. 'The highly intelligent and witty Irishman is yet one more star who emphasises by word and deed the part concentration can play in soccer success.'

Blanchflower was meticulous in his preparations for a game. He owned ten pairs of football boots! He'd often give them to Maurice Norman to wear when he'd finished with them. 'I'd say, "Danny, you can't have ten pairs of boots surely?"' says Norman, who remembers how light they were. Blanchflower had different boots for each occasion and would select the correct pair just before a game, depending on the weather conditions.

During the five minutes before a match Blanchflower would take a ball and carefully run through his repertoire of skills with Mackay and Norman. He would stroke the ball short and long with the outside and the inside of both feet, practise volleying, then try a few back-heels and doing all this with backspin and topspin.

'He drags his boot lazily across the face of the ball for the outswinger; cuts his foot away sharply outside it for the twister the other way. He traps it, kills it with a slack boot, spoons it off the turf, feels it, tries its weight, stabs at it with a toe-end, all to tune himself into an immediate familiarity,' wrote Julian Holland.

Blanchflower was 34 years old and no longer in the first flush of youth. But he was tremendously fit. He always wanted to start training before the pre-season workouts proper had begun. When Nicholson took over as coach, Blanchflower approached him and asked if he could start training a week early. 'I feel I'd like to be a bit fitter than everyone else,' he said. 'Sure,' the Spurs boss replied, 'but when we start you will do the same as everybody else.' After three or four days of pre-season training, Blanchflower approached Nicholson again. 'Bill, don't you think we're doing too much,' he said. It seemed that even Blanchflower had his limits. And Nicholson's training routine was always tough.

Danny had fair hair and eyes that made a woman smile. His tortuous private life – three wives and five children – was testimony to his attraction to the ladies. His personal affairs were as complicated as his football was straightforward.

'We were different,' says his brother Jackie. 'I liked a bet on the horses and a drink. Danny liked to womanise.' Jackie and Danny rarely saw one another in those days, though they played on opposing teams many times both when Danny was at Villa and also at Spurs when they marked each other. 'He used to call me a clown,' says Jackie. 'To me football was just a game; to him it was an obsession. He'd say, "Let's talk tactics" and I'd say, "Aren't they peppermint sweets?" He used to get annoyed.'

According to Ivan Ponting in *Tottenham Hotspur – Player-by-Player* 'the charming but waspishly outspoken Ulsterman was a revolutionary free-thinker, an incurable romantic and perhaps the most beguiling talker the game has known'.

Danny was of average height, but on the pitch his finely chiselled frame gave him a waif-like appearance. He was bony and thin and would walk across the turf on flat heels as though on stilts, ever ready to break into that easy, straight-backed high-elbowed trot of his that took him so often to the ball.

Blanchflower didn't just play football, he dictated the game on his terms. His tremendous ego meant that he always wanted the ball even when, on occasion, someone else was better-positioned to receive it. But he had the skill to lose his marker at crucial moments and rarely lost possession. Once he had the ball he'd look up and dispatch it clinically to one of his team-mates, opening up a defence with short and long passes.

He also liked to mix it and was never afraid of getting stuck into the thick of the action. He wanted to be where the battle was fiercest because that's where he could be most effective. His balance and grace on the ball nevertheless marked him out from the crowd. It was likely you'd notice Blanchflower before any other player on the field.

'His art, his grace, his skill, his coolness, his magnificence in play are incredible,' wrote Ralph Finn in *Spurs Supreme*. 'Watch him as he brings a ball down out of the air as if it were glued to his toe and how, still surrounded by a mass of players, he manoeuvres out of the rut with almost casual effrontery. Watch him as he traps and wheels in one movement. Watch him as he beats a man with a shudder of those slim shoulders and weaves his way upfield, luring the enemy into false positions. His passing . . . is beautiful. That is not a wrong word to use in this text for beauty flows from the play of this prince of half-backs.

Off the pitch, Blanchflower was one of the most intelligent and deep-thinking footballers of his or any other generation. 'Away from the football field, Blanchflower is a born conversationalist,' wrote Holland in *Spurs – The Double*. 'He thinks aloud, riding his ideas like a bronco buster, noting what he can master, flirting with what will throw him. He is as Irish as the Lagan, witty and garrulous, speaking in extremes, voicing the outrageous, even making ridiculous remarks to draw attention to something that suddenly interests him. When challenged with an opposite view which he has at some other time expressed, he will plead that he has the right to change his mind.

'He is emotional, romantic, wildly logical, intuitive, argumentative. He is warm, he is kind, except when honesty demands the cold knife of truth. His intelligence is as lively as his enthusiam for football; his tongue is as facile as his limbs are with the skills of football. Humour bubbles out in his talk as it does in his play. He will concoct epigrams as he will make goal chances; he will smilingly voice paradoxes as suddenly as he will convert defence into attack.

'He will talk about anything for the sheer love of the exercise it gives his excited tongue. He reads avidly and intelligently, digesting his reading with the saliva of discussion. With a glass of abstemious orangeade in his hand, he will even discuss the stimulating properties of good wine. He is the Brendan Behan of the boot, the Wilde of White Hart Lane. He is football's apostle, a muddied oaf with pearls falling from his lips.'

Ralph Finn of *The People* was a big fan of Blanchflower. Week-in and week-out his match reports were full of praise for the Irish genius. 'Clean in his play, scrupulously fair, this meticulous perfectionist has probably done more than any other player in history to lift the regard in which the game is held,' he wrote in *Spurs Supreme*. 'Even those who have never kicked a ball or watched a match in their lives have been impressed by his native wit and eloquence on radio and television, have seen for themselves that at least some of our soccer players have brains and the ability to think for themselves.'

Geoffrey Green of *The Times* was also aware of the intellectual properties which underlay the foundation of Blanchflower's football philosophy. 'Blanchflower practised his profession with all the art, intelligence, craftsmanship and pride at his considerable command. Articulate and persuasive to the point where he might well have taken to law had cirucmstances been different, he was an intellectual, cerebral player. Blanchflower . . . always projected his mind where others projected their bodies because he always thought and talked about it as constructively as he played it.

'He became the master of his craft and as such measured his merit and worth clinically, always being an outpsoken critic of the transfer system and the men who operated it. Precise and tidy of mind and appearance, he could spread out his game similarly before the opposition like some lawyer spreading out his case before a jury.'

Against Everton, Blanchflower had laid out his case and won it with room to spare. He had orchestrated victory against one of the best club sides in the country. And he revelled in 'representing the prosecution' on the football fields of Britain. Spurs always took their game to the opposition. It was their job to defend themselves against it. It was rare that they managed to do so.

Blanchflower was proud of the Tottenham way. He would speak of 'a warm expression' in Spurs' play. And he knew that while opposing fans wanted to see Tottenham beaten, they'd almost prefer their team to lose to the Spurs than to any other side. At least they could enjoy the football if not the result. Dave Mackay was also convinced that the Everton fans had at least been able to appreciate the football Tottenham had served up. 'Whenever I play at Goodison Park I know that I am appearing before people who in every way are sympathetic to good football,' he said.

CHAPTER 27
Christmas Cheers

TOTTENHAM FOLLOWED THE Everton game with a party – their Christmas Party. Everybody agreed it was the best they'd ever had at the club. 'The festive spirit was well in evidence,' according to the match programme for the following Saturday's game against West Ham. They certainly had more to celebrate than any other First Division team.

'The Spurs, on reflection, played their finest football between August and Christmas,' Mackay was to write at the end of the season. 'Every player was at peak form during this period, and we coasted into a ten-point lead and felt grand.'

Spurs were halfway through their League programme and there wasn't a bookmaker in the country who'd take bets on them winning the title. It was already a one-horse race in their book. The balance of the side revolved around the Blanchflower–White axis. White had brought a broader, more urgent sweep to the team. Spurs were better able to vary the pace and power of their game with the talented Scottish midfielder in the side.

Mackay, playing with 'a skirl of bagpipes in his game' according to Julian Holland in *Spurs – The Double*, offered the team the ideal blend of grit and determination to counterbalance his more thoughtful captain. The courageous Jones, with his darting speed, was like an arrow flying through the heart of opposing defences. Dyson had established himself as the number one left-winger having stolen the position from the more skilful but less determined Medwin by offering a unique brand of dash and unorthodoxy. Smith and Allen were a reminder that style and skill may have provided the ammunition but it was goals that mattered most and they knew how to score. Behind them the defence of Brown, Baker, Henry and Norman had bedded down like a rock.

The team's success so far had been helped by having almost all their first-choice players available. Brown, Baker, Henry, Blanchflower, Norman, White, Allen and Dyson were ever present. Mackay had missed one match; Bobby Smith had played 19 of 21, Jones 15, Medwin seven and Saul three with the talented Marchi making just one appearance.

The run of 11 wins which had got them off to a flying start was recognised at the Christmas luncheon. Chairman Fred Bearman presented each of the 14 players who'd played in those opening 11 victories with a silver tray engraved with the scores and the names of their opponents.

The other Christmas awards were more tongue-in-cheek. The diminutive bachelor Terry Dyson was given a copy of the book *Little Women* by Louisa M. Alcott; Bobby Smith received a model of a petrol station because of his reputation for borrowing his team-mates' cars and forgetting to refill the tanks; and 88-year-old chairman Fred Bearman was presented with a copy of the book *Lady Chatterley's Lover* by D.H. Lawrence.

The novel had been banned for 30 years for being obscene, but in early November when a jury at the Old Bailey in London had ruled that it was not, cheers and applause broke out in the courtroom. Penguin books, prosecuted as a test case, sold out 200,000 copies on the first day of publication at a price of three shillings and six pence. The prosecution said the novel contained 13 'bouts' of sexual intercourse between Lady Chatterley and her husband's gamekeeper, Mellors, in many settings 'with the emphasis always on the pleasure, the satisfaction, the sensuality'. On receiving his gift the Tottenham chairman said with a wry smile: 'After I've read it I'll tell you boys all about it.'

Back on the pitch, Tottenham faced two games over Christmas – a crucial period on the soccer calendar and one in which a team could either stamp its authority on the season or lose valuable ground in the title race. Spurs were under no illusions that they had to battle for points over the holiday to maintain their lead at the top.

The League programme had been kind to Tottenham, matching

them with West Ham home and away on Christmas Eve and Boxing Day. The Hammers line-up included John Bond, later the boss at Bournemouth and Norwich, and a young John Lyall, who'd go on to manage the Hammers and Ipswich.

Headed goals by White and Dyson in the first match before almost 55,000 fans at White Hart Lane made sure every Spurs forward had reached double figures in the goalscoring stakes by Christmas. The tally read Cliff Jones (10), John White (10), Bobby Smith (18), Les Allen (12) and Terry Dyson (10). Tottenham had the most feared strike force in the land having scored 73 goals in 22 games.

But Jones was injured against the Hammers, twisting ligaments in his right knee when West Ham keeper Rhodes dived at his feet a minute after the interval. He hobbled around for a while before retiring to the dressing-room with half an hour left. Tottenham keeper Bill Brown would also miss the return match with a swollen right ankle. Terry Medwin was to take over from Jones, while Johnnie Hollowbread deputised for Brown.

Kenny Brown, later to manage Norwich and whose son would play for West Ham, was credited with Tottenham's first goal at Upton Park on Boxing Day after deflecting a shot by Allen into the West Ham net. Allen scored the second with a well-taken strike.

After that, West Ham threw caution to the wind and attacked. The highlight of their afternoon was a fine shot from Bobby Moore which Hollowbread saved brilliantly by leaping to clutch the ball in mid-air.

West Ham played the traditional English way, knocking the ball out to their wingers for the cross into the box and the ensuing goalmouth scramble. It was exciting, but predictable. Tottenham's game flowed much more fluently through an intricate web of fine passes. There was movement, simple passing and clinical finishing.

The third Tottenham goal was fashioned from their own penalty area. Thirteen passes took the ball into the Hammers net as a bemused defence stood and watched White angle a clever low shot in off the far post.

Spurs had produced some of their finest football of the season and after the match Nicholson said the first-half display was the best he'd ever seen from a Tottenham side. And that, coming from a man who was not only careful with his praise but a former member of the great 'push and run' team, was, the players thought, praise indeed.

By the time *Daily Mirror* reporter Ken Jones left Upton Park it was dark. 'I came out of the ground and John White was standing there. Spurs had by now built up a handsome lead at the top of the table and White said to me, "I think the 'double' is really on now." I replied, "The League is on, but you can never tell in the Cup."'

While the Spurs players were still celebrating their second victory over West Ham, misfortune befell their rivals Sheffield Wednesday as they returned from their Boxing Day fixture against Arsenal at Highbury. The coach taking them home after the game was involved in an accident in Huntingdonshire injuring 19-year-old Douglas McMillan, Peter Swan and Tony Kay. Swan and Kay were detained in hospital but made satisfactory progress and were ready to play again in three weeks. McMillan had to have his leg amputated and never played again.

Tottenham's victories over West Ham and a 5-2 thrashing of Blackburn at White Hart Lane on New Year's Eve – achieved without Mackay, suffering from a boil on his leg and replaced by Marchi – meant they entered 1961 with a ten point lead over nearest rivals Wolves. After more than four months of the season they'd lost just one match and had dropped a mere four points. It seemed they would break every League record.

CHAPTER 28

The Cup Campaign Begins

IN THE NEW YEAR, with Tottenham in a seemingly commanding position in the League and the FA Cup ties about to start, the players once more read forecasts that they were a sound bet for the elusive 'double'. But the stories only encouraged other teams to try even harder when they came up against the leaders.

The draw for the Third Round of the Cup, made in the Council Chamber at Lancaster Gate, was favourable for Spurs: they were picked out of the bag to play a home tie with South London neighbours Charlton. It would be the first time the two clubs had met in the competition.

Tottenham had taken 46 points out of a possible 50 in the League. Charlton were a middle-of-the-table Second Division side. More of their fans crossed the Thames to watch Spurs than had attended recent matches at the Valley. The pundits said Tottenham would have an easy ride. But the players were more cautious. 'Too many folk for my liking insisted we were as good as on the road to Wembley,' said Mackay.

The Edmonton gypsies looked in their crystal footballs and came up with the inspiring numbers 1901, 1921 and 1961. The first two years were those in which Spurs had won the FA Cup. The missing figure in the sequence was 1941, but that was an excusable omission as there was no Cup competition that year as a result of the Second World War.

When the day of the game came in early January, Charlton, as Mackay expected, proved to be tough opponents. They were a good side who'd always played attractive football. They'd already scored 55 League goals that season and showed little respect for Spurs' reputation.

Almost 55,000 fans decked out in blue and red were packed into White Hart Lane for one of the most exciting days in the calendar. Some had barely sat down when, after six minutes, a wonderful defence-splitting pass from Blanchflower put Allen clear and Spurs were ahead. The same combination saw Tottenham go two goals up after 28 minutes.

Spurs began to coast on their lead and, despite falling behind so early in the match, Charlton played some delightful football. Their forwards suddenly realised Blanchflower and Mackay had become almost too confident and were leaving the door to the defence wide open.

Charlton captain Stuart Leary took advantage of the gaps in the Spurs rearguard and pulled one back for the visitors after 33 minutes. But Blanchflower, the architect of all Tottenham's best football, could not be suppressed. Three minutes later his pin-point cross deep into the Charlton defence gave the alert Dyson his first Cup goal.

But still it wasn't over. Thirty seconds after the break Charlton's right-winger Lawrie scored. The Spurs defenders were rocked back on their heels as they hadn't been all season. Charlton had exposed a weakness in the Tottenham rearguard: they were shaky under all-out pressure. For 20 minutes the Second Division team bombarded the Spurs goal and seemed certain to equalise.

But Tottenham had the sort of good fortune every side needs if it's to win anything. Charlton's South African international left-half Brian Tocknell let fly with a tremendous shot which no one, including Brown, could have seen. If it had been on target Charlton must have scored. Fate ruled otherwise and the ball went inches past the post.

Eventually Blanchflower restored some semblance of authority to the Spurs side. He went round to his team-mates individually coaxing and cajoling them, trying to gee them up. He slowed the pace of the match to dampen the visitors' onslaught. Tottenham held on, but it was one of their worst displays of the season.

Harry Ditton's report in the *News of the World* the following day summed up just how close the match was. 'Many Tottenham hearts missed a beat as Charlton put up a tremendous fight and more than once went within an ace of forcing a replay. The lads from the Valley surprised us all, not least the Spurs, by their crisp aggressive football.

They refused to be overawed by reputations and right up to the last kick they were in with at least an equal chance.'

After the match one of the Charlton directors told Nicholson: 'You'll win the Cup because the side that beats us always wins it.' If they performed like they did against their South London rivals Spurs would be lucky to reach the Fifth Round. They'd shown little of the cultured attacking play the home fans had come to expect. It had been a tense battle and the fright would unsettle them for many matches to come.

While Tottenham battled through the Third Round of the Cup the dispute between the League and the Professional Footballers' Association over wages and the retain-and-transfer system which tied a player to one club rumbled on. Strike notices had been issued on 13 December with the players due to down boots on Saturday, 21 January.

PFA chairman Jimmy Hill negotiated their first breakthrough on 9 January, two days after Tottenham's Cup tie with Charlton. Following a meeting of First and Second Divison chairmen in London, the League announced it was scrapping the maximum wage from the end of the season – two years earlier than their original proposal.

'Now we have a great chance of matching the Continentals and the rest of the world on their own cash terms,' said Burnley's Irish international Jimmy McIlroy. Fulham chairman Tommy Trinder had already said he'd like to pay inside-forward Johnny Haynes £100 a week.

But the League refused to abandon the retain-and-transfer system. Players were still not allowed to move to a club of their choice when their contract expired, something Hill described as a 'slave contract'. George Eastham, who wanted to move from Newcastle to Arsenal, was challenging his contract in court, arguing it was a restraint of trade.

Not all the players were pleased at the publicity generated by the dispute. Dave Mackay for one believed the cash problem had brought them unwelcome attention unequalled by any other sportsmen. 'For many years now the wage claims of professional footballers have occupied many columns of British newspapers and, overlooking whether or not these claims are just, the position reached a stage when many people were sick and tired of hearing about wage claims. At Tottenham we are fortunate in having so many young fellows who do not waste their time talking about the money they ought to be earning, or whether they are really entitled to be called "football slaves". At "Spurland" our discussions off the field are usually centred around our living – professional football.'

Back on the pitch, Tottenham's next League opponents were Manchester United. The players travelled up to Manchester on the Friday night by train and were booked into the Queen's Hotel, their usual accommodation for matches in the city.

Bobby Smith liked going to Manchester. 'When we were in Manchester we'd go to the dogs, about six of us, or to the pictures. Bill didn't care what you did in your free time as long as you were fit.'

'We used to go to the pictures quite a lot,' recalls Ron Henry. 'The joker there was Peter Baker. We'd be sitting at the back and he'd walk down the front to the ice-cream girl, turn around and shout at the top of his voice, "Do you want a lolly or peanuts?" Everyone used to look round to see who he was shouting at.'

Smith would be joined by the likes of Terry Dyson and Dave Mackay at the Salford greyhound track. 'We used to have a laugh and a drink, though we didn't drink that much. It was fun,' says Smith. Dyson was a cautious gambler and would put his winnings away – if he had any. Smith wasn't as careful with his money and had little success with gambling.

When the players woke up on the Saturday morning they could hardly see out of their hotel windows. 'It was so foggy that we couldn't play the match and had to come back to London,' remembers Baker. The game was re-arranged for the Monday evening, though Baker wouldn't be playing. 'We trained on the Sunday and I pulled a muscle and burst a blood vessel. I couldn't play on the night, though I did travel up with the team.'

Manchester United were not the sort of team to face without all your best players. The daunting task of taking on a side which had taken eleven points from their last six games was made worse by the absence of Jones and Medwin, as well as Baker. Ken Barton came in for Baker and John Smith replaced Medwin who'd cried off at the last minute. Medwin had been selected to replace Jones who'd already been ruled out. It was the first time all season that Spurs had had to play without three of their star players.

Full-back Barton was making his first League appearance. A useful young player who'd joined Spurs from school, he was another in the long line of Welshmen who'd served the club. It was an appropriate time for him to make his full League debut since he was Tottenham's delegate to the PFA! Inside-forward John Smith had joined Spurs in a swap deal that took Dave Dunmore to West Ham in March 1960. At the time, Smith was seen as the long-term successor to Blanchflower. He'd already played for the England Under-23s and seemed to have a promising future.

Spurs stepped out onto the Old Trafford pitch before more than 65,000 fans. The changes forced on Nicholson had left Tottenham exposed. Their old rhythm had gone and they were forced to play the ball square instead of forwards as United pressed forward and closed down the space. Blanchflower struggled to rally his out-of-sorts team by calling and clapping his hands to rouse the players to greater efforts.

United took the lead on 13 minutes through Nobby Stiles. But then their keeper Harry Gregg fell heavily on his shoulder. Just before half-time he aggravated the injury and had to leave the field. Dawson took over in goal but United looked even more dangerous.

Gregg got a great reception when he returned in the second-half, his right shoulder heavily strapped. He took up a position at centre-forward as if he'd wanted to play there all his life. Meanwhile, Dawson was thoroughly enjoying himself in goal and made some good saves, including one that Gregg himself would have been proud of. Ironically, it was a cheeky back-heel into the box by Gregg which set up a second United goal for Pearson.

It was only Tottenham's second defeat in 26 matches. They could have made excuses but it was doubtful whether even with a full side they could have stopped United on this form.

CHAPTER 29

Pièce de Résistance

SATURDAY, 21 JANUARY, was supposed to be the day when the Professional Footballers' Association called all their members out on strike. But it didn't happen. It seemed nothing could stop Spurs' relentless march to the Championship, not even the long-running dispute over the retain-and-transfer system.

On Monday, 16 January, the League had tried to beat the threatened strike by switching the fixtures from the Saturday to Friday, 20 January. This alarmed the small number of clubs without floodlights and there was concern among all clubs that Friday afternoon games would draw much lower crowds. The *Daily Mirror* ran an editorial headlined 'What a way to run a sport!' in which the paper said the League was 'idiotic'.

It soon became clear that the majority of the country supported the players and the League was forced into a humiliating climbdown. After five hours of last-ditch talks on Wednesday, 18 January, the PFA and the Football League resolved the dispute at a meeting with the Ministry of Labour. The League agreed to abandon the regulations that effectively tied a player to one club for life and a new pay charter, including the already-agreed abolition of the maximum wage, was drawn up.

Tottenham were thus given the chance to restore their dented pride against an inexperienced Arsenal side shorn of their first-choice defence by injury. The four defenders in the Gunners' team had played fewer matches between them than Tottenham had already won that season.

But Arsenal did have a dangerous forward line which included David Herd, who'd always been a handful for Maurice Norman, and

George Eastham, who'd finally joined the Gunners from Newcastle in November. Eastham was at the centre of the dispute over the retain-and-transfer system. His stubborn opposition to the rule that prevented a player moving to the club of his choice would result in a High Court ruling in 1963 that the old system was 'an unreasonable restraint of trade'.

A crowd of more than 65,000 – it was to be the biggest home gate of the season – filed through the turnstiles at White Hart Lane to see whether Spurs could do the 'double' over their North London rivals. Arsenal fielded a young right-half called Terry Neill, later to manage both North London teams.

Arsenal began aggressively. Mackay's pal Tommy Docherty got stuck in from the start and began hitting accurate long balls through to his forwards. The Gunners took the lead when a 40-yard pass from Docherty found Henderson as the Tottenham defence was moving out. He spun and drove a low shot into the corner of the net from outside the penalty area.

Stung by the goal, Tottenham really began to play. Blanchflower and Mackay rediscovered the touch that was sadly missing at Old Trafford, Jones had returned from injury and was brilliant, Allen sparkled as he took a leaf out of John White's book and found space where there seemed to be none.

'Tottenham, unruffled and under Blanchflower's cool direction, wove their tapestry of attack in designs of quick surprise, and within a quarter of an hour they were ahead,' was how John Arlott described the fight-back in *The Observer*.

Spurs began to perform at their magical best after those first 20 minutes. Allen equalised with an angled shot from the left after White had switched the play to outfox the Arsenal defence. Then Blanchflower converted a penalty after Neill tripped Dyson.

'On-top Spurs played like peacocks, showing every rainbow feather, aloofly preening themselves before their adoring fans (many of whom had paid an illicit fiver to see the game),' wrote Julian Holland in *Spurs – The Double*. 'It was as though, after Monday's shaking (at Old Trafford), they had determined to refresh themselves, to run over their scales, to go through their practice pieces, to rehearse their exercises. Restored to concert pitch, they were ready, just before the interval to produce the season's pièce de résistance, a breathtaking piece of football that made the huge crowd draw in their breath with admiration and applaud till their hands were as red as Arsenal's shirts.'

Spurs had the ball deep in defence and knocked it around playfully until Mackay kicked it overhead to Norman. It was then passed to Blanchflower, Henry and then Baker while Mackay ran a third of the length of the pitch at full tilt to collect Baker's precise 40-yard pass. It was one of those rare occasions when the Tottenham full-back surprised everyone by knocking the ball long instead of playing it short to Blanchflower. Suddenly the pace of the play had changed. Spurs had moved from defence to all-out attack in an instant.

Mackay swept the ball into his stride, bulldozed his way past an improvised tackle and rolled it casually to Jones. The Welsh winger accelerated towards the penalty area and cracked a shot at goal. The ball rebounded from the Arsenal goal but Smith, struggling to shake himself out of a bad patch, was there to turn it in with one touch and confound the critics who said he was soon to lose his place in the England team.

Remarkably, the big centre-forward was the only Tottenham player in the England side. He'd been awarded his first cap the previous September against Ireland and had kept his place for the matches against Luxembourg, Spain and Wales. Despite widespread Press speculation that he'd soon be axed, Smith battled back to peak form and kept his place in the side for the matches versus Scotland and Portugal.

His goal against Arsenal was the result of a superb Tottenham move. It was also significant, since neither White nor Blanchflower had played much part in the move, although the goal was fashioned in the style the two midfield maestros had championed all season.

Allen added a fine fourth goal for Spurs before Arsenal pulled one back through a deflected cross by Haverty. But by then the game was already over. Tottenham were once again, in the words of John Arlott, 'wearing the air of conscious superiority which is now their accustomed strip'.

CHAPTER 30
Crewe Derailed

THE FOURTH ROUND of the Cup was the next hurdle for the double-chasing Tottenham team. They'd been paired once more with Crewe Alexandra, the team they'd beaten 13-2 in a replay in the same round of the Cup at White Hart Lane the previous season. Smith and Allen were rubbing their hands together when the draw was made remembering the 10 goals they'd scored between them against the same team 12 months before.

When Crewe travelled down to London for that replay in 1960 they arrived at Platform 2 and left from Platform 13 – the exact score on the night. This time around, having caused one of the upsets of the Third Round by beating Chelsea at Stamford Bridge, they were due to arrive at Platform 1 and leave from Platform 4.

The Fourth Division side had developed new tactics to stop the Spurs forwards: they tried to kick them off the muddy White Hart Lane pitch. Crewe's disorganised defenders indulged in hard, clumsy, indiscriminate tackling and aimed their clearances at the second tier of the stands. But Spurs' all-round strength was based on the fact that alongside players with delicate skills, like White and Blanchflower, they also had the raw aggression of the likes of Smith and Mackay. While White was put off his game by the crude tactics, the rest of the Tottenham team dished out as much as they took.

At one point Blanchflower was unceremoniously upended by another wild Crewe tackle. But he got up, his face completely covered in mud, and just stood there grinning. The other Spurs players saw the funny side of it too and began laughing at him. They weren't used to seeing their cultured captain in such a mess. The incident clearly showed that Tottenham were the last team who could be intimidated by crude tactics.

Most of the game was spent in and around the Crewe penalty area and it was as well for the Fourth Division team that their keeper Brian Williamson played out of his skin. His positional sense and instinctive movement frustrated the Spurs forwards until the home fans, knowing their team were safely through to the Fifth Round of the Cup, were cheering his every move. Williamson was supreme and one of the few keepers who could hold his head up while boasting that he only let in five goals. Dyson, Smith, Mackay, Jones and Allen had managed to beat the agile goalie with Tighe replying for Crewe.

Tony Pawson's match report in *The Observer* reflected the majority opinion among the Press on the keeper's performance. 'Williamson, in goal, kept the score within bounds by countless agile saves, three of which were remarkable enough to have won him admission to the Magicians' Circle.' At the end of the match the White Hart Lane crowd rose to applaud the Crewe keeper more than they cheered their own team. 'We were always in the game with a chance,' said Crewe's captain Don Campbell. It was the overstatement of the season.

CHAPTER 31
The First Home Defeat

IT WAS NOT until February that Spurs first faltered on the road to the title. At the start of the month they had a 12 point lead over Sheffield Wednesday, were through to the Fifth Round of the Cup and had scored nine goals in their last two home games.

Just as importantly, they'd survived without any serious injuries from playing in the winter mud. 'Billy Nicholson was never obliged to field an unknown quantity,' said Cliff Jones. 'Spurs were always able to field players with ability and experience, the rhythm of the side was never impaired, the tremendous team spirit never upset.'

Nicholson thought Tottenham's style helped limit the number of injuries. 'If you have a good team the players will play from game-to-game. Good players seldom get injured when they're in a team that plays the short passing "push-and-run" style.'

Tottenham looked destined to go down in history as the most successful English club side of all time. They were heading for a record-breaking season: Arsenal's haul of 66 League points, Aston Villa's 128 goals in a season, the 'double' – all seemed within their grasp.

The point dropped at home to Manchester City in October, defeat at Hillsborough in November and at Old Trafford in January, a draw with Champions Burnley in December and an undignified scramble against Charlton in the Cup were the only signs of weakness Spurs had shown in almost six months.

Tottenham's success had already raised the prospect of an embarrassment of financial riches. 'Spurs fighting for £175,000 jackpot' was the headline in the *Daily Mail*. 'Tottenham, the soccer team of the season, are within sight of the greatest money prize any British side has ever played for,' wrote Roy Peskett. 'From the beginning of this season to the summer of 1962 they could make a staggering profit of £175,000.' They were already one of the richest clubs in the country and had the princely sum of £276,000 burning a hole in their bank account at the start of the season.

The *Mail*'s calculations were based on Spurs winning the 'double'. 'With the Championship of the First Division virtually settled, Tottenham have to win four FA Cup ties to lift the "double",' wrote Peskett. The paper reckoned that two and a quarter million people would watch all Spurs' League and Cup ties. That was likely to bring in a League record £70,000 – £40,000 from League matches and £30,000 from the Cup. If they reached the European Cup final in 1962 they'd get another £60,000. And a successful League and Cup campaign the following season would generate at least £45,000. All of which made up the grand total of £175,000. 'This is a very handy sum to have around when the players negotiate their own wages,' wrote Peskett.

Speculation about Spurs' 'double' chances had begun immediately after the win over Crewe. The players had done their best to steer clear of the issue but now it had to be faced because it had already begun to cause problems. 'I was able to sense a difference in the general attitude of the team almost immediately,' said Cliff Jones. 'We felt we had to win every game, and although I don't think our balance or effectiveness was affected, there was, quite perceptibly, a lot of strain in the side.'

'I made no forecasts, insisting that we would not look beyond the next match,' says Nicholson. 'I believe managers make trouble for themselves when they say they are going to do this, that, or the other. Boasts can be easily destroyed.'

The Spurs boss was unflappable. Not for Nicholson the strain of sitting on the bench chewing his fingernails or puffing on a cigarette. He wanted a better view of the game and sat in the directors' box. 'On matchdays I always sat in the stands because you can't see so well in the dug-out,' he says. 'If I could I would have sat up in the crow's-nest on the roof of the East Stand. You could see the whole plan of the game from up there. We had about 70 seats in the crow's-nest, but I only ever saw a pre-season game from up there.'

Until February 1961 Nicholson had been unable to communicate with the bench from his seat in the stands, but Spurs had now laid a cable under the Main Stand Enclosure at White Hart Lane for a telephone link. Nicholson could now talk to trainer Cecil Poynton down in the dug-out about tactics or an emergency. 'I could get on the phone and give Cecil Poynton instructions if there was an injury to a player for example.'

Down on the pitch another milestone passed away in early February when Leicester City, fresh from a 6-0 win over Manchester United, repelled a last desperate Spurs assault in the closing minutes to hold onto a 3-2 win amid mounting excitement and tension at White Hart Lane. It was Tottenham's first home defeat of the season and ended a remarkable run stretching back five months. The newspapers ran the headline: 'Spurs lose again'.

The Leicester players were more than happy to give their assessment of Tottenham's prospects. 'They'll never win the "double",' some of them told the Press. Their reaction angered Blanchflower. 'They were such a mediocre team they had the right to believe that; after they had beaten us, we deserved to win nothing.'

The evening after the Leicester defeat, Blanchflower had a surprise waiting for him – but it turned out to be an unwelcome one.

The BBC's *This Is Your Life* programme had decided it would like to cover the life and times of the Tottenham captain, such was his fame and following in this remarkable season for the club. He was no longer a mere footballer; he'd become a publicly fêted personality. His television advertisements for a breakfast cereal resulted in an Irish-accented 'Hullo there' becoming a catchphrase.

The programme had rounded up everyone it could find who was connected in some meaningful way to Danny's life and invited them all to the BBC's headquarters in London. 'Spurs were playing at Leicester that day and the BBC sent us down on the two o'clock train so we would not bump into the Spurs players,' remembers Danny's brother Jackie.

The BBC arranged for Danny's parents to come over from Northern Ireland, Jackie had travelled down from Manchester and some of Danny's friends had been flown over from America especially for the programme.

Angus Mackay, the producer of BBC Radio's *Sports Report* programme, was with Eamonn Andrews when he approached Danny and spoke those immortal words: 'Danny Blanchflower, This Is Your Life'. But instead of the usual half-knowing smile from the unsuspecting guest, Danny turned to leave.

'When they said "This is Your Life" and Danny pulled away, Angus grabbed the sleeve of Danny's blazer and as he tried to get away Danny fell backwards down some stairs,' remembers football correspondent Ken Jones. 'You can imagine the trouble the BBC would have been in if Danny had been injured and couldn't play football for Tottenham.'

Angus Mackay walked into the television studio to tell the assembled guests Danny had left in a hurry and was not coming back. 'There will be no show tonight,' he announced seconds before the programme was to have been broadcast. It was the first refusal in the programme's five-year history. 'Eamonn Andrews was upset but we still had a good Irish party,' says Jackie. 'We enjoyed ourselves at the expense of the BBC, but Danny wasn't there.' It cost the BBC almost £1,000 to bring all the relatives, friends and players together.

The story appeared on the front pages of the newspapers the following day. When asked why he wouldn't go on the show Blanchflower said: 'I did it for personal reasons. If I told you what they were they wouldn't be personal any more, would they?'

'He made a great thing of the independence, but he was also bothered about things in his past,' says Ken Jones. Danny and his wife Betty were having problems in their marriage after he'd met a South African model called Averille allegedly in the hotel during Spurs mid-season break in Brighton back in mid-December. 'He probably didn't know which one of the women was going to turn up,' says his brother Jackie.

Sandra Evans, John White's girlfriend, remembers being approached by Betty Blanchflower at a party to celebrate her engagement to John. 'Betty said, "If you have any problems, dear, come to me. I've had them all." She was quite a personality,' says Sandra.

The day after the programme should have been filmed, Blanchflower was given a lot of stick by his team-mates. 'When he came to training the next day we couldn't stop laughing,' says Bobby Smith. '"Where's

Danny?" we said. "Is he here yet?"' Blanchflower was not amused.

But while the players saw the funny side of the incident there were some who believed he was standing up for personal liberty in an age when television was beginning to encroach into people's private lives. Blanchflower, like many footballers, wasn't impressed by television, questioning the assumption that everyone wanted to be on the small screen.

'In walking out of *This Is Your Life* he was making but another gesture – and one of the most effective he has ever made – in bringing dignity to the professional footballer,' wrote Julian Holland in *Spurs – The Double*. 'Calculatedly, he did what no one had done before, to snub this public, soul-baring, orgy and insist that a celebrity, even if he is only a professional footballer, has a right to say no to the public when it wants him to do something he does not like.'

Ironically, when the *Daily Mail* serialised Blanchflower's autobiography *The Double and Before* in November 1961 they capitalised on his refusal to appear on *This Is Your Life*. The publicity said: 'This IS his Life. Danny Blanchflower writes the story he refused to let others tell. Don't miss the most exciting, the wittiest soccer story ever written – the intimate autobiography of Danny Blanchflower. Danny spares no one in a brilliant story of the best and worst of the life that is also his life – BIG-TIME FOOTBALL.'

But Blanchflower didn't shun television or the BBC entirely. Soon after walking out on the live screening of *This Is Your Life* he appeared on a programme called *Face to Face* hosted by John Freeman. And, in any case, the public had sided with him on the right of celebrities to choose whether or not they were laid bare before the public on television.

'His refusal to put himself into the limelight of *This Is Your Life*, his masterly display of argumentative erudition at a *Face to Face* encounter, his occasional radio and TV sallies have endeared him to a vast audience and, in the process, have succeeded in doing more for the good name of soccer and its players than any man, club, League or organisation has managed to do since football began,' wrote Ralph Finn in *Spurs Supreme*.

But Blanchflower was somehow unsuited to television in a way that he wasn't to newspapers. While his career in print journalism, notably at the *Daily Mail*, *The Observer* and the *Sunday Express*, flourished, his later television career on programmes like *Sportsview* didn't last long. He could often be found arguing with producers and directors who wouldn't give him the same creative freedom he'd enjoyed on the pitch at Spurs.

Meanwhile, Tottenham's defeat at home to Leicester had not only cost them two valuable points, but heralded the start of a seven-week period when Sheffield Wednesday began to chip away at their lead, reducing it to just three points. Worryingly, it was at this stage that Tottenham's title bid had faltered the previous season.

It was Aston Villa who'd determine whether Spurs' amazing season continued to blossom. Tottenham had drawn Villa away in the Fifth Round of the Cup and had to play them in the League the week before in what would be a dress rehearsal for the Cup match. The Press wondered if Villa could get a psychological advantage to help them knock Spurs out of the Cup by first winning the League match.

The officials at Villa Park knew they faced a daunting task and the match programme paid tribute to Tottenham. 'It is true to say that the exploits of the present Spurs team have gripped the imagination of the soccer-loving public in a way that no other club has been able to equal for many years. Wherever they go they are a magnet and a most difficult side to hold, as their record shows.'

'Don't treat this as next week's Cup tie,' Nicholson warned his players before the match. 'Remember it's a League match – and that means very different tactics.' But it was no ordinary League game. The players sounded each other out, trying to see what their opponents were made of as they kept one eye on the Cup match to come.

The noise generated by the 50,000 fans at Villa Park was electric but the tough, tense atmosphere affected the quality of the football. Tottenham had a single-mindedness to their play designed to demonstrate their superiority. But the calmness that was their trademark was lost along with their usual confidence and the forward line had lost its rhythm.

The Villa danger men were Gerry Hitchens, the club's leading scorer for the past two seasons, and Peter McParland, the man who'd injured Ray Wood in the 1957 Cup final to deny Manchester United the 'double'. They were determined. But the Spurs' defence shackled them with a ruthlessness that eliminated the danger from the first whistle. The closest Villa got to scoring in the first-half was a hand-ball in the box by Henry which the referee didn't see.

The biggest problem facing Spurs was the treatment Villa were giving Danny Blanchflower. The Villa manager, Joe Mercer, had decided to put Blanchflower out of the game. He ordered inside-forward Bobby Thomson to become an extra half-back, shadow the Spurs captain throughout the match and show no mercy. Some of the Tottenham players wouldn't pass to Blanchflower because he was so tightly marked. 'I took my shadow back into his own defence and advised John White to exploit the space I had left,' said Danny. 'At half-time we could talk about it more.' The players went into the dressing-rooms with the score at 0-0.

Blanchflower had plenty to say about their first-half performance. 'You're not giving me the ball,' he told them. 'But you're marked,' the Spurs defenders protested. Blanchflower was exasperated. 'That's what Villa want! You're doing their job for them. The solution is "push-and-run" isn't it? We're supposed to be good at that aren't we? Give it to me and run forward and I'll knock it straight to you and then you go on with it.' Even a shadow couldn't stop a quick wall pass, thought Blanchflower.

His marker, Bobby Thomson, got frustrated and Villa's whole plan fell apart. Smith put Tottenham in front with a header just after half-time and Dyson got their second with a great shot. Villa pulled one back through a disputed penalty converted by full-back Stan Lynn, but Spurs held on to become the quickest team ever to reach 50 League points.

The victory owed much to Blanchflower and Mackay, players who had the greatest respect for each other. There was just no stopping the Spurs captain. *The People*'s Maurice Smith had never before given a player ten marks in any match. 'I award them here with honours to Blanchflower the Brilliant,' he wrote. The Tottenham right-half had been perfect. His partner, Mackay, was also in superb form. Spurs' human dynamo had 'sparked when so many others spluttered' according to Maurice Smith.

Mackay was the perfect foil for Blanchflower. The ball was always turning up where the Spurs captain happened to be, whereas Mackay always seemed to be turning up where the ball was. The Scot's defensive qualities counterbalanced the Irishman's penchant to attack.

'Mackay would have been my first choice as captain, except that we already had a great one in Danny Blanchflower,' says Bill Nicholson. 'Mackay was a carefree type of person, the opposite to Blanchflower. But they had great respect for each other. They were one of the outstanding partnerships of British football.'

Mackay was prepared to graft and his energy was boundless. 'Here is a dynamic player who moves like perpetual motion through every second of the game,' wrote Ralph Finn in *Spurs Supreme*. 'Here is fire and thrust and dash and not a little skill, too, welded into that human inferno of a footballing frame.'

The Spurs players returned to the Midlands the following Saturday in the knowledge that Villa Park was their Cup bogey ground. They'd lost three post-war semi-finals there through last-minute goals in 1948, 1953 and 1956. But Tottenham had already conditioned Villa for defeat with the psychological advantage they'd gained in their League win. 'If you win this one, you'll win the Cup,' the pundits told the players.

Almost 70,000 fans – the biggest crowd to watch Spurs all season outside of Wembley – packed onto the Villa Park terraces to see the much-discussed tactics the home side said they'd use after a week of secret discussions. But when Villa ran out they were already a beaten side. Whatever their strategy was, it failed to stop an impressive Tottenham team playing some of their best and most inventive football.

It was all over by half-time. 'Aston Villa's contribution was that they provided the ground for the occasion,' wrote Ian Wooldridge in the *Sunday Dispatch*. In the half an hour before the break, Spurs were brilliant. No team in Britain, and few in Europe, could have lived with them. 'Withering runs . . . zany, close-worked passes . . . huge frontal assaults with the ball being crossed from wing to wing and back again,' wrote Wooldridge. 'Again and again the moves stemmed from Mackay. Around him White, Jones, Allen, Dyson, Blanchflower and Norman moved like obedient satellites of an all-powerful planet.'

Mackay was the inspiration. He hassled the Villa players

throughout the 90 minutes. 'On this day he was like some gigantic amalgam of Markova and Marciano,' wrote Wooldridge. 'He performed miracles of delicate ball control, tackling like a battering ram.' At times it seemed he didn't know his own strength, leaving weaker players crumpled on the ground after the fairest of tackles. Mackay was a mighty player.

'He tackles fiercely, at times vigorously, certainly with more bite and menace than any other member of the side,' wrote Ralph Finn. 'And he has been known to incur the displeasure of referees and opponents for his "they-shall-not-pass" attitude.' Managers like Cliff Britton and Charlie Mitten had spoken out against Mackay's tackling. There were even suggestions he should be dropped by Scotland to curb his toughness.

But there was nothing evil about Mackay's tackling. 'Mackay brought many players tumbling to the ground with the ferocity of his tackling, but was always scrupulously fair, always going for the ball,' says Nicholson. 'Dave Mackay had a strict code of conduct. He tackled robustly but always fairly, and expected similar treatment himself. But if anyone went outside the rules he became very angry indeed . . .'

Mackay believed that if a player went for the ball he should go for it with every fibre of his being. That's why he won the ball so often. But there was no vicious intent in his play; and even when opponents lost their temper with him he was slow to retaliate. Mackay had never been sent off and had only been booked twice in almost ten years of first-class football. Indeed, he smiled when other players would have been tempted to strike.

Mackay was but five feet eight inches tall, but you'd never have know it. He was a colossus of a man, a Goliath among Davids, but one who could take any sling-shot aimed at him. Size and power seemed to flow from his every pore. He was in fact a small man. But, as Julian Holland pointed out in *Spurs – The Double*, that was 'as bad a way of describing him as is possible.'

'. . . to imagine Spurs' great '60s side without the vibrant Scot is to picture the Huns without Attila or the Alamo without Davy Crockett,' wrote Ivan Ponting in *Tottenham Hotspur – Player-by-Player*. Indeed, many of the Tottenham team believed Mackay was more important to their success than even the great Danny Blanchflower.

If the Spurs captain was the brains of the side, Mackay was its heart. But he was also a very skilful player whose control was near perfect, whose passing was precise and who could strike a ball as well as any player at the club. In training, he would astound his team-mates by volleying continuously against a wall from 10 or even 15 yards. 'He was a truly great player with far more skill than he was ever given credit for,' says Nicholson. 'He had a delicate touch, two good feet and was such an intelligent reader of the game.'

But there could be no doubt that it was his physical presence opponents feared most; 'muscular thighs and a barn-door of a chest topped by features that were positively piratical,' wrote Ponting. 'The man tackled like a granite avalanche, exuding a passionate will to win and apparently consumed by a devilish, ruthless relish for his work.'

'Crag-hewn out of some bare Scottish hill, he has more pure strength than any other player since the late Duncan Edwards,' wrote Holland. 'A finely-made statue will try to express the human form in terms of stone; whoever made Dave Mackay is trying to express stone in terms of flesh and bone. His thighs are like the granite buttresses of some secure Norman church; his chest is so square and unyielding that it seems he has a second backbone going down the front.'

The goals against Villa came in 30 minutes of super football before half-time. A dazzling left-wing run by White, back at his best, ended seven passes later with Jones crashing a chest-high shot past Villa's new goalkeeper Geoff Sidebottom. The second goal followed a Mackay–Dyson–White–Smith–Allen attack which took the ball across the edge of the penalty area. Jones ran onto it and rifled home an unstoppable shot which was deflected high into the corner of the net off full-back John Neal, later to become the Chelsea manager. The Welsh winger stood there with his arms stretched up towards the heavens.

The game was as good as over. Villa's spirit had been destroyed and Tottenham coasted the second-half. There wasn't the same tension as in the first match and the Birmingham Press accused Spurs of disappointing the big crowd by not pulling out all the stops, though they didn't comment on Villa's poor display. 'You can win them all sometimes, but you can't please them all,' said a resigned Blanchflower.

John Camkin in the *Daily Mail* wrote that Tottenham had shut up the game by tight defensive tactics and that Blanchflower had given the order to get an early goal and then destroy the game with a defensive blockade so Spurs could win the match and go on to do the 'double'. 'It might have been his honest opinion but to us it was a lot of rubbish,' said Blanchflower. 'We believed in attacking soccer at Tottenham and most of the criticism of us over the years – and often by John Camkin – has been that we thought too much of attack.'

Blanchflower knew there were times when an attacking team had their back to the wall and needed to retreat to hold onto the game. If that had happened at Villa Park, Camkin's view might have been fair. But Villa didn't force Spurs to raise their game in the second-half. 'A game of soccer is like a conversation,' said Blanchflower. 'If your companions do not talk very much and you have no need or inspiration to say anything to them the conversation dies. That's what happened in the second-half at Villa Park.'

Tottenham were now chasing Villa's 64-year-old League Championship and FA Cup record. The descendants of that great side of 1897 couldn't protect their forbears' triumph. There were now just three games between Spurs and possession of the FA Cup.

CHAPTER 32
Spurs About to Crack?

TOTTENHAM'S LEAD AT the top of the First Division was eight points when their nearest challengers Wolverhampton Wanderers came to White Hart Lane on the night of Wednesday, 22 February. It was a bigger lead than any of their predecessors had enjoyed. The programme billed the game as a 'Vital Fixture with Wolves'. It was certainly tense.

Spurs had beaten Wolves 4-0 at Molineux earlier in the season and had won on each of the Wanderers' last six visits to the Lane. But Wolves had been playing consistently well and would put up a fight. 'Their style, a successful mixture of strength and finesse, has been remarkably successful for a long time, and few sides in post-war football have a better record than the men from Molineux,' said the match programme.

Before the game, Wolves manager Stan Cullis turned the psychological screw on Tottenham by predicting they were about to crack. Spurs didn't crack but Wolves stole the glory after 90 memorable minutes. The away side chased every ball and tackled tenaciously to throw Tottenham out of their stride. Spurs looked anxious and unusually off colour.

The Wolves half-back line of Eddie Clamp, Bill Slater and Ron Flowers – all England internationals – was hard, fast and tough. Smith and Allen each missed chances for Tottenham and Jones and Dyson 'ran into trouble, and the hard thighs of Wolverhampton's defenders, as though drawn by a magnet,' wrote Julian Holland in *Spurs – The Double*.

But there were also problems behind the forwards. Blanchflower and Mackay were not at their best and the defence was too often caught in possession. Tottenham looked ordinary against a Wolves side that only had ten fit players for three-quarters of the match after Slater injured his ribs in a collision with Smith. He was strapped up, but could only limp along the right-wing for the rest of the match.

Ironically, it was in the opening 15 minutes, before Slater's injury, that Spurs played their best football and threatened to sweep to a spectacular victory. They took the lead after ten minutes with a fine goal by Smith after Blanchflower, Mackay, Norman, Dyson and White had contributed to a brilliant move which took the ball the length of the pitch. They battered the Wolves goal for the next ten minutes but never again reached those heights.

Wolves equalised against the run of play after 22 minutes when a mistake by Blanchflower, of all people, allowed inside-right Jimmy Murray to send the alert Ted Farmer galloping away to score. It was his 22nd League goal in 21 games – an incredible strike rate for the young forward.

Wolves continued to pressure Spurs and were in with a chance of becoming only the second team to win at White Hart Lane right up until the final whistle. In the closing minutes the Tottenham fans gave Wolves the slow handclap as they resorted to the off-side trap to preserve their hard-won point. Donald Saunders of the *Daily Telegraph* thought the Wolves players should instead have been cheered all the way to the dressing-room for their performance.

After Tottenham's successes over Aston Villa the tenseness had returned to their play. The pressure was still on and their challengers, Wolves and Sheffield Wednesday, were breathing down their necks. 'Though Spurs will probably win the League Championship,' wrote Saunders, 'no one is going to convince Wolves of that until the figures are indisputable.'

Spurs recovered their composure to beat Manchester City the following Saturday at Maine Road.

Eric Todd of *The Manchester Guardian* wrote one of the best introductions to a report on a Tottenham game seen in print all season. 'Manchester City's home Football League game against Tottenham Hotspur at Moss Side took ill round about three o'clock, rallied strongly for half an hour, had a relapse at 3.35, and expired at 4.10. At the inquest, a verdict of "accidental death" was recorded.'

City played good football in the first half an hour with versatile inside-forward Denis Law finding time and space all over the pitch. Law was one of Britain's most expensive players having cost around £53,000 when he was transferred to City from Huddersfield.

Law knew how to enjoy life, and in many ways, was similar to Dave Mackay. Law put his heart into everything he attempted and Mackay thought it a pleasure to be around the canny Scot. 'Denis Law makes all who come into contact with him feel that life is worth living, and the only thing he seems to take really seriously is football.'

The same could be said of Mackay. He didn't smoke, but enjoyed a drink, usually a light ale or a glass of stout. He could often be found presiding over the players in the pub after a game ordering 'pints all round' as they discussed some particular aspect of the match. He was the leader of the pack at Tottenham both on and off the pitch.

Mackay drove to White Hart Lane or the club's training ground at Cheshunt in his 3.4 litre Jaguar with a smile on his face. The other Spurs players were as proud of Mackay's Jag as he was himself since they were as likely to be driving it as he was. Bobby Smith, in particular, was always on the lookout for a car to borrow from a team-mate. Mackay was a generous man who'd willingly share anything with his pals. He was one of the boys.

Mackay married an Edinburgh lass called Isobel in 1954. She worked as a shorthand-typist at a large wireworks in Musselburgh. They lived in a house owned by Spurs at East Barnet with their two boys, David junior and Derek, and their little girl Valerie. Dave liked watching television. *Sergeant Bilko* was his favourite programme and enjoyed going dancing with his missus. But his greatest love was golf.

You could often find Mackay on a golf course, as befits a Scot. He liked to go for a practice round with Danny Blanchflower or Bill Brown – both of whom were excellent golfers. All three had in the past qualified for the play-off for the Professional Footballers Golf Competition. They competed as avidly on the golf course as they did on the football pitch. They were determined to win in either sport.

Mackay, like Law, enjoyed his football. He could often be seen laughing as he went to collect the ball for a throw-in, tickled by the reasons for the decision having gone his way. He had a healthy appetite for the game and appreciated the skills of his opponents. Mackay was a very fair player and a good judge of character.

But while Mackay thought Law was a great player, in the second-half against Tottenham on the saturated Maine Road pitch he faded as the City attack ceased to function. The Scottish inside-forward became an anonymous figure in defence as Spurs put City under pressure. It was almost inevitable that Tottenham would score eventually.

The goal came on the hour when Blanchflower flighted an immaculate centre from the right which Medwin met perfectly with his head. The ball went in off the post. It was a solid win and Eric Todd of *The Manchester Guardian* wrote what many already knew: Tottenham were all but assured of the title and would be worthy Champions.

'Even the absence of Jones and Norman (Medwin and Marchi deputised) did not wholly diminish the usual quality of their performance, and the more that opponents see of Mackay and Blanchflower, the more they surely must envy the foundations on which this very fine side is built,' wrote Todd.

CHAPTER 33
Away the Lads

TOTTENHAM TRAVELLED TO Roker Park in the Sixth Round of the Cup for an all-ticket match. Such was the interest in Spurs' attempt to win the elusive 'double' that even other clubs were fascinated by the challenge. The programme for the Manchester City game noted that Tottenham were in with the greatest chance of any team since Manchester United in 1957.

Sunderland, lost in the obscurity of the lower regions of the Second Division for a few years after being relegated for the first time in their 70-year history, were intent on an early return to better company and had suddenly sprung to life. Their young side had lost only once in 20 games over five months. Sunderland's revival, after a mediocre start to the season, had been one of the features of the Second Division. They'd already beaten Arsenal at Roker and Liverpool and Norwich away to get to the Sixth Round of the Cup. Their successful run had rekindled all the old enthusiasm of their tremendous following.

Jack Woods, the northern football correspondent for the *Daily Mail*, freely quoted Danny Blanchflower in an article telling the people of the north-east that Tottenham intended to adopt the same tactics that his colleague John Camkin claimed they'd used against Aston Villa in the previous round, namely to grab an early goal and shut up shop.

'I wonder if the people up there who wrote to me condemning Spurs and myself for planning such tactics realised that they were deceived by the man from the *Daily Mail* – the paper that claims it is so popular because it talks such sense and doesn't ramble whatever the topic,' said an irritated Blanchflower.

Down south those who said Tottenham would win the Cup if they beat Villa were at it again. 'This is the vital game,' they told the players. 'If you beat Sunderland you will win the Cup.' Blanchflower had his own views on such opinions. 'You have to win them all to win the Cup and the truth in their opinions was that they were getting nearer to the truth all the time.'

Roker was packed to the rafters with more than 60,000 fans on that Saturday afternoon. When the players ran onto the pitch the noise was deafening. 'I have never seen such excitement, anywhere, as I did that day at Roker Park,' recalled Blanchflower.

A Cliff Jones goal after only nine minutes had failed to silence the home fans. Once they'd scored, Tottenham slowed the game down. Blanchflower seemed more concerned about having to make the last assault on the 'double' with a tired team than almost anything else. Instead of pulling out all the stops to increase their lead, Spurs casually flicked the ball about as they impudently showed off their skills.

Just four minutes after the interval Spurs were panicked into conceding a corner to gain breathing space, but they didn't get it as all hell broke loose behind their goal. Blanchflower's description of the pressures on Tottenham was worth a Pulitzer Prize. 'That great Roker crowd, starved of glory for so long, could not contain itself. A corner . . . the possibility . . . the equaliser . . . you could feel the tension behind that goal. They shouted and whistled and screamed and fainted with expectancy. The noise was unbearable: I could not feel my senses or clear my thoughts or concentrate properly because of the shrieking din. I was dimly aware that the others around me were shaking in their concentration too, and I shouted at them to rouse them a yard or two this way or that to a better relationship with their task. But it was hopeless. I couldn't hear my own voice. I felt a bit helpless. That great ear-splitting emotional roar was hammering at, and looked like cracking, the invisible links of our defence. It was chewing away at the bonds of confidence between us, and choking the words of encouragement and the shouts of understanding with which we rally one another to keep our lines intact.

'The ball flighted over and there was a wild scramble in the goalmouth. Eighteen of the players engaged in the conflict were packed in our goal area. They jerked about in excited anticipation of the bobbling ball, those trying to get it into the goal and those trying to keep it out. Confusion . . . and then the ball was scrambled behind for another corner. But there was no relief. The intensity grew as the delirious crowd sucked in its breath to raise the din. Another corner . . . the possibility, the equaliser had been dangled in front of their noses like a carrot and now they were straining themselves all the more to get a bite at it. Over came the ball for the same treatment with the same result – another corner. The pandemonium increased . . . Over it came again . . . and in the frothing panic it was smashed into the net. The equaliser.'

Sunderland's centre-half Charles Hurley had joined the attack, Norman-style, for much of the second-half and it was his header from the corner that enabled 18-year-old inside-left Willie McPheat, only passed fit just before the match, to score. His shot went in off captain Stan Anderson's leg. Pandemonium broke out inside Roker.

Mackay was witnessing the kind of scene he'd read about taking place abroad but never imagined could happen at home. 'When Sunderland scored a well-merited equaliser thousands of people invaded the pitch to personally "thank" their heroes. Fair enough. But when one lad, as goalkeeper Bill Brown turned to pick the ball out of the net, cheekily ran forward and asked him for his autograph, we all thought the joke had gone a little too far! But then, in football, one has to be prepared for anything.'

The scene calmed and Sunderland's efforts calmed with it. 'Sunderland put us under pressure with a succession of corners but we held out,' remembers Nicholson. 'A less-experienced side might have surrendered.' Spurs eventually got a grip on the match and guided it to the final whistle, and a replay, in their more familiar cultured style.

The insurance cover for the first-team squad on their return flight from London to the north-east was £600,000. It would have cost much less to insure the Sunderland side. That difference in class certainly showed in the replay.

Tottenham never gave a team a second chance in the 1960–61 season. They beat every side they played at least once. Mackay told his team-mates he couldn't see anyone, not even Burnley, stopping them after their luck at Roker Park. He felt certain they'd account for Sunderland at home.

There were so many people trying to get to White Hart Lane on the night of the Sixth Round replay that even the players were caught up in the crowd. The police had to help some of them to get to the ground. As each player finally reached the dressing-room, the tales of what was going on outside became more and more elaborate.

Bobby Smith couldn't get near the ground. Fortunately, a police motorcyclist recognised him and told the Spurs centre-forward to get on the back of his bike. 'I had to dump my car at the side of the road at White Hart Lane,' recalls Smith. 'My wife had to get out of the car and walk down White Hart Lane. It took her ages to get to the ground.'

The policeman told the fans: 'Look, I've got Bobby Smith on the back, let us through'. But they still couldn't negotiate a way past all the people. 'I'd never seen a crowd like it,' remembers Smith. It took the policeman 25 minutes to get him to the ground. They arrived at 7.20. The game was due to kick off at 7.45.

The gates were locked with 64,797 fans inside. Hundreds of ticket-holders couldn't get in. The scramble outside had started so early that schoolchildren on their way home got caught up in it. In future, the local schools would have a half-day when Spurs played a big match at home.

Tottenham were confident about the replay. The team that wins the Cup cannot fail; at most it can have a momentary lapse. Spurs had already had their loss of concentration in the first game. They were in no mood for further mistakes and wouldn't fail again, not in front of their own fans. 'This time the vast crowd would be on our side,' said Nicholson, 'though the noise might not equal the Roker sound.'

Sunderland were without left-half Jimmy McNab who was injured in the first game. Their most influential player, right-half and captain Stan Anderson, had to abandon his attacking role behind the forwards and cross over to try to snuff out the irrepressible John White. The tactical shift left Sunderland lacking their earlier thrust up front.

Spurs took the lead when Allen hammered in a goal from the left after 27 minutes. Just over half an hour had gone when Smith got the second after Sunderland keeper Peter Wakeham could only parry a shot from Jones.

Seconds before half-time Jones set up a third goal for Dyson to put the match beyond any doubt. Tottenham had calmly pulled Sunderland apart with the arrogance of a team that knew it was destined for greatness.

There was no let-up after the interval as Spurs, arrogant and dominant, retained the ruthlessness they'd shown in the first half. Sunderland tried bravely to mask their nerves. 'They tried to fathom the mind of White who, with Danny Blanchflower, fashioned the fantasies of soccer which streamed from Spurs,' wrote Clive Toye in the *Daily Express*.

It was a thankless task. Tottenham taught Sunderland the lesson they'd given Crewe the previous year: it was folly to upset, for however short a time, so resourceful a team. Sunderland had already endured 65 minutes of torture when Tottenham turned the screw once more. 'Almost unnoticed there suddenly danced into the Sunderland penalty area a white-clad figure, the ball obedient at his toe,' wrote Julian Holland. 'Delicately he picked his way past not one or two of the red-and-white striped defenders, but four before he slipped the ball inside for Dyson to hammer home the fourth goal. For once the heavy, frowning uncertainty left Les Allen's face. His grin, as his colleagues mobbed him with their salty-lipped congratulations, seemed to reflect perhaps that he was worthy after all to rank as an equal in this team of stars.' Five minutes later Mackay cracked home a left-foot shot to round off the scoring. It had been a convincing 5-0 victory under the White Hart Lane floodlights.

'The twin towers of Wembley were looming nearer and we were still comfortably situated in the League,' recalled Blanchflower. Spurs were one game from Wembley.

CHAPTER 34
The Semi-final

SPURS LOST A League game at Cardiff on the Saturday which they should have won. They were twice in front but each time allowed the Welsh side to pull back and eventually score the winner. Cardiff were mobbed by some of the excited fans among the 46,000 who filled Ninian Park.

Nicholson and his players were disappointed to lose a game that had been switched to the Saturday evening to avoid clashing with a rugby international being played that afternoon. Still, the most important game came next: the FA Cup semi-final against Burnley. Blanchflower tried to look on the bright side after the defeat in Wales. 'We reckoned we were due to lose one and it was better at Cardiff than in the semi-final,' he said.

Spurs' League form had suddenly become inconsistent. They'd been averaging just a point a game since the New Year and by the time they faced Burnley in the semi-final of the FA Cup at Villa Park their twelve-point lead had been cut to just four points by Sheffield Wednesday.

Jones had been missing throughout the end of December and most of January with an injury, White had lost his form and Mackay was burning himself out as he tried to compensate for his team-mates' frailties.

It was not a good time to have a bad patch. The FA Cup semi-final against Champions Burnley would be a tough game. 'When we heard the draw for the semi-final – Spurs versus Burnley at Villa Park – we knew our biggest challenge lay ahead of us,' remembers Cliff Jones.

Burnley had, of course, held Tottenham to a 4-4 draw at White Hart Lane back in December after being four goals down. 'The memory of their fightback at White Hart Lane was never far from us,' said Jones.

It was during the tense few days leading up to the semi-final that the 'double' became an official target when it was mentioned for the first time during a team talk. The first-team squad was taken to the pretty seaside town of Mumbles next to Swansea, the home town of both Cliff Jones and Terry Medwin, for some training beside the golf course.

The two wingers had spent a lot of their childhood in Mumbles, little knowing that years later it would be the scene of a historic address by the captain of Tottenham Hotspur. For it was in the sun lounge of the Caswell Hotel that Blanchflower talked about Spurs' 'double' chances.

'The "double" hasn't been done this century, but let's face it, we've got a very, very good chance to pull it off. We're just 180 playing minutes from winning the Cup and we need less than a dozen points from ten games to clinch the Championship. I think it's on.' The others agreed.

'That's the first time I thought we could do it,' says Jones. 'Up until then nobody wanted to bring it up. We thought we'd probably won the Championship by then and that if we could beat Burnley the "double" was a real possibility.'

Burnley were a clever team, well drilled and methodical. They had players like the great Irish international Jimmy McIlroy, Ray Pointer and Jimmy Robson 'whom we knew could transform a game with one stroke of impish ingenuity' said Jones. 'Of one thing we were sure: Burnley were our biggest obstacle to pulling off the "double".'

The result is always more important than the quality of football or the entertainment in an FA Cup semi-final. They're mostly rugged affairs full of safety-first spoiling tactics. The occasion at Villa Park was further undermined by the newspapers who'd decided it was an 'unlucky' ground for both teams. Spurs had lost three semi-finals there since the war, while Burnley had a terrible scoring record at Villa Park.

Spurs were supremely confident about beating any team at Wembley where the players knew the conditions and the space would suit their style of play, but Villa Park wasn't Wembley. 'I don't think we would have worried unduly if Burnley had been our Wembley opponents,' said Jones. 'But meeting them in the semi-final . . . Well, that was different.'

Spurs and Burnley were evenly matched. The Champions had greater individual skills, while Tottenham worked better as a team. Burnley were the only club in Britain who could match Spurs' adventurous continental-style attacking game.

The Lancashire side had begun the season chasing the treble of European Cup, League Championship and FA Cup. But it was a good time to play them since they'd concentrated too much effort on Europe and lost 4-1 to Hamburg just three days before.

Tottenham had the home dressing-room and Blanchflower kidded McIlroy about it before the semi-final. 'We've got the lucky dressing-room and you never win at Villa Park,' he told his Irish international team-mate. 'We've not been here in our own jerseys yet,' McIlroy replied. Burnley had always had to wear a change strip at Villa Park because of the clash of colours when they played Aston Villa.

'We've never lost against those jerseys here,' quipped Blanchflower, reminding McIlroy that Tottenham hadn't lost a League match at Villa Park since the war. 'Where did you stay last night?' he asked. 'Droitwich,' the Burnley inside-forward told Blanchflower. 'Poor sods,' smirked Blanchflower. 'We stayed there before our 1956 semi-final here and lost.' McIlroy smiled at Blanchflower's insinuations but the Spurs captain hoped they had made him uncomfortable.

Nicholson and his players knew it took a good side to win the League and a lucky one to win the Cup. Lady luck shone on them at Villa Park where the game failed to live up to unrealistically high expectations. The conditions didn't help, but there's no doubt that the tension felt by both sides also contributed to a less-than-spectacular game.

Some 22,000 Tottenham fans made the journey from North London to the Midlands for the match. It was a bright day but a strong swirling wind, light bouncing ball, hard ground and the nerves that always accompany a semi-final dragged the game down to a keenly contested but rather ordinary level. It was by no means a classic.

Only Blanchflower and McIlroy, close friends who shared the scheming role for Northern Ireland, had the skill and nerve to beat the difficult conditions. But it was Burnley, marshalled by McIlroy, who dictated most of the play. They'd have won if the breaks had fallen evenly. But they failed to turn their superiority into goals. The Spurs forwards weren't firing on all cylinders but they had the fortune.

'We began with a strong and gusty wind in our favour, but for 30 minutes Burnley promised to cement a grip on the game that would take a lot of breaking,' recalls Cliff Jones. 'For the first half-hour Burnley had more possession of the ball than we did,' recalled Blanchflower, 'although they did not penetrate in relation to it.'

Nevertheless, Burnley had Spurs on the rack. They were not only the cleverer side but also the cooler team. It was the defence that saved Tottenham in those early exchanges. 'There was Brown, like one of the Harlem Globetrotters, picking the ball off the heads of the leaping Burnley forwards,' wrote Julian Holland in *Spurs – The Double*. 'There was Henry keeping his head and his feet against the guile and speed of [John] Connelly. There was Norman blocking every thrust of Pointer with breath-taking judgement. There was Baker blotting out Harris and making time to cover his colleagues. There was Mackay, with the most difficult task of all, ever at McIlroy's elbow. And at their head there was Blanchflower, like a schoolboy hero, leading his men ever back into attack, on legs that seemed now to be made only of sinew, bone and muscle.'

Blanchflower was ice cool in his brand-new black and white football boots when Spurs were in trouble. When the rest of the defence in turn seemed under pressure it was their captain who came to the aid of first Baker, then Norman and even Mackay. How Tottenham needed his calm influence during those first hectic 30 minutes.

Then suddenly the whole complexion of the game changed when, in one of their first real raids, Tottenham had their first stroke of luck. As the Villa Park clock struck half past three, Jimmy Adamson, Burnley's big and thoroughly dependable captain and centre-half, so often the hero in the past, tried to intercept a flick from Les Allen. There was nothing difficult about it and nine times out of ten he would have met it on the half-volley. But this was the tenth time. Somehow the wind forced the bouncing ball past his outstretched foot and Bobby Smith raced round him to drive the ball with his trusty right boot past the helpless dive of Burnley keeper Adam Blacklaw.

Smith deserved the credit for taking his chance so well on such a big occasion. But it was Burnley's mistake that had cost them dearly against the run of play. 'It was a gift goal and one, quite frankly, that we didn't deserve,' says Jones. No team could afford to hand out goals on a plate to this Tottenham side.

It was a triumph for Smith and marked the moment when his luck returned. The big-hearted centre-forward had been repeatedly criticised for his performances at Spurs and in an England shirt over the past few months. To his credit, Smith had never allowed the attacks to get him down even when all the footballing gods seemed to have deserted him. He knew he wasn't playing well. 'I seem to have lost a lot of the goal edge,' he'd told Maurice Smith of *The People* a few days before the semi-final. But Smith was not a player to give up without a fight.

The goal made him the hero of the hour. From then on Spurs were in control of a match that minutes before looked to be swinging in Burnley's favour. At last their defence, superbly marshalled by Blanchflower, was given a rest from the exhausting task of shackling the tormenting McIlroy, eager Connelly and lurking Robson.

'We then saw Blanchflower, enjoying one of his greatest hours, switch to the offensive,' wrote Donald Saunders of *The Daily Telegraph*. 'Tantalising passes gave his indifferent forwards chance after chance to sweep to victory. But, with Jones and Allen right out of touch, and White making only occasional contributions, Smith and Dyson could not, on their own, shake the Burnley defence.'

Just before half-time they should have had a second goal when full-back John Angus punched out a header from Dyson from under the bar after it had beaten the keeper Blacklaw. The referee didn't see it and the Tottenham fans resorted to booing him in their frustration. But the fates had not turned around and had not finished with Burnley yet.

They began the second 45 minutes searching for the equaliser, but just two minutes into the second-half, Tottenham had their second stroke of luck. Alex Elder curled a long free kick into the Spurs goalmouth, Jimmy Robson leapt high, flicked his head – and the ball was in the Tottenham net. The Spurs defenders turned dejectedly and Jones thought the goal might turn the tide. '"That's it," I thought to myself. "We're in for it." And judging by the long faces of my team-mates we all felt the same way as the whole Burnley team went into a dance of triumph. But, suddenly, I knew something was wrong. The crowd fell silent for a split second, and then roared with anger or joy – depending on the colour of the rosette they were wearing – as they saw the referee Ken Collinge of Altrincham, signalling a free kick.'

The 46-year-old referee had spotted Robson using Maurice Norman's back to climb for the ball. '. . . Although I must admit from where I was standing it had looked a perfectly good goal,' said Jones. The referee had a different view. 'I saw it clearly,' said Collinge. 'I'm surprised there was so much fuss for the whistle had blown before Robson even headed the ball.'

Immediately afterwards Ron Henry saved the ball with his hands as clearly as Angus had in the first half. '. . . [he] definitely handled the ball on the goal-line,' said Blanchflower. 'He didn't do it intentionally but it definitely hit his hand.' The boos rang out from the Burnley fans when the referee didn't give a penalty.

Burnley could not fight this kind of thing, though they tried. The Lancashire side kept up the pressure and three of their shots had just been blocked on the goal-line when Tottenham broke and were awarded a free kick in the 49th minute. Blanchflower curved the ball towards the Burnley goal, Elder headed a weak clearance and there was Smith to hit a sweet right-foot volley from just inside the box. It flew into the net before Blacklaw could move.

There was a delighted roar from the Spurs fans. Smith, the most attacked and underrated member of Tottenham's record-breaking team, had hammered a two-goal claim to keep his England place. Before the match he'd told Peter Lorenzo of *The Daily Herald*: 'I've just about had enough of this "He's no good for England" business. I don't mind people criticising me, but not every time my name is mentioned. If only I could score three goals this afternoon, or even two.'

Smith had battled and chased every ball to get what he wanted. His goals were another example of his value to Spurs and allowed Blanchflower and his team to dictate the course of the game. The watching England manager Walter Winterbottom couldn't fail to be impressed with Smith's performance.

Burnley continued to make a game of it but made a tactical mistake in the second-half when they repeatedly played the long ball through the middle. These tactics were meat and drink to Norman. Tottenham's tall, commanding centre-half was contesting the man-of-the-match award with Blanchflower. He had completely marked Pointer out of the game.

Tottenham enveloped their penalty area to protect their lead. Burnely made tenacious efforts to drag themselves back into the match. Even Adamson joined the attack in the hope of redeeming himself for his earlier mistake. But Spurs would not give way now.

The game was all over when Dyson and White set up the unmarked Jones. He hammered the ball home with his left foot for Tottenham's third goal almost on the final whistle. Some people thought Smith had scored that one too, but he admitted he hadn't. 'I was up with the ball but didn't touch it,' he said after the match. 'It was Jones's goal alright.'

Hundreds of Tottenham fans ignored appeals for them to stay off the pitch and chaired Smith off at the finish. The players retreated to their dressing-room to reflect on the match. Ron Henry rated the victory as one of the games that stood out in that 'double' year. 'I can remember coming out of the dressing-room into the long corridor at Villa Park and seeing my wife standing at the other end. She was very excited. "You'll be playing at Wembley," she said. I don't know how she got in there and nor does she, but she was there.'

Burnley couldn't complain about the result even though the luck fell Tottenham's way. But Jones was counting his lucky stars that Robson's equaliser had been disallowed in the second-half. 'So shall I always maintain that if Robson's goal had been allowed, Burnley would have beaten us. The spark went out of Burnley when Bobby Smith put us two up – but had they equalised I think they would have hit us for four.'

Blanchflower was also humble in victory. 'I thought Burnley had some bad luck that day, although I felt that we still deserved to win – one more easily remembers the ill-luck of the losing team, as it seems pointless to account for the negative moments of the team that finished with the positive result. I wondered afterwards if Jimmy McIlroy was thinking about my doom-laden prophecies before the match.

Tottenham were going to Wembley and the players had cause to celebrate on the way home. 'I remember the train journey back from Villa Park was unbelievable,' says Terry Dyson, who, by his own admission, had not played well against Burnley. 'We had a big compartment booked on the train and the champers flowed. We realised we'd almost got the "double".'

CHAPTER 35
The Title Race Goes On

SPURS WERE ONE game away from winning the Cup. Their opponents would be Leicester, sixth in the First Divison, who eventually won the other semi-final after two replays against Sheffield United 'Now, we all knew, only 90 minutes, and Leicester City, stood between us and the achieving of the soccer summit,' said Mackay.

'We didn't feel the pressure,' remembers Nicholson. 'We were on top of the world after winning so many games. We were coming to the end of the season and we'd already won our semi-final and had almost got the Championship. We could forget about the Cup final. We were there and nobody could stop us; nobody could take that away. We had a bloody great chance of winning the League. It was in our hands if we kept at it. We were in the Cup final but we hadn't won the Cup yet. If we wanted to win anything it was the League so we went for the title.'

Spurs' next League game was at home to Newcastle on the Wednesday night following the semi-final. The game was originally scheduled for the Saturday but, of course, Tottenham were otherwise engaged at Villa Park against Burnley. Newcastle were third from bottom having won only eight of their 33 League matches so far. They were desperate for points.

If Spurs had been lucky at Burnley their good fortune deserted them against Newcastle. They should have scored between 10 and 20 goals depending on which journalist you chose to read. Julian Holland thought they could have had a lead of six goals by half-time and should have won 10-0 or 12-0. Laurie Pignon writing in *The Daily Sketch* believed Tottenham should have scored 20 goals. In fact, they managed only one.

Spurs scored when Jones just saved the ball from crossing the goal-line before centring for Allen to put Tottenham ahead. They'd totally dominated the first-half and the one goal was scant reward for their efforts. In the ten minutes before half-time at least half a dozen shots and headers stuck on the goal-line and were desperately cleared by the Newcastle defence.

Dave Hollins, the Newcastle keeper, playing his first match since a £12,000 transfer from Brighton a week before, led a charmed life. He made more than 20 great saves, some by good judgement and others by sheer luck. The ball seemed to strike him as often as he saved it. And it hit his colleagues too, sometimes on their hands. The ball was even blocked on the line by Tottenham's own players getting in the way. Among the misses was a Blanchflower penalty, the only spot-kick Spurs had missed all season.

Julian Holland takes up the story of the match. 'Spurs played superb football up to the penalty area. In midfield, all their artistry was at its most evident. Never did a player find himself with the ball for more than a second but there were three colleagues circling around him waiting for the pass. The ball moved the length of the field in staccato nine-men moves, foot-punched from unmarked man to unmarked man, and never within intercepting length of an outstretched Newcastle leg. Wisely, the Newcastle defence funnelled back to their penalty area, crowding the final assault.'

'Newcastle had taken a bigger hammering than a blacksmith's anvil in the first 45 minutes,' wrote Pignon of *The Daily Sketch*. 'It seemed pointless to come out for the second-half. Spurs' half-backs and forwards were carving them up and eating them alive.'

But as the game wore on a hint of desperation crept into Spurs' play 'like the panic of a surfacing diver who is too long in breaking water,' according to Holland. 'Faster and faster they made their ploys, their control slipping as the hard ground bounced the ball out of instant obedience. Forgotten were the famous changes of pace, the lulling, stupefying, casual, midfield inter-passing, followed by the sudden dart for goal. White, Jones and Dyson resorted to long-running, individual sorties, Smith hobbled with an injury, Allen, once the gauche forward of the line, looked in astonishment at the temporary demoralisation of his colleagues, impotent himself to make the goals that would have restored order. It must have seemed for those 11 Tottenham men as they raced faster and faster, like fish in a tank outside some Paris restaurant, perked into galvanised life with overdoses of oxygen, that the truths of life were being denied, that night was day and that their system of victory was in reality as haphazard as a forecast on the pools.'

It seemed like everything had been turned upside down and black was white as an unmarked Ivor Allchurch equalised in the 64th minute with a free header and Albert Scanlon, bought from Manchester United in November, scored the winner an unlucky 13 minutes from the end. Scanlon had picked up a clearance, raced up the left wing and, from midway between the penalty area and the touch-line, lobbed a cross over the bemused Brown in the Tottenham goal. Those two breakaway attacks, and a couple of others by Allchurch in the first-half, were all Newcastle could muster on the night. But it would prove to be enough.

'Like a kitten enmeshed in a ball of string, Spurs' frantic, panicking struggles served only to wrap them more tightly in the web of frustration in which two successive defeats against indifferent teams had enfolded them,' wrote Julian Holland in *Spurs – The Double*.

In the last few frantic minutes Spurs threw everything at Newcastle. Every Tottenham player except the two full-backs and Bill Brown had at least one shot at the Newcastle goal and Bobby Smith must have had at least a dozen. As Newcastle clung on to their slender advantage keeper Hollins and centre-forward Len White collided and were knocked out. White was taken to hospital with a suspected broken ankle. But Newcastle held on to secure a famous victory. It was one of the shocks of the season and only the second home defeat inflicted on Spurs.

When Spurs went to Craven Cottage to play Fulham on the following Saturday it was clear all was not well. They were no longer working hard enough to find the space they needed to play their open, fluid attacking football because they were dog-tired. White hadn't been at his best for a few months, at least in the League matches, and Mackay had had to push himself even harder to get through the extra work.

Blanchflower had also raised his game. He led by example, urging team-mates to greater efforts when they were flagging. 'He must have lived wholly on his nerves as the fatal time of Easter approached,' wrote Holland. 'His football was all head, his brain and his will whipping his body into the effort that he knew had no end until May 6th. '

'Danny was not the fastest player,' said goalkeeper Bill Brown, 'but one complemented the other: Dave would play the two positions until Danny got back and vice versa. They were worth two players each. But these weren't things that were talked about, they were things that happened automatically. Everybody covered for everyone else. We had a system; we always played with ten men because, I don't care what you say, like in an office there will always be someone that comes in with the Monday morning blues even on a Friday! So now you're a body short. We went out the same every time; there was a feeling you had to give 110 per cent; you always had to give that little bit extra because there was always someone who was going to have a bad day. Now, of course, if a player is having a bad day you can bring on a fresh one.'

Mackay's extra workload had done him some damage and he was lacking his usual fire. He was burned out. 'His coals no longer glowed, his flames no longer danced and leaped,' wrote Holland. He'd lost his spark. Against Fulham the contrast with Johnny Haynes, by his own admission the most difficult opponent Mackay faced in his career, was striking as the England inside-forward had a splendid match. Ironically, White was the only player anywhere near his regular form, but even he faded.

The game finished goalless, but Tottenham were lucky to escape their third successive League defeat. They hadn't won a League match since 25 February and had collected just eight points from their last nine games. Meanwhile, their closest rivals Sheffield Wednesday were beating Manchester United 5-0 at Hillsborough.

'We are not playing too well,' said Nicholson. 'We haven't been for a few games now. We used to enjoy our football because we were working hard. There is no substitute for effort in this game. We have got to get back working. Nothing else will do.'

They'd struck one of those bad patches that can hit a club at any time. The goals weren't coming, tension was building up and the team's rhythm was being affected again.

Tottenham now faced a similar situation to the previous season:

two home games against teams in the bottom half of the First Division. It was two successive home defeats against Manchester City and Chelsea at Easter that cost Spurs the Championship in 1960. Easter was the Cup Final of the League programme and they were struggling once again.

Nicholson was as aware of the danger as anyone. He called the team together for a crisis talk. 'The defence is doing very well – just as they did last year,' he said. 'But the forwards are going to have to finish a lot better if we're not going to repeat last season's disappointment. You're not doing enough work – and that's a criticism I don't want to make again.'

As always, Nicholson was right. Tottenham's whole pattern of play was built on work. Everything depended on the support given to the player in possession. The more passing options they made available the better Spurs played.

Their first fixture this time was, ironically, against Chelsea on Good Friday. Mackay and Smith were injured so Marchi and Saul got another chance to play a role in Tottenham's title bid. But this was like Newcastle all over again. Spurs should have been five or six goals ahead by half-time and had dominated the match even more than against Newcastle.

There were no goals when the referee blew his whistle for half-time. It meant Tottenham hadn't scored in the League for 190 minutes. The home fans in a 65,000 crowd were beginning to think they'd never find that back of the net again.

But five minutes into the second-half a move on the right involving Blanchflower drew the Chelsea defence and, when the cross came in, Jones fournd himself all alone in front of an open goal. He ran the ball into the net with the care of a player expecting something to go wrong at any moment. The goal completely changed the mood among the players.

Tottenham did almost as they pleased. 'It was wonderful to watch the way Spurs slowed the game down and dictated the pace,' wrote Ralph Finn. 'As they ambled, Chelsea chased, looking like carthorses galloping like mad to try to keep up with the trotting thoroughbreds.'

Marchi had a great game against Chelsea's dangerous striker Jimmy Greaves, snuffing him out completely. 'Certainly on this form Marchi is almost as good as Mackay at his best,' wrote Finn. 'And if Marchi lacks Mackay's bite in the tackle, he is perhaps the stronger defensive player.'

Tottenham were now in complete command and their superiority was clearly shown when Henry raced forward to take a short corner to Marchi. The thought of covering for his attacking full-back hadn't entered Marchi's head. His only concern was pushing for more goals.

Jones was superb and added a second goal to his first, while Allen and Saul (who looked a very promising young player) scored another two. Two late goals from Chelsea made the score look more respectable than it should have been.

After the doubts that followed his transfer to Spurs Cliff Jones had more than justified Bill Nicholson's judgement that he would be a great asset to Tottenham. He had blossomed into one of the best wingers in the country, if not Europe. His speed was spellbinding.

'Like a hungry cheetah at full stretch on the trail of its hapless prey, Cliff Jones running towards goal was a spectacle to take the breath away,' wrote Ivan Ponting in *Tottenham Hotspur – Player-by-Player*. 'The Welsh dasher was that rare and glorious being, a speed merchant with ball control, and he was undoubtedly the most thrilling, eye-catching entertainer in Spurs' greatest team.'

Former England manager Terry Venables stood on the Tottenham terraces as a boy and Jones was one of his heroes. 'Of my time supporting Tottenham, and Bill Nick might agree, Cliff Jones was possibly the best winger the club had. I thought he was absolutely magnificent.'

Jones had a reputation for being courageous and carries the scars to this day which prove how brave he was. Dave Mackay describes him as the most fearless player he's known. His bravery was most noticeable in the air where, if there was the slightest chance of scoring, Cliff would throw himself in among the boots regardless of the personal danger.

'He was not a big guy, yet he was able to get across defenders consistently with powerful headers,' recalls Venables. 'He must have had so many cuts on his face.'

Nicholson had no doubt that during the 1960–61 season, Jones was the most courageous player in the team. 'There was no braver player in the game than Cliff, and for a small, slight man he scored some memorable goals with his head.'

Jones played without shin pads because he believed he could run quicker if he didn't wear them. He ignored all the knocks and bruises he'd collected so he could more easily outpace defenders.

His markers, with one or two exceptions, weren't intentionally rough on him, but, as Mackay knew well, he was so quick that a player could quite accidentally find himself hitting Jones's leg in a tackle.

Although Cliff could play on either wing he was particularly effective cutting in from the left before heading for goal or opening up space for a team-mate along the touch-line. But he was most dangerous when he was streaking through the middle of the park.

He was brilliant at taking on defenders, but he didn't dazzle them with intricate dribbling; his art was speed and surprise which often left players chasing shadows. He'd go past markers before they had a chance to make a fair tackle. 'Defenders would take a gamble when confronting him,' says Venables. 'They could either bring him down or watch him go by. His pace and change of direction made him such a tricky winger.'

Dave Mackay was also impressed with the Welsh winger's skills. Mackay had faced the daunting prospect of trying to stop him in international football when Scotland played Wales, as well as trying to set him in motion at Tottenham. 'Jones, as I have noticed so often, does not appear to run over the ground. The lithe Welshman seems to skim the surface as he glides past opponents, often sending a defender going the wrong way with a shrug of the shoulders or flick of his foot.'

Jones had a very long stride which helped him to cover the ground at a tremendous pace. Mackay thought he was the fastest man since Stanley Matthews was at his peak and that he was easily the quickest player in Europe, if not the world, when running with the ball.

'The power and pace of Jones has proved a nightmare to some of the best backs in the game for, like other great players, he is a man full of ideas – original ones – which he produces in his efforts to outwit the opposition,' says Mackay. 'Jones's ability to hit the ball freely with both feet is something else which commends him.'

If he was fouled, Cliff would fly through the air like an arrow for yards afterwards. But he never retaliated or showed any emotion. 'Like Tom Finney and Stanley Matthews, who have also had plenty of experience in being sent flying, he has control of himself and his temper,' says Mackay. Cliff opposed any kind of violence on the pitch. 'Football was never meant to be a game of biff and bang,' he once said.

'Jones is the complete modern footballer, equipped with all the skills of the game and invested with a rare, tactical intuition,' wrote Julian Holland in *Spurs – The Double*. 'He goes where the play dictates, able at all times to contribute a major part in any stage of the game. He is the outrider in Nicholson's crack army. More than any other player, he has made Blanchflower's old age comfortable and filled with renown. There is no higher compliment.'

The following day that famous old club Preston came to White Hart Lane on a wet and miserable Saturday afternoon. They were bottom of the League and it showed. Tottenham thrashed them 5-0. White scored the first after just three minutes with a speculative 25-yard drive that slipped under the body of Preston's Irish goalkeeper Kelly on the slippery pitch.

The second goal, Spurs 100th of the season, was masterly. Blanchflower, superb throughout, started the move that progressed through Marchi to Allen near the corner of the penalty area. The Spurs inside-forward checked the ball and palmed it under his boot before calling Blanchflower back from an offside position and then rolling the ball onto the penalty spot for Jones. The Welsh winger changed feet twice before he had the ball where he wanted it and then he fired home.

Saul scored the third with a header and then Blanchflower indulged in some Irish blarney for the fourth goal. The Spurs captain stepped up to take a free kick after a foul on Allen. But he hesitated before chipping the ball over to Jones on the right. The Preston defence were still wondering what Danny was up to when the ball hit the back of the net. Jones' third – and Tottenham's fifth – was a sparkling overhead kick.

Marchi, again deputising for the injured Mackay, was faultless and was given 10 out of 10 by Ralph Hadley of *The People*. He showed off all the skills he'd learnt in Italy and revelled in the freedom he was given by the Preston midfield. When Blanchflower paused for breath, Marchi took up the gauntlet and confidently directed the attack.

But it was Blanchflower who shone brightest. At one point, surrounded by three Preston players, he turned four times in the same spot before threading the ball to Marchi. Mackay's replacement had stood there watching and waiting, admiring his captain's intricate ball skills.

'We have four plans for short free kicks,' Blanchflower told Ralph Hadley of *The People* after the game when asked about Spurs' well-worked fourth goal. 'Sometimes they work, sometimes they don't. This one did.'

Preston's Cliff Britton knew it had worked all right. His team had one of the best defensive records in the League but they couldn't hold the Tottenham goal machine. 'Any team would have been beaten by Spurs on their form today,' he said.

CHAPTER 36
Married to the Team

IN BETWEEN SPURS' home game with Preston on Saturday and their match at Stamford Bridge on Easter Monday was a very special event involving all the players: Maurice Norman's wedding.

'Monty' was to wed a 20-year-old student called Jacqueline Knight of Old Park Avenue, Enfield. The ceremony was held at the picturesque country church of St Thomas à Beckett perched prettily on the edge of the village green at Northaw in Hertfordshire.

Terry Medwin was the best man and, like Norman, he wore a top hat and tails. Jacqueline wore a dress of Nottingham lace with a classic line bodice, a crinoline skirt and short train. Her short veil was held in position by a coronet of lily of the valley with satin leaves and crowned with two white roses. She carried a bouquet of gold roses and lily of the valley.

But getting married to a famous footballer wasn't all roses, as Jacqueline already knew. Norman suffered with tonsillitis all season but he couldn't have his tonsils out because the team needed him so much. It was to be a very eventful week for Norman.

Spurs had a fight on their hands at Stamford Bridge. They had to come from behind in front of a packed crowd of more than 65,000 who were willing their team to win.

Smith, back in the team after injury, scored the first goal with a powerful header. But Chelsea fought every inch of the way despite losing Peter Brabrook with a dislocated shoulder after 33 minutes following a collision with Norman.

Then Greaves was booked for protesting after he thought he'd pulled Chelsea level. The referee gave offside. But the equaliser came just three minutes later through Frank Blunstone and Greaves did score a wonderful goal in the 56th minute after running from the halfway line to put Chelsea ahead. Greaves had scored his first-ever League goal for Chelsea against Tottenham on his debut in 1957 in a 1-1 draw.

Spurs looked to be heading for a defeat that would have reopened the Championship race. They needed to score quickly, and they did through a Medwin header. Then Blanchflower motioned to newlywed Norman to join the attack for a free-kick. Mackay swung the ball in, Norman rose and the ball was in the net. It was a masterful move by the Spurs captain.

In the past Blanchflower had been criticised by other managers, notably Jimmy Anderson, for changing the team during a game. This time he had no reason to worry. Nicholson had given his captain more responsibility than he'd known before and he appreciated the value of Blanchflower's improvisations during games. It had worked this time.

Spurs had the Championship in their sights and the double over Chelsea had virtually assured that they'd win the title. 'When I scored that header I knew we'd won the League,' says Norman. It was a remarkable week for the big centre-half. He'd never know another one like it.

CHAPTER 37

Champions!

TOTTENHAM'S LEAD OVER Sheffield Wednesday had narrowed to just three points after the draw with Fulham at Craven Cottage. It had shaken Spurs up to see their ten point cushion eaten away. But Easter had been the crucial test and Tottenham had come through with flying colours.

Spurs had taken a maximum six points from their Easter games and now held a five-point lead with a goal average which was worth another point. There were just five games left.

Wednesday had gone 19 matches without defeat but, just as the strain of being chased had proved too much for Tottenham the year before, now the strain of chasing was proving too much for the Owls. They'd only managed to stay within striking distance of Spurs because of their water-tight defence marshalled by captain Tony Kay who hadn't missed a game all season. They'd conceded only 39 goals in 38 League games – the lowest in the First Division and nine fewer than Spurs.

When the Sheffield team came to White Hart Lane on Wednesday, 17 April it was their last chance to halt Spurs' relentless drive for the title. The Owls needed to win to keep their Championship hopes alive. A draw would seal the title for Tottenham.

Wednesday had lost only three times on their travels, winning seven and drawing eight of their fifteen away games. Their last defeat was at Everton way back on 3 December.

So many journalists wanted to cover the match that some couldn't get into the press-box. The *Daily Mirror*'s Press pass was taken by the paper's chief football writer Bill Holden, leaving Cliff Jones's cousin Ken Jones without a ticket for the match. Cliff told him to come down to White Hart Lane early and said he'd get him a place by the track.

It was a tough, bruising match in which silky skills were sacrificed in the win-at-all-costs atmosphere. The fiercely contested battle was fought in front of 62,000 frenzied supporters. They'd been queuing outside White Hart Lane since the early morning to see the match.

The opening half an hour was played at a fierce pace in which little was seen of Blanchflower, Mackay and White. Blanchflower was not at his best, lost in the turmoil swirling around him, White was struggling without his captain's usual flow of passes, and Mackay was fully occupied by his personal battle with little inside-right Bobby Craig.

For once the defence was without its usual cover and the attack without its inspiration. Only Jones's mazy solo runs had breathed life into a flagging team. Wednesday, the club which ended Spurs' 11-game winning streak at the start of the season, were fighting for every ball.

The Owls started mixing it and the tackling became terrifying. The referee, 'Smiler' Tommy Dawes of Norwich, was one of the busiest men on the pitch. 'I certainly knew I had refereed a match,' he said after the game. Dawes repeatedly blew his whistle and seemed to be constantly talking to players on both sides to try to stop the match getting out of hand.

Then, in the 19th minute, Wednesday's inside-left John Fantham fell down before Norman had got within two yards of him. For some strange reason the referee, seemingly affected by the occasion as much as the players and the fans, awarded a free-kick. The decision led to a storm of booing and a bottle was thrown onto the pitch.

Wednesday's powerful left-back Don Megson strode up to slam the ball against Tottenham's defensive wall. When it came back to him his cannonball left-foot shot flew past the helpless Brown into the net. Laurie Pignon in *The Daily Sketch* described the goal as 'the biggest bit of night-light robbery I have seen'.

Wednesday were now in the game only in breakaways, but they were still dangerous. In the 42nd minute, centre-forward Keith Ellis headed firmly against the post. It was a lucky escape for Spurs since another goal then could have finished them off and opened up the Championship race.

That close call was followed a minute later by 50 seconds of Tottenham at their majestic, unstoppable best when they dramatically turned the game upside down. There were just three minutes left until half-time when Baker hit a 40-yard clearance. Dyson, the smallest player on the park, incredibly outjumped Megson, a man nearly a foot taller than him, to head the ball backwards to Smith. The England forward, with an astounding piece of juggling, lobbed it over his international team-mate Peter Swan with his right foot and then ran round him to smash the ball into the roof of the net with his left. Smith was whirling a dance of delight into the arms of his team-mates as the crowd went crazy. It was the goal Spurs so desperately needed.

A minute later, before the roars of the home fans had died down, Allen incredibly put Tottenham ahead. They were awarded a free-kick deep in the Wednesday half. Blanchflower, regaining his composure with every minute, slowly walked up to take it, motioning Norman into the penalty area. The Spurs captain placed the ball perfectly, his tall centre-half leapt to head it sideways to Allen 15 yards out and the inside-forward crashed the ball past England keeper Ron Springett with a superb shoulder-high right-foot volley. The crowd's roars turned into a crescendo.

The Tottenham players went into the dressing-room at half-time on a high. But they had their wounds to tend to from the battle on the pitch. Most of the Spurs forwards had suffered some hard knocks from trips and crash tackles; Mackay had suffered a couple of vicious challenges in the first half; and Jones had two stitches in his knee, though neither Wednesday nor the crowd knew about his injury. The winger would miss Wales's forthcoming World Cup match against Spain in Cardiff.

In the second half, Blanchflower was back at his best and took control of the match. He slowed the game down, lowering the tempo and taking the sting out of Wednesday's attempts to strike back. He began once again to prompt his forwards with searching passes.

The clashes out on the pitch became even more ferocious with Wednesday coming off worse. Springett was charged into a post by Smith and badly hurt his back. He had to be replaced for four minutes by full-back Peter Johnson while he was given treatment on the touchline. 'Smith hit Springett so hard they reckon his shoulder blade is still in the goal at White Hart Lane,' said Tottenham fan Les Gold who never missed a game all season.

Then Wednesday centre-forward Keith Ellis was knocked out late in the game and had to be led off the field. He couldn't hear the deafening crowd because of all the buzzing in his aching head.

Mackay had his name taken along with Wednesday's Peter Johnson and the referee also gave stern lectures to Tony Kay and Brian Hill. This was clearly not a game for the soccer purist or the faint-hearted. The stakes were high and the commitment of the players unrelenting.

Mackay was nothing if not a great character. Even in the cauldron of White Hart Lane on that steamy April night he was still able to give the affair a sense of perspective. At one point, as he was running towards the Tottenham goal with the ball, he pulled his leg back as if he was going to blast it past Brown. Sixty thousand fans almost had a heart attack.

Ken Jones sat on the touchline that night more or less level with the 18-yard box at the Paxton Road end. He remembers how cool Mackay was. 'The ball went out of play where I was sitting for a throw-in to Spurs. I put my foot on it as Mackay came across to take the throw. Just before he took the throw he said to me, 'You can have 6-1 that Smithy won't get his head to this'. It was amazing that in the midst of such an important game he would think of chatting to me on the touchline.' Smith didn't get near Mackay's throw which was headed away by Wednesday centre-half Peter Swan!

The countdown to the final whistle was nerve-tingling and the tension distracted Spurs from their usual brand of flowing football. They hesitated, made mistakes and were clearly affected by the importance of the occasion. It was 'a heart-lifting, blood-pounding period of fear for Spurs' hysterical fans as Wednesday fought on and fought on . . . [in] the shredded-nerve atmosphere built up by the baying-for-victory crowd' was how Clive Toye described those last minutes of the game in the *Daily Express*.

There was no more scoring for the fans to roar and Les Allen's late first-half strike proved to be the goal that won the Championship. It was a strike of considerable skill and complete confidence. With it he'd convinced Wednesday of the impossibly long odds against them winning the title and made sure the trophy would go to White Hart Lane.

Five thousand crazy supporters, drunk with success, brushed the police aside to gather in front of the directors' box. 'We want Danny! We want Danny!' they yelled for ten minutes. Clearly they'd decided who the architect of Spurs' great triumph was.

Blanchflower was the inspiration behind Tottenham's achievement, though Mackay was almost equally as important. It was difficult to pin down how Blanchflower had made it all work. He was part of the team, not a product of it; essentially he was the deputy manager. And while, in the past, his insistence on having his own way wasn't tolerated by his managers, Nicholson had the sense and the confidence to harness Blanchflower's independence instead of fighting it.

When the Irishman eventually led his all-conquering team into the directors' box, the ear-splitting roar that had gone on before seemed but a whisper as the crescendo of cheering reached a new high, even for White Hart Lane, the scene of so many tremendous achievements in this momentous season. 'The crowd was delirious – the 5,000 on the pitch and the other 57,000 still rooted in the stands and on the terraces. They didn't care tuppence if they never got home,' wrote Toye in the *Express*.

The players threw their bath towels into the crowd and stood smiling with tears of pride in their eyes. They returned to the dressing-room eventually where the champagne was already bubbling in anticipation of the deserved celebrations that would follow. The Wednesday captain Tony Kay clinked a champagne glass with Blanchflower in the Spurs dressing-room to toast Tottenham's triumph.

Up in the press-box Clive Toye was penning the words Spurs' fans had hoped and prayed all season that they'd read all season. 'Tottenham Hotspur became Champions of England last night. And the grey, gaunt, two-tiered stands of Tottenham can scarcely have gazed down on moments drawn so tight with nerve-tugging tension. Or moments so filled with the magic impulse that makes Spurs the great team, the great goal machine, the great champions as the 120 seconds of sheer, incisive, savage soccer which threw back the final challenge from Sheffield Wednesday.'

Blanchflower had his own theory on what he'd contributed to Tottenham's triumph. 'I could change the rhythm, change the pace, slow it down if necessary, speed it up when we needed to. I also had the ball much more often than anyone else – so I should have done something with it shouldn't I? And I was a lot older than the rest – 34. I had learned how to play by then, and, at Villa, how not to play.

'Most of all I could read the team as players and as men. I think I knew how to bring out the best. I would never, for instance, direct Maurice Norman openly on the field – I'd ask Peter Baker or Ron Henry to talk to him. But with Dave Mackay you never had to worry about confidence or ego. I remember Terry Medwin getting injured once, being unhappy about staying on. Dave and I suggested Terry go out to the right wing, where we used to put people who'd been in the wars, for a few minutes till he recovered. Five minutes later he came haring back. "Did you say go on the right wing? I was on the right wing!" I think I knew the team.'

Tottenham were eight points ahead with three games to play. They needed just three points to set an all-time record for the First Division to add to the one they already held for the Second Division (70 in 1920). 'Now we are going for the record number of points,' said Nicholson after the Wednesday match. He was ever the perfectionist.

CHAPTER 38
Countdown to Wembley

TOTTENHAM HAD SCALED the highest peak to secure the Championship, but there were still three more home games and almost three weeks before the Cup final against Leicester at Wembley on 6 May. The only target left in the League was Arsenal's record of First Division points.

In truth, though, the rest of the League campaign was an anti-climax. Spurs went to Burnley in a match billed as 'The Battle of the Champs' and let a two-goal lead slip. Baker strolled half the length of the pitch unchallenged to score with a speculative shot from 20 yards and Smith added a second with a header. But Burnley fought back, as they had at White Hart Lane in their thrilling 4-4 draw back in December. Tottenham lost 4-2, though the defeat would have been heavier but for some amazing saves by Brown.

Tottenham then beat a promising young Nottingham Forest team at home thanks to a goal scored by Medwin, the only player in the team who wouldn't be in the Cup final line-up. They'd equalled Arsenal's record of 66 points set in 1931 with one match still to play.

The final game of the season was at home to West Brom in front of 52,000 fans. Les Gold was in the crowd, though not in his customary position on the Shelf. He'd saved his pennies to buy a ticket near the directors' box so he could catch a glimpse of the players being presented with the Championship trophy and their medals.

'They were expecting to see more than the Championship trophy being handed to us by the League president, Mr Joe Richards,' says Cliff Jones. 'A win by Spurs would have taken us past the First Division points-scoring record set up by Arsenal 30 years before.'

But West Brom, who themselves only just failed to win the 'double' in the 1953–54 season when they won the Cup and came second in the League, played Tottenham at their own game and, on the day, played it much better.

Former Arsenal star Joe Hulme was in the press-box reporting the match for *The People*. 'I watched Spurs trying to improve on Arsenal's record with mixed feelings . . . I was in that Arsenal team 30 years ago when they created the record with 66 points. Spurs never looked like going one better.'

Tottenham could have been four goals behind at half-time instead of just one. Blanchflower and Mackay wandered, leaving huge holes in the defence and so much open space that Albion's forward-line was using the match for shooting practice. They couldn't fail to score eventually.

Inside-forward Derek Kevan scored the first and Bobby Robson, later to become the England manager, struck the second from 25 yards. Brown was so surprised he didn't move. Smith got one for Spurs four minutes after half-time, but it wasn't enough. Tottenham would have to be content with equalling the points total set by their North London rivals.

After the match there were tremendous scenes in front of the Main Stand as thousands of supporters raced across to see the League president, Joe Richards, handing over the magnificent First Division trophy to Danny Blanchflower.

Tottenham's devoted supporters were all there at White Hart Lane to see the crowning of their idols. There was 'Johnny-the-Sticks', so-called because of his walking sticks, and 'One-armed Lou', who between them had virtually cornered the black market in Tottenham tickets; Fred Rhye, an ex-boxer and North London bookie who'd followed Spurs for almost 30 years and was probably their most faithful fan; Morris Keston, a much younger and wealthier supporter who'd made his money in the rag trade; and, of course, Les Gold, then in commercial printing, but who, years later, would launch Les Gold Promotions and organise testimonial dinners for players like Bobby Smith and Jimmy Greaves.

'There were some real characters who used to hang out with the team,' remembers Tony Marchi. 'They were life-long Spurs fans and followed the team everywhere. Fred Rhye was a smashing guy. He was a bookmaker so when we were playing away he just took a holiday to come and watch us. Morris Keston was another one who went everywhere. If you went up to Manchester, say, they'd be there. You'd get in the hotel and they were booked in there too. You'd have a beer with them at night. They were not hangers-on; they were good blokes.'

Cliff Jones was also aware of how important the loyal Tottenham fans were to the club's success. 'Spurs' real supporters are among the most loyal and knowledgeable in the country. They are fantastically proud of their club and, equally important, they are devoted to good football – no matter which side produces it.'

When Danny Blanchflower stood in the directors' box on that marvellous night to express his gratitude to the 'wonderful supporters' after receiving the League Championship trophy, every single member of the Spurs team agreed wholeheartedly with the sentiment. The support they'd received during the season was often worth an extra player. 'I, for one, shall never underestimate the huge part played by our followers,' says Jones.

But Spurs had their critics after that home defeat by West Brom. 'Had their thoughts not been so firmly on the coming Cup final (it was only a week away) there is little doubt they would have added the points record . . .' wrote Julian Holland in *Spurs – The Double*.

Cliff Jones had his own views on the criticisms handed down to Spurs. 'Albion played some magnificent football and goals by Derek Kevan, their very big and very dangerous striker, and Bobby Robson enabled them to beat us, most deservedly, by 2-1. A few critics were quick to claim that we had played at half-pace to avoid any chance of injury, while others said we had completely lost our touch. Neither viewpoint was remotely near the truth. We would very much have liked to have eclipsed that Arsenal record and we certainly didn't pull any punches. And to say that Albion won because we were off-colour is doing a famous Midland club much less than justice. We played quite well in patches – well enough, probably, to have beaten most teams – but the fact remained that Albion played so much better. They looked far more like Champions than we did.'

But Danny Blanchflower probably gave the most honest assessment of the match. 'Of course we wanted to win. But we did not want to win so much as we did, say, when we played Sheffield Wednesday.'

Tottenham had clearly taken their foot off the accelerator after they clinched the title. 'We eased up after the winning post,' acknowledged Blanchflower. 'Another win or two and it would probably have been an all-time record, but we were not thinking about records then. Our eyes were only on the Cup final.'

Spurs were halfway to the 'double'. The Cup final was their last challenge.

CHAPTER 39
Final Build-up

TOTTENHAM DIDN'T QUITE regard the Cup final as a 'normal game' but they prepared for it as if it was. Their routine didn't vary one bit. The club believed that 'special training', while useful on occasion, did not achieve a great deal if used too often. That's why they didn't go away to prepare for the final.

The players reported at White Hart Lane at 10 o'clock every morning, as usual, and the only concession was one extra visit to the training ground at Cheshunt. They wanted to play a practice game on a surface with grass of similar texture to Wembley's and the nearest they could find was one of their own little-used pitches.

The semi-final saga between Leicester and Sheffield United had stretched boringly and inconclusively across three dreary, defensive matches before City clinched the tie. It had taken them nearly 14 hours of football to reach Wembley and they'd allowed lowly Barnsley to take them to a replay along the way. Leicester had enjoyed a fine spell of methodical football in the mud during the early part of the year, but they faded with the spring.

Nicholson told his players that if they played the same kind of game which had earned them the League Championship, and made maximum use of Wembley's open acres, they'd be good enough to win.

Tottenham's ability to improvise was one of their biggest weapons. They'd start off in a recognisable formation, but once the whistle went the numbers on their backs counted for little. They played to a double spearhead of Smith and Allen with Blanchflower, Mackay, and White acting as the brains of the team. The defence played a pivoting game with Henry and Baker always ready to cover Norman whose own job was really that of a third back. Dyson and Jones were given a free rein.

The players adapted their game to the demands on the pitch. It was possible to see Henry trying a shot from inside the other team's penalty area, Allen defending alongside Norman, or Dyson covering Blanchflower. At any time, you might find any player in almost any part of the field.

The main line of attack was through the centre because they'd decided long ago that the centre-to-far-post theory was outdated, although there were times when the traditional cross was worth trying, especially if the defence was suspect in the air. The aim was to keep the other team's defence stretched by creating space and making the ball do the work. Then, at the right moment, they'd play the ball through to the strikers.

The Tottenham players felt the main threat from Leicester would come from their lively captain Jimmy Walsh and from centre-forward Ken Leek, a Welsh international who played alongside Cliff Jones and Terry Medwin for his country. Walsh had scored twice and Leek once when Leicester ended Spurs' unbeaten home run in mid-February.

Norman, in particular, wasn't looking forward to marking Leek whose ability, fierce shooting with either foot and strength in the air had done much to get Leicester to Wembley. Norman didn't normally worry, but when he did have doubts about anything it usually upset him, sometimes with disastrous results. And Norman was worried about Leek.

But Leicester manager Matt Gillies shocked everyone when he announced that he'd decided to leave Leek out of the Cup final team and bring in a talented, but inexperienced, 21-year-old Scot called Hugh McIlmoyle. Norman was over the moon. Nicholson was also pleased. 'I never knew why he made the change, but the critics said it would weaken Leicester because Leek had scored some important goals and his aerial power would be missed.'

At midday on the Friday before the final the players booked into the Hendon Hall Hotel, the nearest large hotel to Wembley at the time. It was conveniently situated on the North Circular Road about 15 minutes' drive from the 'Venue of Legends'. Nicholson wanted to make sure the players got a short break from the hundreds of well-wishers and autograph hunters, to say nothing of last-minute ticket requests.

Most of the players had steak and chips for lunch after they arrived that Friday and then relaxed in their rooms or wandered around the hotel grounds. Some of the squad played for pennies on the hotel putting green.

After an hour or so the players were taken by coach to Wembley for a close look at the unique playing surface. There was less than 24 hours to go before the Cup final began.

As they arrived the sun seemed to be smiling on the vast stadium with its famous twin towers. Inside last-minute preparations were being made everywhere. The television engineers were making final adjustments to the sound and vision and the ground staff were scurrying around. Everyone seemed to have something important to do.

The players strolled out onto Wembley's immaculate green grass with some of the journalists who'd be covering the game the following day. Cliff Jones walked out with John White and as they stepped onto the pitch he noticed the rest of the team looking up at the huge, empty terraces. Cliff looked up as well and somehow was able to visualise exactly how it would be the next day with 100,000 faces staring down at him. He could almost hear the roar of the crowd.

Cliff and John were wandering down to the goal near the mouth of the tunnel which leads to the dressing-rooms when the canny Scottish inside-forward suddenly stopped about seven yards out, grinned and said: 'If I get the ball right here tomorrow I shall move forward, like this, and swing my right leg, like this, and, hey presto, the ball will be in the back of the net. Nothing to it,' he added as he finished his impeccable little demonstration. 'More than likely you'll hit it out of the ground,' Cliff told him.

After their Wembley preview the party returned to the Hendon Hall Hotel for a light tea. During the meal Nicholson told the players he'd arranged for them to see an excellent film called *The Guns of Navarone* at the Odeon Cinema in Leicester Square.

Quite a few people were surprised they went to the pictures on the eve of such an important game. But it was a very wise move by the Spurs boss for two reasons. First, going to the film stopped the players lounging around talking about football and the Cup final in particular. Second, they all decided to go to the late show which didn't finish until after 11 o'clock; by the time they travelled back to the hotel, had supper and climbed the stairs into bed it was past midnight and they were all pleasantly tired. 'We went straight to sleep and thus escaped those restless, endless "small-hour" thoughts which I think most people have when something momentously big and exciting is due to happen the following day,' says Jones.

CHAPTER 40
Smith Goes Missing

THE PLAYERS USUALLY shared a room with their best pal in the team. Jonesy was with John White; Mackay with Bill 'Hovis' Brown; Blanchflower shared with Tony Marchi; the two full-backs, Ron Henry and Peter Baker, were together; and big centre-half Maurice 'Monty' Norman stayed with Bobby Smith.

As they closed their eyes that night some of the players were worried about more than the opposition they'd face the next day at Wembley in the form of Leicester City. Three of the Spurs stars were carrying injuries which were playing on their minds.

Blanchflower had appeared in 42 League matches and six Cup ties for Tottenham as well as four international games for Northern Ireland and a representative match for the Football League. 'I had taken some stick in most of these,' he said. 'Every ambitious hatchet man was after me.'

In the last two League matches of the season 'the callous boot of an opponent' had bruised his right ankle and 'a vicious tackle from behind' had twisted his right knee, straining his ligament. 'These niggling injuries weren't enough to "bench" me but they slowed me down and created a little Wembley doubt in my mind,' he said.

Dave Mackay had injured his right shin after being accidentally kicked during an international match against England when he didn't wear shinpads. His injury remained a secret until after the Cup Final. Fortunately, Mackay had rested for several days and that, plus expert treatment from trainer Cecil Poynton, meant he'd be fit enough to play.

Smith had also picked up a bad injury. He'd twisted his knee in the final League match against West Brom at White Hart Lane the Saturday before the Cup final. But Smith didn't know he was really in trouble until he kicked the ball during a mid-week practice match. 'That's when it really started to cause me pain,' he says.

Smith decided to keep the injury quiet. 'Bill didn't know; in fact, no one knew,' he says. 'Bill wouldn't have let me play, but I thought, "I'm not going to miss this one for the world," so I didn't tell anybody.'

Smith decided to see his own doctor in Palmers Green on the Friday morning before that day's training session in which Nicholson would check the fitness of all his players before picking the team to play in the Cup final. The doctor gave Smith an injection.

'Bill looked at us all and I was running about and kicking the ball,' says Smith. 'We only played for about 20 minutes on the Friday morning and Bill must have thought, "He's OK".'

Smith went back to his doctor on the Friday night for more treatment and was told: 'Come down early in the morning and I'll give you an injection; then you've got to return at lunchtime for another one before the kick-off.'

On the Saturday morning trainer Cecil Poynton was given the job of making sure all the players were awake and getting ready for breakfast. Maurice Norman woke up before Poynton had reached the room he was sharing with Bobby Smith, but when he looked across at his room-mate's bed he saw it was empty and looked like it hadn't been slept in.

'I guessed he must have been out on the town all night and I shuffled his bedclothes to make it look like he'd slept there,' says Norman. 'I knew he had to live like that, it was the way his adrenaline flowed. Nevertheless, Norman was angry that Smith had not got a good night's rest before such an important game. He decided to say nothing until after the Cup final, but then he'd give Smith a piece of his mind.

Meanwhile, according to Smith, he'd got up at seven o'clock and climbed out of the window. He then drove his car back to the doctor's at Palmers Green for another injection in his knee at around 9.30.

After Smith had left, the other players began to wake up. Cliff Jones and John White, befitting the start to one of the greatest days of their lives, tackled their breakfast of fruit juice, scrambled egg and bacon, toast and tea in bed. Mackay was not one of those energetic types who, on the morning of a match, liked to climb into a tracksuit and go racing round a track. He preferred to conserve his energy for the game and so, on that Cup final morning, he also stayed in the room he shared with Bill Brown.

Ron Henry vividly remembers waking up on the morning of the Cup final even though it's almost 40 years ago. 'It was a lovely morning. Peter and I were laying in bed in a downstairs room in the hotel. The window was open and three little boys leaned through and said, "Can we have your autographs?" So we got out of bed and gave them our autographs.'

The only players who didn't have breakfast in bed that morning were Bobby Smith, Maurice Norman, Danny Blanchflower and Tony Marchi as well as Bill Nicholson, of course.

Blanchflower had woken up when he heard a door slam somewhere. His curtained windows were an orange glow; the room he was sharing with Tony Marchi full of shadows. Blanchflower looked at his watch. It was 8.15. He'd slept well.

'I seemed to hear noises from the crevices of the hotel interrupting my dozing moments like voices in a tunnel,' he remembered. 'A baby's cry, a man singing, other men's voices. I was warm and comfortable and dozed off again. It was surface sleep and I gradually awakened.'

Blanchflower heard Ron Henry's voice and thought he seemed bright and cheerful. Then he heard the chink of cups in the corridor and a woman saying to someone, 'Tea or coffee, sir?' He looked at his watch again: 8.50. Marchi, in the other bed, seemed to be asleep. Then the telephone rang and the man said: 'It's nine o'clock, sir.' 'Congratulations,' Blanchflower replied, and then got up.

A couple of newspapers lay on the floor just inside the door. The *Daily Express* said Blanchflower had spent the night before happily telling stories to the other players to keep their minds off the worrying day ahead. The *Daily Mail* reported that Blanchflower looked tense and strained.

The door lock rattled and a grey-haired woman with glasses poked her head round the bedroom door. 'Are you getting up for breakfast, sir?' she asked. 'Yes, thank you,' said Blanchflower. A mumble came from Marchi's bed. 'Are you getting up for breakfast?' Blanchflower shouted across to him. Another muffled groan from the heaped bedclothes. 'Yes,' interpreted Blanchflower and the woman retreated, not very convinced.

Blanchflower got up and pulled back the curtains. He was greeted by a bright morning and a dry and cool day. The Spurs captain washed and dressed as quietly as he could since Marchi was still hiding in the other bed.

When Blanchflower got down to the dining room it was almost empty and some of the staff were having breakfast. Nicholson was there and he joined him. Blanchflower ordered grapefruit, cereal, tea and toast. He'd just finished the grapefruit when a man slid onto the seat beside him. 'We're from Burnley,' he said. 'You'll know Jimmy McIlroy. We've come down for the match. We go to all the Burnley home games.' The Burnley fans told Blanchflower that after Spurs' semi-final win the Cup was as good as theirs. 'We know you'll not want to be bothered; we know what it's like. We'll not bother you. Would you just sign this . . .' The man stuck an old Burnley programme between Blanchflower and his cereal. When the Spurs captain had signed it and the man had gone off not to bother someone else, Tony Marchi at long last joined Blanchflower for breakfast.

Meanwhile, after his 9.30 injection, Smith drove the 20 minutes back to Hendon Hall where 'I had to show my face,' he says. When Norman saw Smith he approached him immediately. 'I wondered where you were,' Norman said agitatedly. Smith explained he'd been to see his doctor in Palmers Green, 'but don't say a word to anyone, especially Bill.'

The other players had emerged in ones and twos throughout the morning. Most of them were in the television room by 11.15 when the BBC's *Grandstand* programme started setting the Cup final scene.

Blanchflower noticed that the newspapers had covered themselves both ways. 'You know the dodge: one staff man plumps for one team and another man for the other team. Then after the event the one who has backed the winner is promoted big in the paper with that "I told you so" build-up and the paper is right once again.'

The *Grandstand* team were taking it cautiously. David Coleman opened the proceedings from the Royal Box. Kenneth Wolstenholme had arrived at Wembley at 10 o'clock that morning and interviewed fans in the Green Man pub before roaming Wembley Way looking for fans arriving early to contradict one another about who would win the Cup.

Wally Barnes stood on the Wembley turf around the spot where he'd been injured in the 1952 Cup final, wondering if there would be another injury and explaining why he thought Leicester would win. He mentioned the Tottenham attacking wing-halves and predicted they would leave gaps for the Leicester forwards to exploit. Later Mackay and Blanchflower joked about it.

Mackay and Brown were still absent from the television room. They'd stayed in their own room playing records until it was time to emerge for lunch at around 12 o'clock.

Just before lunch Bobby Smith told trainer Cecil Poynton he was going for a walk. 'Well, don't be long,' said Poynton, 'lunch is at 12.30.' Instead of walking, Smith got in his car and sped back to his doctor at Palmers Green for another injection.

Terry Dyson had really gone for a stroll within the grounds of Hendon Hall. 'I remember I walked around the grounds before lunch on the Saturday and that's when I really started thinking about the game,' says Dyson.

Just before 12.30 the players sat down for a light lunch. Most had steak, rice, toast and tea, but Blanchflower ate an omelette instead of the steak. Smith returned from his trip to the doctor's just after lunch had started. 'Where have you been?' the players asked him. 'Out for a walk,' he told them. 'It's lovely out there walking.' They shrugged and carried on talking. The players were very relaxed as they chatted over lunch. Nobody seemed to be unduly worried about the approaching game.

Blanchflower felt confident. 'I had a look at the faces around me . . . Bill Brown, Peter Baker, Ron Henry, Maurice Norman, Dave Mackay, Cliff Jones, John White, Bobby Smith, Les Allen and Terry Dyson. I felt very proud of them. I felt that we would win at Wembley and be the first team of the century to do the "double" – but if something happened and we didn't do it then I would still feel the same afterwards – glad to belong with them.'

After lunch the players went back to the television room and watched the BBC's version of how both teams had got to Wembley. The big pre-match news had been the dropping of centre-forward Ken Leek of Leicester. The television highlights showed that Leicester's path to the Cup final had been a bit hesitant. The one notable feature was the number goals scored by the head of Ken Leek. The Spurs players were glad he'd been left out, especially Norman.

The Cup final build-up was followed by some hazy film of the first American in space: Alan B. Shepard Jr., a commander in the US Navy. He'd managed a 15-minute sub-orbital flight that took him 115 miles above the earth where he'd carried out some manouevres with his Mercury spacecraft. Shepard had then landed in the sea near the Bahamas, 360 miles from the Cape Canaveral launch site.

The players got ready and boarded the coach for Wembley at 1.40 p.m. When Mackay got on he felt full of enthusiasm for the test ahead. 'I simply could not get onto the field quickly enough to play my part in trying to help Spurs achieve the "impossible",' he says.

The coach left the hotel a few minutes before two o'clock. It was soon nosing steadily through the crowds. Whatever the noise outside, inside everything was very quiet. 'That's when we were left with our own thoughts,' says Dyson. 'I wanted to win, but I also didn't want to have a bad game. Your pride comes into it.'

Cliff Jones sat next to Ron Henry but the Tottenham full-back didn't say a word. Henry was usually a bit nervous when given time to think before a big match. Jones thought that wasn't such a bad thing; it showed he was properly keyed up – although, of course, on the pitch you had to relax.

Coming up to the stadium the players heard a strident voice demanding, 'Repent in the Lord'; Dixieland jazz from the kerbstones; strange sights and sounds. It was all part of the wonder of football. 'The Cup final seems like a fair, or bazaar or something,' thought Blanchflower.

CHAPTER 41
The Cup Final

AT FIVE MINUTES past two the Spurs players hung their coats in the Wembley dressing-room. There were telegrams on the table, the business of preparation, a mixture of noises, some of them distant, some just above the players' heads.

Nicholson came around to have a word with all the players. He usually sat down beside each of them in turn and discussed the man they had to watch. He never wasted valuable words. His guidance was direct. The basis of all Nicholson's talks was to prepare his players for any possibility on the pitch. The result was that they took the field confident, relaxed and determined to really enjoy themselves.

Mackay, for one, had found through experience that the information Nicholson gave him about specific players was completely accurate. 'It is the smaller and vital parts of an opponent's make-up that Nicholson is so good at detecting,' said Mackay. 'He will, for instance, notice that a player, when in a certain position, invariably moves to the same corner of the pitch. He may also remind me, for example, that the inside-forward I have to watch has developed a technique of moving into an open space far away from where he ought to be.'

Nicholson suggested the players take another look at the Wembley turf and get accustomed to the stadium's unique 'electric' atmosphere. He also wanted them to kick a ball in the air to see how it bounced and to appreciate its pace off the pitch. Although both teams had been to Wembley the previous afternoon to get a feel of the playing surface, they hadn't been allowed to take a ball on the field. Nicholson was thorough in his preparations. His approach to the game had played a major part in Tottenham's success.

Blanchflower joined the others to get the feeling of the atmosphere and to judge the conditions, like the wind and sun, rather than to inspect the pitch, which he'd done the previous day. However, after agreeing there was rain about, the players decided not to wear the rubber studs they'd selected the day before, but to revert to leather studs. A gusty, swirling wind promised to make life difficult and they were going to need every bit of grip they could get.

In the Wembley dressing-room Mackay noticed a certain tenseness for the first time since he'd joined Spurs. 'Usually, I think we were a rather noisy crowd as we prepared for a game,' he says. 'On this occasion we were most quiet; no one said very much. Inwardly, I suspected we all felt we'd let everyone down if Spurs did not win and so achieve the "double" which had become an obsession for us all.'

The players with injuries were busy considering how they felt and whether they'd cope during the game; they were taking precautions to make sure they didn't have any further problems. Although Blanchflower's injured ankle wasn't giving him any pain, he was strangely aware of it. He wondered if it might go at some point in the match and, if so, when. Mackay had a thick sponge pad – specially made for him by trainer Cecil Poynton – around his injured right shin and wore thick shinpads over the top. The sponge pad was an extra precaution. Mackay was taking no chances today. Smith couldn't have played without the injections, but now he felt like everything was fine. 'I could take a lot of stick,' he says, ' and had played with a lot of injuries.'

The big striker had promised himself that if Spurs got to Wembley he'd walk to the bottom of the tunnel before the kick-off and listen to 'Abide With Me' – one of his favourite hymns. So, at 2.20, as the crowd sang the famous football anthem on the eve of the 1961 FA Cup final, England centre-forward Bobby Smith could be found at the mouth of the Wembley tunnel. 'The atmosphere was fantastic,' he remembers.

The time passed quickly enough and before he knew it Blanchflower was walking up the tunnel behind Nicholson alongside the Leicester City team. Although the Cup final was the showpiece of the season, and the game was destined for an important place in every book of sporting records, the Spurs players lined up in their customary way before walking onto the pitch. Brown came after Blanchflower, Jones went behind White, Mackay carried a ball and Norman was last. The Leicester team were led out by captain Jimmy Walsh who was followed by goalkeeper Gordon Banks. The Spurs players didn't talk to their opponents as they moved towards the pitch. They were focused on the task ahead – making history.

Peter Baker remembers the light at the end of the tunnel. 'Walking along the tunnel you could see this bright light, but it seemed miles away. You think you'll feel intimidated by the roar of the crowd, but you don't. You don't really hear it; you just get the volume of it. But the hardest thing is trying to get your team-mates to hear you when you're playing.'

Despite the large crowd, Blanchflower wasn't the only Spurs player who was disappointed by how he felt before the game. Most of them had been underwhelmed by their Wembley experience so far. Jones knew a Cup final appearance was every footballer's ambition and that a schoolboy dream was about to come true. He also believed it was usual to be overcome, or spellbound, by the occasion and the atmosphere. But he wasn't. In fact, he was very disappointed with all the trimmings of the 1961 Cup final.

Jones thought that perhaps he'd expected too much, but, whatever the reason, the occasion, the atmosphere and even the huge crowd seemed to be lacking something. He was a little nervous, but far from overawed. 'So this is Wembley on Cup final day,' he said to himself.

Like Blanchflower, Jones thought the earlier rounds of the Cup had generated more excitement among the supporters. 'Our semi-final with Burnley at Villa Park had much more atmosphere, mainly, I suspect, because almost everyone there was either a Spurs or Burnley fan.'

Jones wondered how many businessmen and their 'clients' were making their first visit to a football ground that season. He thought the FA had to do something to ensure genuine fans came before people who had more money, contacts and influence, than a love of the game. He'd spoken to many Spurs fans who'd seen nearly all their matches, home and away, in all weathers, but couldn't get a ticket for the final. 'I think the 1961 Cup final struck me as exactly what it is – a gigantic social occasion,' he said.

But Bill Nicholson thought there was little wrong with the principle of giving tickets to those who keep the game going at the lower levels. 'As a national event it needs to be seen by the whole nation, not merely the fans of the two clubs,' he said.

Ron Henry wasn't nervous before the final. He just wanted Spurs to show people how well they could play. 'It's everybody's dream to play at Wembley,' says Henry. 'And I thought if I don't play well I'll not only let myself down but my family too, because I knew they were up in the stands, and I wasn't going to do that. All the other players' families were there as well.'

Blanchflower still felt calm as he walked across the green turf and took up a position at the head of the team as they lined up in front of the Royal Box. Before the game both sides were presented to the Duchess of Kent, or Princess Marina as she'd become known.

The teams were: Tottenham Hotspur: Brown, Baker, Henry, Blanchflower, Norman (M.), Mackay, Jones, White, Smith, Allen, Dyson.

Leicester City: Banks, Chalmers, Norman (R.), McLintock, King, Appleton, Riley, Walsh, McIlmoyle, Keyworth, Cheesebrough.

There were no substitutes, although each team had one player on standby before the match in case of injuries or illness. Tony Marchi had been on standby for Tottenham, though his slim chance of appearing in the final had gone the moment the teams walked onto the pitch. He wouldn't even get a medal (Cliff Jones would become the first substitute to receive a Cup Winners' medal in 1967 when Spurs beat Chelsea 2-1).

Princess Marina was introduced to the Leicester players first. As she walked across the short stretch of red carpet towards the Spurs team Blanchflower noticed that her eyes and face were expressionless and still. Near the end of the line, before reaching Norman, she stopped, turned slowly, and said to Blanchflower: 'The other team have their names on their suits.' 'Yes, ma'm,' the Spurs captain replied, 'but we know each other.' He certainly didn't want to be undermined before the game had even begun.

Spurs were the biggest favourites to win at Wembley since Wolverhampton Wanderers were beaten by Portsmouth in 1939. It was only the memory of that shock result and the overwhelming odds against the 'double' that had cast any doubt on Tottenham's ability to win the Cup. They were the fourth League Champions since the turn of the century to reach the Cup final in the same season. The other three – Sunderland, Newcastle and Manchester United – had all been beaten by Aston Villa, the last 'double' winners. It was as if the men from Villa Park were destined to protect the achievement of their forbears.

Up in the commentary box the BBC's Kenneth Wolstenholme set the match up nicely with the million-dollar question: '. . . can Spurs break the voodoo that always hangs over League Champions when they play in a Cup final?'

Tottenham, of course, had already disposed of Aston Villa in the Fifth Round. But whatever the bookies or the fans thought, the 'double' wasn't in the bag yet. Blanchflower thought Leicester certainly stood far more chance of beating Spurs than Aston Villa had been given of stopping Manchester United's 'double' attempt four years earlier.

Leicester had enjoyed a good season and one of their characteristics was a tendency to raise their game against top-class opposition. They'd also been able to put out a settled team which had helped their consistency. Leicester had beaten six top League sides – including Tottenham at White Hart Lane, Spurs' first home defeat of the season. They'd also slaughtered Manchester United 6-0 in January after the Reds had recorded six successive wins in League and Cup matches. Leicester were no pushovers.

The whole country was about to witness the game they'd been anticipating for weeks. Those not lucky enough to be inside Wembley Stadium were watching on television in homes and pubs across Britain. The match was also being seen live in 12 European countries and recordings would be sent to many other nations around the world including America.

Just before the toss, the BBC switched to their radio camera on the other side of the Wembley pitch to give viewers a better picture of Danny Blanchflower and Jimmy Walsh standing by the centre circle waiting to toss up. Blanchflower tossed the coin and Walsh called. 'That was a pretty neat trap,' said Wolstenholme as Walsh controlled the coin when it landed on the turf. Tottenham would play with the wind and rain behind them in the first half, while Leicester had the kick-off.

Spurs approached the Cup final in a more conservative frame of mind than for any other game that season. It was the only match in which Norman didn't go up for all the corners. For Tottenham it had been a season of Cup finals because every team was desperate to beat them and their opponents had raised their game time after time. That was why Blanchflower's ability to slow the pace of a match, absorb pressure and consolidate gains, was so important.

Mackay thought the Wembley pitch was by far the best he'd ever played on. 'Any footballer ought to be able to produce quality football on its lush surface and if a team is able to settle down quickly – after playing upon well-worn pitches – they enjoy a wonderful experience.'

But Tottenham took a long time to get a fine touch on the ball and Mackay fouled McIlmoyle after just a few seconds. Spurs moved well enough in the early stages, but Blanchflower thought they didn't pass as accurately as usual. The players misjudged their distribution on the slower tempo of the Wembley turf.

By the time experience should have enabled them to adjust to the slow Wembley pitch it had started to rain heavily and the players were faced with different conditions. 'If the same applied to Leicester then the expectations of their play were not so complex and they did not have to adjust to the same degree,' said Blanchflower.

Just eight minutes had gone when Mackay took a long throw near the corner flag. The ball was headed back to him by a Leicester defender. Mackay got to the byline and sent over a beautiful cross which Dyson laid into White's path. The Scot received the ball in exactly the position, some seven or eight yards out, that he'd stood in the previous day with Jones when he'd promised to move forward, swing his right leg and plant the ball in the back of the net. Nine times out of ten he'd have scored. Unfortunately for White, Jones's prediction, and not his own, came true: he blasted the ball high, and not so handsomely, over the bar. It ended up on the greyhound track which circled the pitch. 'Chance number one goes a-begging,' said Wolstenholme.

Leicester were very much in the game in the early stages and might have scored on three occasions. They were inspired by their skipper Walsh, while young McIlmoyle, playing deep in his first Cup match, to try to draw Norman out of the Spurs defence, justified his inclusion in the side. He repeatedly twisted and turned his way past the flailing legs of the Tottenham defenders.

Leicester's raking three-man moves were threatening to unlock the Spurs defence. Their first clear chance came after a dazzling Walsh dribble, past Mackay and Blanchflower, had set up McIlmoyle. His first-time shot flashed across the Spurs goal. Then McLintock had Tottenham reeling when he swept a wonderful cross-field pass to Riley. The right-winger put over a difficult, swirling ball in the high wind to McIlmoyle who scooped it over the bar. It was just a half-chance really and the young Scot did well to get on the end of it. 'I doubt if Ken Leek could have done better,' wrote Alan Hoby of the *Sunday Express*.

Leicester looked dangerous when they attacked and were getting on top. Meanwhile, Tottenham were struggling. Blanchflower looked slow and was mistiming his tackles. The Spurs skipper wasn't playing well. In fact, Jones, regarded as one of the most dangerous wingmen in the whole of Europe at the time, was the only bright spark for Tottenham. After about 15 minutes he caught Walsh's boot full in the chest and Cecil Poynton came on to plunge a cold sponge on his chest. The 'magic' sponge seemed to do the trick.

Shortly afterwards Walsh cut through the Spurs defence and slid the ball to 'Box-of-Tricks' Riley. He put over another pinpoint cross and Cheesebrough, hurtling in like a rocket, seemed certain to score. But Tottenham's ice cube of a right-back Peter Baker appeared from nowhere to bravely head the ball clear from inside the six-yard box. Unfortunately, Cheesebrough's boot hit him full in the face and Baker was knocked out. He was unconscious and lay flat on his face on the edge of the six-yard box. It took a few minutes before a groggy Baker got to his feet. 'They said I got kicked but I think the ball hit the top of my head instead of my forehead,' says Baker. 'I was fine afterwards.'

At that point Tottenham looked anything but the Pride of London or the Team of the Century. 'Bedraggled and faltering, leaving large gaps in the middle, they looked at this point artisan; blue-shirted Leicester the artists,' wrote Hoby of the *Sunday Express*.

But the game was doomed to be a disappointment from the moment the Wembley injury jinx struck again right in front of the Royal Box in the 19th minute. Baker had only just recovered from his bang on the head when McLintock played the ball towards Len Chalmers. It slipped through Smith's feet and the Leicester right-back, disputing possession with him, seemed about to clear when Les Allen raced in to challenge for the ball with the outside of his right foot. Chalmers tried to pull it away, but they clashed and he was caught. He fell to the ground, writhing in agony, his face creased with pain – an all-too familiar sight in Cup finals of the era. For the seventh time in nine years the Wembley hoodoo had struck.

McLintock dropped to right-back from right-half, Ken Keyworth moved from inside-left to fill his position and outside-left Albert Cheesebrough switched to the right-wing so Chalmers could limp out to the left. But the injured Leicester full-back would now play little part in the match. 'It looks as if we can say that Leicester now have ten men unless Chalmers makes a miraculous recovery,' said Wolstenholme. For most of the game he limped about on the left-wing, a virtual passenger.

Allen, obviously under the strain of having caused the injury to Chalmers, now played at half-pace; Spurs seemed to be almost as much put out by the episode as Leicester. '. . . the incident spoiled my game too,' said Allen afterwards. 'I was quite upset.'

As so often happens, the ten men tried harder, Tottenham relaxed slightly and it became more difficult for the favourites to win. Leicester found more space and used it well. They played inspired football and, to their credit, made Spurs work very hard. 'Ten men not only fight just that little bit harder, but their whole game, logically, becomes more defensive,' says Cliff Jones. 'And at Wembley . . . we certainly found it very hard to make our way through the very brave Leicester defence.'

Leicester moved the ball longer distances and often into more penetrating goal-worthy areas of play than Spurs. But, while they had their fair share of the ball, the underdogs never looked like scoring. Brown didn't have a real save to make in the match, while Banks was constantly in action. Nevertheless, with Blanchflower off form – he was often caught in possession by the Leicester forwards – and trying to slow the game down to a pace Leicester wouldn't allow, and Mackay never quite as dominating as he can be, Tottenham lost their cutting edge. They allowed themselves to be panicked by Leicester's grim fight against the odds, and they were more nervous than their opponents as a result.

The result was that for a long time the reshuffle made little difference to a calm Leicester defence. Time and again their cool Scottish centre-half Ian King, 'as craggily tough as a Highland peak' according to Hoby of the *Sunday Express*, flung back the challenge of the League Champions. Leicester's magnificently drilled defenders brushed aside Tottenham's stuttering raids with almost nonchalant insolence.

Only occasional runs from Jones, the one Spurs forward who consistently reached his true form, troubled the Leicester defence. 'The Welshman set the crowd alight every time he got the ball,' wrote Ralph Finn in *Spurs Supreme*. 'He relieved pressure with bursting, searing runs that retrieved yards of lost ground. He tore through the defence, side-footing and turning opponents the wrong way, and more than any other forward helped to shake the stolidity and soundness of a fine Leicester defence. So helpless were Leicester against Cliff's dazzling runs that they were forced to foul him seven times to stop him.'

At one point Jones flew down the left-wing onto a through ball from White only to be sent tumbling over the photographers behind the goal-line. 'The speed of this man is fantastic,' said Wolstenholme. Jones was also proving a handful in the air. 'Remarkable how Cliff Jones, a very slight player, can get up to such heights when the ball comes across,' said Wolstenholme. 'He's scored many a goal this season with his head.' It was not so remarkable considering the hours of practice Jones had put in under the direction of his father all those years ago in Swansea. The effort was now paying off big time.

Tottenham generally began to improve towards the end of the first-half with Jones making darting runs, Blanchflower, at last, starting to win his tackles, and Dyson beavering away on the left-wing. But the threat from the two Spurs wingers and their captain wasn't the only problem facing Leicester. The redeployment of their forces after the injury to Chalmers may not have upset their defence too much, but it had greatly affected their forward-line. They could only attack down one wing and were thus deprived of the element of surprise. Leicester also lacked the extra firepower another striker would have given them.

But the Tottenham forwards weren't doing much better at this stage. 'Certainly, there's nothing in the Tottenham finishing to suggest that they're League Champions so far,' said Wolstenholme. 'In fact, both defences have been so much on top containing the forward-lines that neither goalkeeper has been troubled and we've been playing now for 37 minutes.' All that was about to change – dramatically.

A minute later Blanchflower knocked the ball through for Allen on the edge of the 18-yard box; he passed to Dyson on the right-wing and his low cross was rifled into the net with the side of his foot by Jones on the far post. The crowd roared and the Welshman raised his arms in triumph. 'I made no attempt to hide my tremendous delight,' he says. 'I had scored in a Wembley Cup final . . . or so I thought.' One moment he was on top of the world, the next it was as if someone had poured a bucket of cold water over him. The linesman had immediately put up his flag for offside and Jack Kelly, an experienced international referee, blew his whistle to disallow the goal.

'It was a ridiculous decision,' says Jones. 'There is no other word for it. I ran at least seven yards to get to the ball and at the moment Dyson played it I was fully four yards onside. Frank McLintock was just one of the defenders nearer the goal than me.' The linesman flagged only when Jones reached the ball; he'd apparently not seen him racing through to meet it. Bill Nicholson was one of the thousands who thought that Jones's goal was a good one. After the match the Spurs manager would complain that too many linesmen were concentrating entirely on the man with the ball so that when they finally spotted the key player in the attack – the one without the ball – moving through they automatically ruled him offside. 'Moving off the ball is an art which we concentrate on and its use provides for entertaining football. But it is frustrating to the players to find themselves unfairly penalised by bad offside decisions,' Nicholson said. He believed that although it was primarily the linesman's decision to watch for offsides, more referees should be prepared to ignore the waving flag. 'Often they are in a better position to spot exactly when the man without the ball begins to move through than the linesman.'

After that the Spurs players probed nervously, missed chances, passed inaccurately and even ran into each other. Maurice Smith of *The People* described them as a 'stammering, shadowy impersonation of the great side we know. Gone was their pin-point accuracy. Gone their split-second timing. Gone, too, their deadly finishing.'

Just before half-time Cheesebrough turned Jones and played the ball wide to a blue-shirted Leicester player. It was Chalmers. When Cheesebrough saw he'd passed to the injured full-back he threw his hands in the air in frustration. It summed up Leicester's predicament. They'd done well to hold out until half-time. Their performance had been nothing less than heroic. The question was could they keep up the pace on the strength-sapping Wembley pitch with only ten fit players?

Blanchflower was now caught up in the mechanics of the play and nothing else. He'd earlier thought the crowd remote, not as intimate as it was at White Hart Lane. But the intensity of the task at hand meant he'd completely blocked out the fans on the terraces. His thoughts were solely on the match. Leicester, with the wind behind them in the second-half, didn't make too many demands on themselves.

On 55 minutes a Blanchflower free-kick was headed down by Norman to Allen but he missed what looked like a reasonable chance by slicing the ball left of the goal and almost hitting the corner flag from five yards out. 'That was a wonderful chance of getting a Cup Winners' medal in your pocket,' said Wolstenholme.

Smith had a great chance to restore Tottenham's pride when he ran on to a lovely through ball from Dyson. Unfortunately, the only thing that ended up in the back of the net was McLintock as he collided with a post trying to clear the ball. Leicester responded with a shot from Riley which almost caught Brown in two minds as it whistled past the left hand post.

Then Dyson on the halfway line flicked the ball forward to Jones who ran through the middle. The ball broke to White who crossed to the far post for Smith to nod it back to Dyson. The diminutive winger headed the ball over the top while standing almost underneath the crossbar. It was a golden opportunity and Dyson knew he'd missed a sitter. It would have been easier to score. 'No wonder the Tottenham players hold their heads in their hands,' said Wolstenholme. 'That was one of the few times Spurs have been able to open up this brilliant Leicester defence.'

Leicester held out bravely until the 69th minute. Then, with exhaustion and the heavy pitch taking their toll of the players' flagging limbs, Spurs went in front. The move that led to the goal started with Henry who tackled Cheesebrough on the right-wing and knocked the ball along the line to White, to Smith who passed inside to Jones, to Dyson, out to the right-wing for Allen who turned inside the full-back near the corner flag before knocking the ball with the outside of his right boot back for Dyson. 'The goal roar from the Tottenham thousands packed into the stands and terraces rushed up and clutched us by the throat as left-winger Terry Dyson, who had moved into the middle, suddenly sent a glorious through ball into the Leicester goalmouth,' wrote Hoby of the *Sunday Express*. Dyson had played an inch-perfect pass to the unmarked Smith who was lurking on the right near the penalty spot. The rugged, broad-shouldered Spurs centre-forward, looking very much an accomplished international, had about half a yard to play with. He controlled the ball with his right foot and, in one movement, turned past King for only the second time in the match, dummied the centre-half, feinted and swivelled to hit the ball on the turn. Boot met ball with a thud and the brown blur rose at an acute angle before crashing into the back of the net with the superb young Leicester keeper Banks going the wrong way as he dived to his right in vain.

It was as if the Wembley pitch was made-to-measure for Smith since no matter who the opposition he always seemed to get vital goals there; he'd scored in every international under the shadow of the twin towers and indeed anywhere else that he'd donned an England shirt.

As soon as Smith's shot hit the net, Blanchflower and Mackay were both convinced Spurs had won the Cup. 'That could be it because Leicester are really up against it now,' said Wolstenholme. 'Smith is the hero of the hour. The "double" is beginning to look a reality now.' The Spurs fans certainly thought so and began to sing: 'The Cup is going to Tottenham.'

In the brief moments left, the blinding cheetah speed of Jones, the sly positioning and passing of John White, described by Wolstenholme as 'a superb player; the great link man', and the sudden surges of left-winger Terry Dyson had the crowd gasping and enthralled. Spurs had done little to justify their tag as the 'Team of the Century' until the last half an hour when tiredness had taken its toll on a City side which had battled helplessly against the odds. Leicester had fought until their legs became lead and their hearts and lungs grew limp. 'The Leicester defenders now must be absolutely leg-weary,' said a sympathetic Wolstenholme. They'd been worn down by the combined burdens of knowing that, unlike most underdogs, they wouldn't be popular winners – most neutrals wanted Spurs to triumph – understandable apprehension about their opponents and, by far the most relevant, playing with a man short.

At last Tottenham had begun to play like their old selves. Wolstenholme noticed the difference up in the commentary box. 'Spurs are beginning to play with their usual confidence now. Spurs are doing their inter-passing – keeping in the same position but trying to draw a defender. That's the object of it all. Trying to find an opening.'

In the 77th minute the unfortunate Chalmers, who at one point had collapsed and was reduced to crawling on his hands and knees, just couldn't get the ball away and pushed a pass inside that went astray. It was intercepted by Allen who knocked it forward for Smith. He played a one-two with White before taking it along the wing. With infinite poise he looked up and saw Dyson unmarked 15 yards from the far post. Smith sent over a precise cross and you could almost see the muscles in Dyson's neck as he deliberately placed a bullet header wide of Banks's reaching hand from just outside the six-yard box. 'It's in the net; it's in the net. That's a beautiful goal by Dyson,' said BBC radio commentator Raymond Glendenning. 'Spurs are now two up with 14 minutes left to play. They're well on their way towards something that hasn't been done since 1897, the Cup double.'

Dyson threw up his hands and did his familiar war dance of victory. 'I remember Colin Appleton saying, "Well done, Terry," as I ran past him after I'd just scored,' recalls Dyson. 'It was unbelievable.' The jubilant Spurs fans were cheering and waving their wooden rattles. They could taste victory. Dyson's goal confirmed the view of

Blanchflower and Mackay that the Cup belonged to Spurs.

Blanchflower looked up above the Leicester goal and saw for the first time that day the huge scoreboard the television cameras focused on. It read: TOTTENHAM HOTSPUR 2 LEICESTER CITY 0. Although there was still some time to go, he somehow felt that would be the final score. That glance up at the scoreboard was the thing Blanchflower would remember most about the 1961 Cup final.

The game was now all over bar the shouting. 'It will be interesting to see what sort of fantastic scenes they're going to witness at Wembley when the whistle goes in about 30 seconds from now with everyone wishing to pay tribute to this wonderful side which has done so much for English football this season and, we hope, will do even more next season when they play in the European Cup,' said Wolstenholme.

The classy multi-passing among the jubilant Spurs players was brought to an end by the referee's final whistle. 'An ear-splitting racket of sound rose from the giant bowl of Wembley Stadium,' wrote Alan Hoby of the *Sunday Express*. 'It was a roar of triumph and joy and it came from the mighty host of Tottenham fans in the 100,000 crowd. For at that moment . . . Tottenham Hotspur became the first club of the century to win the fabulous Cup and League double.'

After a long, hard season they'd found the glory. Spurs had achieved the impossible. Cliff Jones knew what it meant. 'The "double" – the Everest, the four-minute mile of soccer – had been done. And I was a member of the team who had achieved it,' he said.

At the final whistle, Blanchflower thought only about climbing the stairs to take the Cup. For so many people that seemed the whole point of the afternoon. Nicholson waited for his team to come off the field so that he could shake hands with each and every one of the players who'd done him so proud. He seemed to linger a moment longer with man of the match Ron Henry. The Tottenham full-back had been at the club longer than any of the others and had played with the Spurs boss. They were close. Nicholson congratulated Blanchflower last of all just before his captain climbed the 39 steps to the Royal Box where he was to be presented with the Cup by the Duchess of Kent. Tottenham's Welsh winger Terry Medwin, who scored in his only appearance in the Cup way back in the Third Round against

Charlton, sat just beside the Royal Box. He looked on proudly as Blanchflower moved along the presentation balcony.

Nicholson wasn't too excited by the moment of triumph. 'If I won a million pounds on the pools or in a newspaper competition, I would not jump for joy,' he wrote in his autobiography many years later. 'If something has been your ambition and you have achieved it, then that's fine. If anything, I felt a slight sense of dissatisfaction. I had wanted us to play well and show how good we were, but the match had not been particularly entertaining.'

After the presentation Blanchflower and Smith carried the Cup down to the pitch. The Spurs players ran round the field with the trophy held high in time-honoured fashion and saluted their loyal fans. Blanchflower, named Footballer of the Year for the second time just two days earlier, realised the lap of honour was part of the day, but he hadn't much heart for waving the Cup around. He didn't like it. He didn't dislike it. He just did it. 'I looked upon it as a duty rather than an enjoyment. The achievement as far as I was concerned was over. I was satisfied and happy that we had done it, but I had no desire to go dancing round about it. Neither had I any desire ever to stop those who want to do it. The whole point to me wasn't in winning the "double". It was in believing we could win the "double". For the player the reality of a Cup final can never live up to the dream, the promised land, anyway. The dreams are for the fan, not the player, for the lover of the game who will never know what it is like out there. Cup final day is the fans' day.'

In the warm glow of victory the Tottenham dressing-room was all champagne, back-slapping, laughter and reporters' questions. Allen and Jones slipped across to the Leicester dressing-room to see how Len Chalmers was getting on. 'Les Allen came in after the game to say how sorry he was,' remembers Chalmers. But, understandably, the full-back was so disappointed and emotional that the apologies and sympathy didn't seem to get through to him.

Nicholson wasn't conscious of being caught up in any euphoria. The players felt the same. 'In those days you weren't mobbed by television reporters or the Press,' he says. 'There were no press conferences or countless interviews with radio reporters. I do not remember giving a press conference, although I did speak informally to some reporters afterwards. In those days the game did not need to sell itself. Grounds were full at clubs which were successful.'

The injury to Chalmers had raised inevitable questions about whether Spurs would have won if he hadn't been injured. The Spurs players had their own views on how the injury had affected the match. Jones thought the theory that they would definitely have lost was quite wrong. 'If Leicester, with a full team, had scored first I believe they might have won – narrowly; but if we had scored first when City were at full strength I think we might have managed four or even five. I am convinced the side scoring first was destined to win this match.'

Mackay didn't get half as much pleasure in beating ten-man Leicester as he'd have done against a complete team. 'No one, after he has played his heart out, likes to have people suggest to him that the result might have gone the other way had the opposition been at full strength.'

Mackay thought that in showpiece matches like the Cup final substitutes should be allowed since otherwise it was unfair to the fans who paid big money to watch two teams at full strength and to the winning team. 'One day the rulers of the Football Association will decide to have substitutes in the one match which season after season is ruined in this manner,' wrote Hoby in the *Sunday Express*. 'They will decide that the Cup final is a show spectacle between two equal teams – not an exhibition of pluck and guts by one hopelessly crippled side. When?' It was to be another four years before Charlton's Keith Peacock became the first substitute used in English football.

Whether Leicester would have beaten Tottenham if they'd been at full strength no one will ever know. The point was to be debated heatedly for a year or two as each Cup final came round. Then, when the precise details of the disappointing match became blurred by time, all that remained clear in the memory was the indisputable fact that Spurs in 1961 created soccer history. 'We can only applaud Tottenham for writing an imperishable page in the fables book of soccer and sympathise with Leicester for being one more victim of the Wembley hoodoo,' wrote Hoby.

It might have been the worse match the 1961 team had played for Spurs, but it was good enough to clinch the 'double'. 'Bad matches teach you more than good ones,' said Blanchflower. 'This one confirmed that our team could play well below par, disappoint all our expectations, and still beat average teams like Leicester. Some people might call that "coasting" or "idling" or maybe "rubbish", but it's part of a good professional's make-up that he can have a below-average or plain bad day and still beat the average teams. The trick is to know your own capabilities, and to recognise a bad day when you see one, to ride along with it, taking fewer chances and minimising errors. When you can do that you're a real pro.'

Nicholson was as disappointed as his captain. 'The match did not live up to its pre-match publicity. Cup finals rarely do. I believe it is because the players are loath to take chances. They wait that extra split second before releasing the ball and that gives defenders time to intercept or make a tackle. Even experienced players are affected by the tension and do not play as well as they usually do in League matches.'

Many years later, after he'd had time to reflect on the triumphs of the 1960–61 season, Nicholson was more positive about his team's achievements. 'Looking back now the "double" was fabulous, but there was also disappointment for me when we did not put our "double" feat right out of anybody's reach – remember that Arsenal caught up with us ten years later – by doing it for a second year in succession. Which we should have done.'

CHAPTER 42

The Celebrations

TOTTENHAM HAD DONE the 'double'. It was the last day of a season to remember. A time to celebrate. Later that night their triumph bubbled to a climax with a celebration dinner. Everyone at the club, and many associated with it, turned up at the Savoy Hotel in London.

The players from the 'push-and-run' side were there along with the employees from the Spurs office, like Alan Leather and Barbara Wallace, and more glamorous guests including a sprinkling of celebrities from stage and screen and famous names from the world of soccer.

The hotel had received a lot of telegrams congratulating the team, but there were also a few bitter ones. Les Allen was still upset about the injury to Chalmers and, although happy Spurs had won the 'double', felt the edge had been taken off his celebrations. The evening only really came to life for him after he received a telegram which read: 'Forget about it. Congratulations. Len Chalmers.'

Cliff Jones for one was impressed with Chalmers' attitude to the affair. 'Soccer would be a much better game if every player would learn to accept defeat and bad luck with such good grace,' he said.

Meanwhile, Nicholson was still not overjoyed at his team's historic achievement. 'I do not recall being over-elated . . . at the banquet after our victory. I looked on our success as an honour that meant more to the club than to any individual.

Ken Jones clearly remembers how upset the Tottenham manager was by his team's failure to reach his high standards on the biggest stage of the season. 'It's really got me down today that,' Nicholson told Jones. 'We did nothing. We didn't play. We didn't even start to play.'

Dave Mackay also remembers how disappointed Nicholson was with his team's performance. 'I'm sure any other manager in the League would have just been delighted to have won the game,' says Mackay. 'But Bill was a bit of a perfectionist and he was disappointed that we didn't do it in style. The players were just happy and elated to have done it.'

A large group of John White's relatives had come down from Scotland for the game and in good Scottish tradition thoroughly enjoyed themselves after the match. But White's fiancee Sandra Evans wasn't quite so happy. 'I was disappointed at the Savoy because I wanted to stay the night. I had always wanted to stay in a London hotel, but we didn't.'

Meanwhile, Nicholson was also worried about how the men he'd played with in the 'push-and-run' team felt on this night of celebration for his current side and the new and even more successful system in a completely different era. 'Bill was concerned with his "push-and-run" team,' recalls Alan Leather. 'They may have felt they were in the shadow of the "double" side.'

Nicholson was also less than happy with his salary. 'At the time, I was earning little – around £1,500, about twice the national average wage but no more than the top players – though I did receive a small bonus later as an acknowledgement of my work.'

The players received a set of suitcases from Spurs as a gift to mark their achievement in winning the double. They, in turn, chipped in to buy Bill Nick a Remington shaver as a token of their appreciation for all his work during the season. It probably meant far more to him than his 'small' bonus from the club.

All the employees received a bonus after the 'double' success. They had all, in their own way, contributed to the most successful season in the history of Tottenham Hotspur Football Club.

Alan Leather was given a year's salary as his bonus. At the time he was earning £10 a week, which was half the amount the players got. He used the money to buy a Triumph 2000 – his first big car. 'I couldn't believe it. It was the size of a tank.'

Some of the players also bought cars with the proceeds of their 'double' success. Ron Henry had been earning £16 and eight shillings a week that season, but with his win bonuses he could afford to put a down payment on a car. 'After we won the "double" we bought a car,' recalls Ron. 'It was a Vauxhall Victor. We had to have the car on the tick.'

Despite their phenomenal success the players were still not well off. It was an era before commercialism had touched the nation's number one sport and the words 'promoter' or 'agent' had not yet found their way into the vocabulary of football. 'I used to say to Les Allen, "We've got to win today. Mum and Dad are coming round for tea and we need some salad!"' says Ron Henry. 'We never earnt a penny outside the game.'

But Tottenham's 'double' winners wouldn't have changed anything for the world. 'I have no regrets at all,' says Dave Mackay. 'When I look back at football, before and after, I played at the best time, in my own mind anyway. It was the best era of football when it was played a bit slower, with a lot of skill; not so much hustle and bustle and pressure on players; no use of the elbow and that sort of thing. The game was much better and easier to play, and certainly more entertaining.'

'Today they play for the money,' says Bobby Smith. 'We played for the glory.'

CHAPTER 43
Epilogue

SPURS SHOULD HAVE gone down in history as the first team to complete a double of 'doubles'. But that distinction would have to wait more than 30 years for the Manchester United team of the 1990s.

Tottenham failed to complete two 'doubles' on the trot because of one match in 1962. Ironically, the game was against an Ipswich team managed by a former Spurs star. 'We should have won the "double" for a second time in the 1961–62 season and we would have done but for my old Tottenham team-mate Alf Ramsey,' says Nicholson.

Spurs lost 3-2 at Portman Road and were also beaten in the return match at White Hart Lane later in the season playing the same way, this time by 3-1. 'If we had picked up two of those four points, we would have won the Championship because our goal average was superior to that of Ipswich who won the title for the first and only time,' says Nicholson.

Spurs did get back to Wembley in 1962 where they beat rivals Burnley 3-1, thanks to goals from Jimmy Greaves, Bobby Smith and a Danny Blanchflower penalty. They fielded the same team which had played in the 1961 final with the exception of Jimmy Greaves, who replaced Les Allen, and Terry Medwin, who was selected ahead of Terry Dyson.

It was their second successive FA Cup triumph. More importantly, it guaranteed Spurs a place in the European Cup Winners' Cup. Nevertheless, the fans had hoped to see Tottenham become the first British team to win the European Cup. After a gallant effort their European adventure was ended by Benfica in the semi-final.

The following season Tottenham did become the first British team to win a European trophy – the Cup Winners' Cup. Danny Blanchflower was again the inspiration behind their success. He came back from injury to lead his team to an amazing 5-1 victory over Atletico Madrid in Rotterdam.

The margin of victory remains the biggest in the history of the Cup Winners' Cup – a competition which started in 1960. It was to be Blanchflower's last really big game for Spurs and was also the last major trophy lifted by the 'double' team.

Danny Blanchflower finally hung up his boots on 5 April 1964 at the age of 38. He'd played 382 games for Spurs and scored 21 goals. The Tottenham captain was also capped 56 times by Northern Ireland.

Danny moved into journalism, writing a weekly column for *The Observer* and then the *Sunday Express*. He also worked, briefly, as a TV commentator. Bill Nicholson wanted his former captain to succeed him after he quit in 1974, but the board had other ideas and surprisingly appointed former Arsenal defender Terry Neill.

Blanchflower finally became a manager in June 1976 when he took over Northern Ireland. He also took over as boss of Chelsea in December 1978. They were in severe financial trouble and Blanchflower failed to keep them in the First Division. After nine months he resigned.

Blanchflower suffered with Alzheimer's in his 60s. After entering hospital for a check-up in 1993 he fell over and broke his hip. His condition deteriorated and he fell into a coma. Danny Blanchflower passed away at a Cobham nursing home on 9 December 1993 at the age of 67. His gravestone reads:

'To the Glory of Robert Dennis Blanchflower. Beloved Father & Grandfather. 1926 – 1993. To thine own self be true.'

Terry Medwin played just enough games in the 1960–61 season to earn a Championship medal but he missed out on a Cup Winners' medal in 1961 because of the form of Terry Dyson. But Medwin played in the 1962 final instead of Dyson and got his medal after helping to beat Burnley.

Medwin was the first of the 'double' team to suffer a career-ending injury when he broke his leg in a game against South Africa's national team in Cape Town in 1963. He played 215 times for Spurs and scored 72 goals.

He left Tottenham to become a coach at Fulham and then joined Swansea as assistant manager to John Toshack. He still lives in Wales.

Bobby Smith was the first casualty when Tottenham brought Jimmy Greaves from AC Milan in 1962. He returned to the first team in place of Les Allen, but the years of punishment on the pitch were slowing him down.

Bobby fell out with Spurs and asked to be put on the tranfer list when they refused his request for a rise. Tottenham sold him to Brighton in May 1964 for £5,000. Smith had played 317 games for Spurs and scored 208 goals, as well as netting 13 times for England in 15 internationals.

When his football career ended, Bobby became a painter and decorator and drove a mini-cab. He now lives on a disability pension after suffering from heart trouble as well as having a hip replacement. Bobby still lives in Palmers Green, North London.

John White was struck by lightning on a golf course on Tuesday, 21 July 1964, at the age of 26. His tragic death heralded the break-up of the 'double' team. White had played 219 games for Spurs and scored 47 goals.

At his funeral both chapels were packed and there was also a large congregation outside listening to a relay of the service. How great a player he would have become no one will ever know.

Goalkeeper John Hollowbread remained a faithful understudy to Bill Brown and got a short spell in the first team during the spring of 1964 when Brown was injured. That summer, with Pat Jennings about to sign for Spurs, Hollowbread joined Southampton for £2,000. He had made 73 appearances. Hollowbread retired through injury in 1966. Today he lives in Spain.

Mel Hopkins tried his best to break into the first team after the 'double' season but couldn't dislodge Peter Baker. After five years in the reserves he followed Bobby Smith to Brighton in October 1964. He had played 240 times for the first team at Tottenham. Hopkins left Brighton for Northern Ireland side Ballymena before moving on to Bradford Park Avenue in 1968. Today he lives in Wales.

At 24 years old Les Allen seemed to have the world at his feet and a long career at Tottenham ahead of him after the 'double' success. Indeed, many people thought he'd soon add full international honours to his Under-23 cap. But just seven months after Spurs lifted the FA Cup at Wembley they signed Jimmy Greaves from AC Milan.

Allen finally lost his place for good when Alan Gilzean arrived from Dundee in December 1964. After 137 games and 61 goals for Tottenham he joined Third Division QPR for £21,000 – a record fee for that club – the following summer. When he hung up his boots in 1969 he took over as Rangers' manager for one season. In 1972 he became boss of Swindon but left football when he was dismissed two years later.

Allen then worked as a model-maker for an Essex firm. Today he's more famous as the father of former striker, Clive, now Tottenham's reserve team manager and a television pundit. His other son, Bradley, has played for QPR and Charlton.

Tony Marchi finally re-established himself in the first team after 1962. His biggest moment came when he replaced the injured Dave Mackay in the 1963 European Cup Winners' Cup final in Rotterdam.

Marchi was badly injured at Anfield in a League match against Liverpool in 1964 when he was 32 years old. He left Spurs the following year after making 260 appearances and scoring seven goals. Marchi became player-manager of non-League Cambridge City, but played only one game. In 1967 he was appointed manager of Northampton and lasted one season.

After that Marchi quit football and bought a wallpaper and paint shop in Maldon, Essex.

Terry Dyson left Spurs for Fulham in June 1965 having made 209 appearances scoring 55 goals. He played 22 games for the Cottagers, netting three times. In 1968 he joined Colchester United and played another 56 League games, getting on the scoresheet four times.

Dyson played part time for Guildford and then became a manager with non-League Dagenham and Boreham Wood. He also began teaching PE at Hampstead High School and then at a special school for expelled children in Bushey, West London.

Peter Baker continued to play superbly for Tottenham after surviving a challenge from Welsh international Mel Hopkins. He was still extremely fit when a young Cyril Knowles arrived to take his place. When he left to become player-manager of South African side Durban City in 1965, Baker had played 342 games for the club.

He remained in South Africa when his football career was over to start a successful furniture business. He still lives there with his family. 'Even today I'm asked for autographs and people still write to me,' he says. 'The interest has always been tremendous. I've met many players who say the 'double' side was the finest they ever played against.'

Ron Henry became the only man to have played with and under Sir Alf Ramsey when he represented England in 1963. But that was to be his only cap. He also briefly took over as captain at Tottenham after Blanchflower retired. Knee trouble ended his first-team career in 1965 but he carried on playing for the reserves and the 'A' team.

Henry played 287 games for Spurs. His only goal came in a League match against eventual Champions Manchester United at White Hart Lane in February 1965 when he delighted the crowd by scoring with a speculative 35-yarder.

Today he runs a market garden from his base in Redbourn, Hertfordshire and still coaches youngsters at Tottenham.

Bill Brown was the first-choice keeper at Tottenham until the spring of 1964 when injuries and the arrival of a young Irishman called Pat Jennings threatened his position. Brown and Jennings played an almost equal number of games over the next two seasons.

In October 1966 Brown made way for the young pretender when he joined Northampton after playing 262 games for Spurs. He joined Canadian team Toronto Falcons the following year.

Brown stayed in Canada and worked for a Toronto property developer until joining the Ontario government's Land Department in 1975. In 1988 he had a heart attack, which persuaded him to cut out the 40 cigarettes he smoked each day. In 1994 Brown was diagnosed with prostate cancer but survived that, too. He retired in 1995 and continued to live in Simcoe, Ontario.

By 2004, when he was inducted into the Tottenham Hall of Fame with the rest of the double-winning team, Brown had been ill for some time. He died on 30 November 2004, aged 73, leaving his wife Elaine, two daughters and his son, who had become a detective.

Maurice Norman played 23 times for England and continued to give sterling service to Spurs. But in 1965 he suffered a horrific injury in a friendly against a Hungarian Select XI, breaking his leg in five places.

Maurice finally retired after a two-year battle to recover from his injury. He had played 411 gaves for Spurs scoring 19 goals.

Maurice worked at a petrol station in Friern Barnet before opening a wool shop at Frinton-on-Sea in Essex. When the business collapsed he returned to the land as a gardener at Wickham Market in Suffolk.

Frank Saul was just 18 years old when he played for Tottenham in the European Cup against Feyenoord in 1962. He seemed to have a bright future, but never quite fulfilled his potential. Nevertheless, Saul's versatility enabled him to play at least 20 games a season.

Only 24 years old when he left for Southampton in January 1968, he was the makeweight in a £40,000 deal that took Martin Chivers to Spurs. Saul played 125 games for Tottenham and scored 45 goals.

Dave Mackay broke his leg in a second-round Cup Winner's Cup tie against Manchester United at Old Trafford in December 1963. Nine months later he fractured the same leg in a comeback match.

Mackay recovered from his injuries to become captain of Tottenham after Blanchflower retired and he led the team to victory in the 1967 FA Cup final against Chelsea. In July the following year he joined Brian Clough at Derby for a token £5,000. Mackay had made 318 appearances for Spurs and scored 51 goals as well as earning 22 Scotland caps in his career.

In his first season, Derby won the Second Division Championship and Mackay shared the Footballer of the Year award with Manchester City's Tony Book. He made 122 appearances for the Midlands club, scoring five goals.

Mackay finished his distinguished career as player-manager of

Swindon in 1971. He briefly took over at Nottingham Forest in 1972 before rejoining Derby the following year as Clough's successor. In his second season as manager they were Champions.

Mackay left the Rams in 1976 and took over at Walsall the following year. He was then lured to the Middle East on a lucrative contract where he won five league titles and one Gulf Cup with Al Arabi. He spent nine years in the Gulf (1978 to 1987).

Mackay returned to England and became boss of Doncaster Rovers, but he resigned in March 1989. The next month he became manager of Birmingham City but after two seasons he quit and returned to the Middle East where he steered Zamalek, one of Egypt's top two teams, to the title in both his two seasons there as coach.

Cliff Jones matured into possibly the best winger in world football and Juventus offered an astronomical £100,000 for his services. He was not for sale.

Cliff was the last member of the double-winning side to play for the first team at Spurs. He was 33 years old when he joined Fulham in October 1968 after playing 370 games and scoring 159 goals. Apart from Ron Henry, who was still coaching, he was the last of the 'double' team to leave the club. He was capped 59 times by Wales, his last appearance coming in 1969.

After his Football League career was over, Cliff joined Southern League Kings Lynn before moving on to Wealdstone, Bedford and Cambridge City. When he hung up his boots Cliff became a porter at Covent Garden before returning to his old trade as a sheet metal-worker. In 1972 he became a PE teacher at Highbury Grove School in Islington. Cliff was made redundant in 1993.

Bill Nicholson did his best to replace the players who'd reached the dizzy heights of success in the early 1960s. The new players he brought into the side enabled Spurs to lift more trophies. Tottenham won the FA Cup again in 1967 and in the following decade they captured the League Cup (1971 and 1973) and the UEFA Cup (1972).

At the start of the 1974–75 season Spurs lost their first four League games – matching their worst-ever start to a campaign 62 years before. They were also slaughtered 4-0 in the League Cup against

Middlesbrough at White Hart Lane. A 2-1 defeat against Manchester City in the fourth League game was the last straw. That night, after 38 years at the club, the last 15 as the most successful manager in its history, he resigned.

Nicholson was disappointed both that Tottenham didn't retain him in some capacity and that they ignored his advice to appoint Blanchflower as the new manager. He didn't return to Spurs for two years after he quit, although he still lived within walking distance.

Nicholson's services to football were recognised in 1975 when he was awarded the OBE by the Queen Mother at Buckingham Palace. He returned to the club as a consultant to Keith Burkinshaw and became responsible for professional and non-League scouting at Spurs.

In 1983 Nicholson was belatedly given a testimonial and the following year was awarded the Professional Footballers' Association Merit Award. Previous winners included Bobby Charlton, Denis Law, George Eastham, Bill Shankly, Tom Finney, Sir Matt Busby, Joe Mercer and Bob Paisley. In 1991 his contribution to Tottenham was at last recognised when he was appointed president.

Nicholson is one of only four men who have won the Championship as a player and a manager with the same club – Kenny Dalglish, Howard Kendall and George Graham are the others. 'There is no dispute, absolutely none, that he makes the grade as Tottenham's All-Time Great Manager,' says Harry Harris of the *Daily Mirror.*

Nicholson passed away peacefully in a Hertfordshire Hospital on the morning of Saturday, 23 October 2004, aged 85, after a long fight against illness. He was surrounded by his family, including his wife Darkie and two daughters.

The tributes poured in from around the world. But those from his players would have been the most important to the great man who was never comfortable in the limelight.

'I've cried already today,' said Dave Mackay. 'He's been ill for some time, but when things like this happen it's sad. He did everything for the club. They were fourth from bottom when he took over and within a year and a half we had won the double.

'Bill was a marvellous manager, one of the top five in the game over the past fifty years. He always wanted us to play football and sometimes we were winning games 5-1 and then drew 5-5. He always wanted us to go forward. That is the type of manager and man he was.'

'Bill was absolutely straightforward,' he added. 'When he said something, he meant it – he would never go back on his word. He never let us forget we were out there to entertain the public. He was 100 per cent honest and 100 per cent Spurs.'

Nicholson's death brought an outpouring of emotion from former players and the thousands of fans who had lived through the glory years and were so grateful to have seen the fruits of Bill Nick's hard work on the pitch performing miracles for the Lilywhites during the 1960s and early '70s.

Tottenham chairman Daniel Levy mourned Nicholson's passing and praised his achievements. 'Bill's death is a tragedy for the whole of football but particularly for his family and all of us at Spurs,' he said. 'He was loved by everyone at White Hart Lane and there is no doubt that he, in turn, loved this club. He will never be forgotten.

'He lifted Spurs from mediocrity to the sublime, as we became the first British club to win a European trophy, and to so many wonderful achievements such as that special double of 1961.

'Throughout it all, as player and manager, he did things his own way. His teams played with his own brand of attacking flair, entertaining all the way. Indeed, he made our famous old Spurs cockerel crow with pride.

'He was a giant of the game and was deservedly held in high esteem and with intense respect throughout football. He was our club president and a man that we all looked up to and whose presence we sought.

'We at Spurs owe it to Bill, and his memory, to maintain his vision and to ensure his achievements remain our inspiration in the years to come.

'Bill Nicholson devoted his whole life to Tottenham Hotspur and to our fans, and will never be surpassed as the greatest individual in our history. He set unbelievable standards and gave the name Tottenham Hotspur a global dimension with his own unique and wonderful style of football.'

On the day he died, Tottenham were fittingly due to play a team steeped in tradition – Bolton Wanderers. Nicholson's influence overwhelmed everything about the sad occasion at White Hart Lane.

The autumn rain was unrelenting, but the bouquets and sodden cards were slowly growing outside the entrance to the ground as fans came by quietly to lay their tributes. They knotted their scarves on the guard rail or scribbled a homily to Nicholson, whose name was synonymous with Tottenham Hotspur for 60 years.

Many were simply addressed to 'Mr Tottenham'. 'Goodbye, Sir Bill,' said another, referring to the deeply held belief among the fans and at the club that Nicholson deserved a knighthood. 'Thank you for the glory years' was a sentiment that summed up the sense of gratitude.

While the skies wept, with flags at half-mast, Spurs paid a moving tribute to Nicholson, a manager for whom the diehards at White Hart Lane retained a deep affection 30 years after his retirement. The club had clearly prepared for this sad event.

The afternoon began with a scene of floral and spoken tributes, as sombre music played and a parade of old legends prepared to address the appreciative crowd of young and old alike.

Many of Nicholson's players had returned to pay homage. The list included veteran Tommy Harmer, inside-forward and team-mate of Nicholson in the mid-'50s, Mel Hopkins and Les Allen from the double team, and Martin Chivers, Ralph Coates, Martin Peters, Phil Beal and Pat Jennings from the '60s and '70s, plus many others from later years, including Paul Gascoigne.

The former players lined up to pay their respects and shared memories that were uniformly respectful: 'A very hard man, straight, honest, effective, a perfectionist.'

'When I arrived,' recalled former Spurs captain Alan Mullery, 'most of the "double" team were still playing and the esteem in which they held Bill was unbelievable. He never lost a [domestic] cup final, he was a genius as far as football was concerned.'

Tottenham's former goalkeeper, Jennings, said simply, 'The team he put together in 1961 was impossible to follow.'

There was a half-hour tribute to Bill Nick on the stadium's giant video screens, showing footage of his team's finest moments. Black-and-white images and some colour footage showed Danny

Blanchflower, the elegant, eloquent Ulsterman, and others all in white diving into the mud before holding silverware aloft – the glory, glory years. Mackay, whose defensive skills were supplemented by a thunderous shot, then Smith, a raging bull of a centre-forward. Glimpses of the double winners were followed by snatches of the first team to win a European trophy. Goals from Dyson and Greaves lit up the screen. 'What a game,' declared the commentator.

It was emotional and inspiring and showed a time when Spurs were a byword for style and excellence at home and abroad. Every now and then, Nicholson was shown speaking of his memories, his philosophy.

In the stands, middle-aged supporters wiped away a tear and told their sons of the days when Tottenham's cockerel crowed over the land. They reminisced over the double team and remembered the European trophies Nicholson's vision had brought them. They cheered as the screen filled with film showing the white double-decker bus ferrying some of Nicholson's heroes along Tottenham High Road with another haul of silverware.

When Nicholson's image was projected onto the big screens to a backdrop of his many trophies, there was prolonged applause from Tottenham and Bolton supporters alike which lasted until the words 'Bill Nicholson 1919–2004' filled the screen.

During the minute's silence before the game, which was observed with true dignity, all that could be heard was the rain hitting the roof. It fell like a veil of tears, but not one jacket collar was raised to keep out the damp. A fan's banner said it best: 'Sir Bill Nicholson – Mr Tottenham.'

When the match got underway, the current crop of Spurs players seemed to try too hard and could not live up to their heritage as they lost 2-1. Afterwards, the dejected Tottenham players wished they had provided a more fitting tribute to their club's greatest manager.

'My granddad probably tells me more than anyone about Bill Nicholson,' said Tottenham midfielder Jamie Redknapp. 'They were great players and he was a great man. I just wish we could have paid tribute to him better.'

Bolton's former Spurs striker Les Ferdinand recalled, 'I met him on a few occasions and obviously we all know what Bill means to Tottenham Hotspur. It's a sad day.'

Spurs Welsh winger Simon Davies added, 'The game was secondary today. We wanted to give him a good send-off and the only way we could do that was with a win.'

Martin Samuel wrote in the *News of the World*: 'If the fans left defeated, the memory of Bill Nicholson meant they were not downhearted. They made their way into the bluster and drizzle hoping for a brighter future, and for a leader who would one day restore the glory, glory to Tottenham Hotspur. They left hoping for the second coming of Bill.'

Despite the rain, many fans lingered to read the floral tributes by the main entrance. There were sons whose fathers were not even born when Nicholson retired in 1974. Twenty minutes after the match, a small boy stood in sombre mood in front of the makeshift shrine. The youngster looked at the flowers, scarves and shirts and read the tributes. He seemed to understand.

The messages conveyed a sense of paradise lost. 'To Bill, the best we've ever had. RIP. Frank Craig.' Another just said, 'Sadly Missed.' Among the bouquets, the brightest had the sweetest message: 'Bill Nick. The Greatest Spur Ever. From Sarah.' A Spurs jersey draped over a barrier said, 'Sir Bill Nick, Your Glory Will Never Fade.'

By now, even more of the notes attached the missing 'Sir' to Nicholson's name. There was still great resentment that his achievements had not been recognised by his country. A knighthood was the only honour missing from Nicholson's career.

Tottenham fans had petitioned for such an honour right up until his death. On a website dedicated to the Nicholson knighthood campaign, the last message was posted just eight days before he passed away. It read: 'We have been contacted by the Government department responsible for honours, and they have sadly told us that Bill will not be considered for further honours. With this in mind, we have decided that there is no longer any point in collecting signatures for the petition.'

Supporters' Trust spokesman Daniel Wynne said, 'The "Knight Bill Nick" campaign didn't achieve its aim, but to us he was Sir Bill.

Bill Nicholson was the father figure of our club, and we are mourning the loss of a man who is very dear to us all. We will never forget him and he will always have a very special place in our hearts.'

Mackay also felt Nicholson should have been honoured by the Queen. 'I am amazed he wasn't [knighted]. He did so much for the game and the club, and people forget that he lived in Tottenham for 60 years. He did so much for the community.'

Cliff Jones added, 'There was a strong campaign for him to be knighted and I am amazed he wasn't. He did so much for the game and the club. He drilled into us that the most important thing was the club and its fans, and I would put him alongside the greats such as Brian Clough, Bill Shankly, Sir Matt Busby and Sir Alex Ferguson.'

Tottenham MP David Lammy also paid tribute, saying, 'I was brought up with the deepest respect and affection for Bill. He was the greatest manager Spurs have ever had, not only winning trophies but also doing it in dazzling style. He will never be forgotten.'

Nicholson's standing among the fans was clear to see from the hundreds of floral tributes, scarves and shirts, as well as messages of condolence, left by the pitch at White Hart Lane both before the Bolton match and through the days following his death.

After the match, the tributes left outside the ground were moved to pitch-side and the stadium remained open all week so the fans could sign a book of remembrance and pay their respects.

Two weeks after Bill Nick died, Tottenham organised a simple yet elegant memorial service at White Hart Lane on Sunday, 7 November. On a grey, calm morning, it was a dignified celebration of his life: poignant and emotional but not ridiculously sentimental.

All his family were there, of course, along with almost 10,000 fans, which again was hardly surprising. He was revered by generations of supporters, many of whom laid shirts, scarves and wreaths beside a huge blue-and-white banner proclaiming, 'Glory, glory Tottenham Hotspur 1961.'

The cast list for football's farewell to one of the great post-war managers said everything about his stature. Members of the double-winning side were again in attendance, mingling once more with players from Nicholson's teams of the '70s, to pay homage to a man whose name will forever be associated with Tottenham Hotspur.

Harmer, Smith, Mullery, Peters, Chivers, Kinnear, Beal, Jennings, Coates, Saul, Robertson, Clemence, Perryman, Pratt, Neighbour, Hoddle, Mabbutt, Miller, Shreeve, Pleat, Keane, Defoe, Carrick – the players and personalities covered every twist and turn in the Nicholson years and beyond.

The present-day millionaire players, immaculately dressed in club blazers, may not have known the man they were honouring, but they were fully aware that his spirit still stalked the corridors of White Hart Lane – the world famous home of the Spurs, thanks to Nicholson.

It was like a convention of Tottenham's great and good, and only one man could have got them together in the same place at the same time. His players loved him. They may not have thought so at the time they played for him, but it was clear enough as they paid their personal tributes.

It was a poignant weekend on which to remind everybody associated with the first club to win the double in the twentieth century of the standards that produced that remarkable achievement. Nostalgia hung heavy in the air as images of the Nicholson era once again flickered on the giant video screens positioned high on the stand roof at each end of the ground.

On a makeshift stage in the middle of the pitch, some of the star-studded names that epitomised Nicholson's reign took to the podium – Jimmy Greaves and Cliff Jones from the '60s, Martin Chivers and Steve Perryman from the '70s, Glenn Hoddle and Gary Mabbutt from the '80s.

Each of them spoke eloquently of his qualities: loyalty, passion, teamwork and, above all, respect for the fans. Each talked with affection, recalling a time in football history when values were different and clubs recognised success was built on stability and loyalty.

The sprightly Welshman Jones and portly Englishman Greaves, who had joined Tottenham just after the double season, walked arm in arm along the blue carpet (red was out of the question) to the podium so they could address the fans gathered behind the Paxton Road Stand goal. The two representatives of a triumphant past were given a heartfelt standing ovation.

'From the day he [Nicholson] took the helm at White Hart Lane, he was the great man of the club,' said Greaves, standing right above the penalty area where he had displayed his skills as a goal poacher in the 1960s. 'He gave a generation of fans something they'll never ever forget.

'He arrived at my flat in Milan wearing a trilby, tweed coat and thick gloves, and from the day he signed me from AC Milan I had nothing but the deepest respect for him and I can safely say that's a fact for all my team-mates, too.'

Greaves, of course, embodied the kind of player Bill Nick loved because he was an entertainer. Speaker after speaker emphasised that Nicholson's great strength was putting the fans first.

Greaves added, 'He was a dour Yorkshireman – on the outside. But he was a great man with many values who did have a humourous side. Like all great managers, he was one of the lads when he wanted to be and the boss when he needed to be.'

He recalled Nicholson's waspish sense of humour when Jones went to the Spurs boss and asked him to raise his wages to £100 a week. 'I want £100 a week because I'm the best winger in the world,' Jones had told him. 'That's your opinion not mine,' was Nicholson's instant reply.

Greaves also recalled Bill Nick's final dressing-room instruction before every match: 'Remember, you are going to run out in front of the people who pay your wages. Their expectancy of you is high, their value of you is high and their opinion of you is high. So do not let them down. Entertain them and you can only do that by being honest with yourself, respecting your team-mates and your opponents, and by, as a team, playing as one.'

Jones, one of the greatest and quickest wingers of all time, recalled how economical Nicholson was with compliments. 'I remember feeling really pleased with myself after playing a good game. He patted me on the back and said, "Well done, Jones." I replied, "Steady on boss," to which he remarked, "Remember, son, a pat on the back is only two feet away from a kick up the arse."

'He didn't waste words, but he paid attention to detail. He managed the club from the boot room to the boardroom. He insisted that the most important people at the club were not the directors, management or players but the supporters. He would say they come through the turnstiles to pay your wages and Tottenham is an important part of their lives.'

Energetic midfielder Perryman, whose 17-year career was launched by Nicholson in 1969 and whose integrity as captain mirrored his manager's philosophy, revealed, 'The first thing he taught me was to play quick, easy and accurate.'

Perryman, one of Nicholson's longest-serving players, recalled some of the manager's favourite maxims, like, 'Play the way you are facing,' 'When the game dies, you come alive,' and 'Don't spectate, and if you do, go and pay your admission money.'

'I never saw a hair out of place. He had the shiniest shoes, creases in his trousers that you could cut with – and a hatred of anything red!' This touched a chord as the crowd laughed. Among the special guests even Arsenal's vice-chairman David Dein and director Ken Friar smiled wryly.

Perhaps the most fitting tribute came from former centre-forward Chivers, who remembered Nicholson's reaction after Spurs had beaten Wolverhampton Wanderers to win the UEFA Cup in 1972. 'We were all waiting to drink the champagne, but Bill walked straight into the Wolves dressing-room to congratulate them on being the better team.'

Playmaker Hoddle, an apprentice in Nicholson's final year as manager, remembered being told off even after a fine performance. 'I'd scored a hat-trick for the youth team and the following morning the manager said, "Young Hoddle, your third goal – you took a big risk with that. You should have passed."'

Nicholson, the last Tottenham manager to win the title in that fabled double year of 1961, set a standard that all his successors have tried to emulate. He wanted not just to win but to win with style. 'He gave a generation of fans something they will never forget,' said Greaves.

The film on the big screens at White Hart Lane had evoked memories of the Nicholson legacy. Those fans old enough remembered what it used to be like when the Lilywhites ruled.

At the end, the tributes were brought to an emotional finale by Bill's daughter, Linda, who thanked everyone – particularly the fans. 'We know Dad loved you as much as you loved him,' she said.

A final prayer and blessing, and then Brian Alexander, a solemn and sensitive MC, triggered the release of 85 white doves from the centre circle to honour each year of Nicholson's life.

As the fans left the stadium, the words of Julia Ward Howe's ballad, which had been adopted by Tottenham fans decades ago, rang around the famous old ground:

> He has sounded forth the trumpet that shall never sound retreat,
> He is sifting out the hearts of men before his judgement seat,
> Glory, glory, hallelujah!

'The hour-long tribute hit just the right note and would, I suspect, have earned the endorsement of the tough, uncomplicated Yorkshireman looking down from above for any quivering lips,' wrote Michael Hart in the London *Evening Standard*.

Many of the fans present never knew Nicholson or saw his teams play, but as chairman Daniel Levy said, 'It was the greatest period of our history cascaded into a kaleidoscope of success after success. He did so much for the club, we must never let his legacy fade. He must be our inspiration as we strive to ensure a new era dawns at White Hart Lane.'

There's a bust of Nicholson in the main entrance to the West Stand at White Hart Lane like the one of Herbert Chapman that stood for years inside Arsenal's famous marble halls across North London at Highbury. The road leading to the main entrance to the ground was renamed Bill Nicholson Way in his honour and the nearby Northumberland Arms pub now also bears his name. It's the least Nicholson deserved after dedicating his life to Tottenham Hotspur.

The Results

Road to the Championship

Date	Opponents	H/A	Score	Spurs scorers
Aug. 20	Everton	H	2-0	Allen, Smith
Aug. 22	Blackpool	A	3-1	Dyson (2), Medwin
Aug. 27	Blackburn	A	4-1	Smith (2), Allen, Dyson
Aug. 31	Blackpool	H	3-1	Smith (3)
Sept. 3	Man. Utd	H	4-1	Smith (2), Allen (2)
Sept. 7	Bolton	A	2-1	Allen, White
Sept. 10	Arsenal	A	3-2	Saul, Dyson, Allen
Sept. 14	Bolton	H	3-1	Smith (2), Blanchflower (p)
Sept. 17	Leicester	A	2-1	Smith (2)
Sept. 24	Aston Villa	H	6-2	White (2), Smith, Dyson, Allen, Mackay
Oct. 1	Wolves	A	4-0	Jones, Blanchflower, Allen, Dyson
Oct. 10	Man. City	H	1-1	Smith
Oct. 15	Nottm. F.	A	4-0	White, Mackay, Jones (2)
Oct. 29	Newcastle	A	4-3	Norman, White, Jones, Smith
Nov. 2	Cardiff	H	3-2	Blanchflower (p), Dyson, Medwin
Nov. 5	Fulham	H	5-1	Jones (2) Allen (2), White
Nov. 12	Sheff. Wed.	A	1-2	Norman
Nov. 19	B'ham	H	6-0	White, Dyson (2), Jones (2), Smith (p)
Nov. 26	West Brom.	A	3-1	Smith (2), Allen

Dec. 3	Burnley	H	4-4	Norman, Jones, (2), Mackay
Dec. 10	Preston	A	1-0	White
Dec. 17	Everton	A	3-1	White, Allen, Mackay
Dec. 24	West Ham	H	2-0	White, Dyson
Dec. 26	West Ham	A	3-0	White, Allen, o.g.
Dec. 31	Blackburn	H	5-2	Smith (2), Allen (2), Blanchflower
Jan. 16	Man. Utd.	A	0-2	
Jan. 21	Arsenal	H	4-2	Allen (2), Smith, Blanchflower (p)
Feb. 4	Leicester	H	2-3	Allen, Blanchflower (p)
Feb. 11	Aston Villa	A	2-1	Smith, Dyson
Feb. 22	Wolves	H	1-1	Smith
Feb. 25	Man. City	A	1-0	Medwin
Mar. 11	Cardiff	A	2-3	Allen, Dyson
Mar. 22	Newcastle	H	1-2	Allen
Mar. 25	Fulham	A	0-0	
Mar. 31	Chelsea	H	4-2	Saul, Allen, Jones (2)
Apr. 1	Preston	H	5-0	Saul, White, Jones (3)
Apr. 3	Chelsea	A	3-2	Norman, Smith, Medwin
Apr. 8	B'ham	A	3-2	White, Smith, Allen
Apr. 17	Sheff. Wed.	H	2-1	Smith, Allen
Apr. 22	Burnley	A	2-4	Baker, Smith
Apr. 26	Nottm. F.	H	1-0	Medwin
Apr. 29	West Brom.	H	1-2	Smith

League Scorers: Smith 28; Allen 23; Jones 15; White 13; Dyson 12; Blanchflower 6; Medwin 5; Mackay 4; Norman 4; Saul 3; Baker 1; Own Goal 1. Total: 115

League Appearances: Brown 41; Hollowbread 1; Baker 41; Barton 1; Henry 42; Blanchflower 42; Norman 41; Marchi 6; Mackay 37; Jones 29; Smith (J) 1; White 42; Smith (R) 36; Saul 6; Allen 42; Dyson 40; Medwin 14

Spurs attracted 2,037,671 people to their 42 League games.

Football League Division I Final Table 1960–61

	P	W	D	L	F	A	Pts
Tottenham Hotspur	42	31	4	7	115	55	66
Sheffield Wednesday	42	23	12	7	78	47	58
Wolverhampton Wanderers	42	25	7	10	103	75	57
Burnley	42	22	7	13	102	77	51
Everton	42	22	6	14	87	69	50
Leicester City	42	18	9	15	87	70	45
Manchester United	42	18	9	15	88	76	45
Blackburn Rovers	42	15	13	14	77	76	43
Aston Villa	42	18	5	19	67	71	41
West Bromwich Albion	42	18	5	19	67	71	41
Arsenal	42	15	11	16	77	85	41
Chelsea	42	15	7	20	98	100	37
Nottingham Forest	42	14	9	19	62	78	37
Manchester City	42	13	11	18	79	90	37
Cardiff City	42	13	11	18	60	85	37
West Ham United	42	13	10	19	77	88	36
Fulham	42	14	8	20	72	95	36
Bolton Wanderers	42	12	11	19	58	73	35
Birmingham City	42	14	6	22	62	84	34
Blackpool	42	12	9	21	68	73	33
Newcastle United	42	11	10	21	86	109	32
Preston North End	42	10	10	22	43	71	30

Road to Wembley

Date	Round	Opponents	H/A	Score	Spurs scorers
Jan. 7	3rd	Charlton	H	W 3-2	Allen (2), Dyson
Jan. 28	4th	Crewe	H	W 5-1	Dyson, Smith, Mackay, Jones, Allen
Feb. 18	5th	Aston Villa	A	W 2-0	Neal (o.g.), Jones
Mar. 4	6th	Sunderland	A	D 1-1	Jones
Mar. 8	6th (r)	Sunderland	H	W 5-0	Allen, Smith, Dyson (2), Mackay
Mar. 18	SF	Burnley	Villa	W 3-0	Smith (2), Jones
May 6	F	Leicester	Wemb	W 2-0	Smith, Dyson

FA Cup Scorers: Dyson 5; Smith 5; Allen 4; Jones 4; Mackay 2;. Own Goal 1. Total: 21

Cup Appearances: Brown 7; Baker 7; Henry 7; Blanchflower 7; Norman 7; Mackay 7; Jones 6; White 7; Smith (R) 7; Allen 7; Dyson 7; Medwin 1

Tottenham were watched by 474,363 people during their seven Cup games . . . more than had watched any other club at any other time.

For the Record

First team to win the League Championship and FA Cup in the same season this century

Football League

Eleven successive wins at start of season

First Division

* 31 victories in 42 games
* 16 away wins in 21 games
* Equalled Arsenal's record of 66 points in a season
* Equalled Arsenal's record of 33 points from away games
* Unbeaten for 16 games from start of season
* First team to gain 50 points in only 29 games
* Equalled Manchester United's (1956–57) and Wolves' (1958–59) record number of 'doubles' by beating 11 clubs twice

Club

Most League goals in Tottenham's history: 115

WE ARE TOTTENHAM

Voices from White Hart Lane

by Martin Cloake and Adam Powley

ISBN 9781840188318
Now available as a Mainstream
paperback (£9.99)
www.mainstreampublishing.com

Rodney Marsh once infamously dubbed them 'the worst fans in Britain', but 'fickle' is the more familiar label applied to supporters of Tottenham Hotspur. But who are these seemingly forever unhappy fans, the caricatures beloved by the media and the marketing men? Are they a disparate group of people whose only real connection is a shared love for their club? More importantly, what have they got to say for themselves?

We Are Tottenham puts Spurs supporters at the centre of the tale of a dramatic season at White Hart Lane, one in which fans' hero Glenn Hoddle was axed after only six games, and the club faced a fight for its reputation. Rather than deliver a mere roll-call of games in a season vital to the club's future, *We Are Tottenham* uses the events and themes of the 2003–04 campaign to address the issues that matter to many football fans today, from the dominance of money to the passions of a local derby. It is a compelling account of the joy, frustration and absurdity of following a Premiership club.

> 'Martin Cloake and Adam Powley's review of Tottenham's 2003–04 season is an unexpectedly light-hearted and amusing read, as well as being an acute summary of Tottenham's most recent campaign of low points'
>
> – *Sunday Times*

Ten years after the launch of
Mainstream Sport we are proud
to present

Mainstream Sport Classics

THE GLORY GAME

The New Edition of the British Football Classic

by Hunter Davies

ISBN 9781840182422
Now available as a Mainstream Sport Classic paperback (£7.99)
www.mainstreampublishing.com

When the first edition of *The Glory Game* was published in 1972, it was instantly hailed as the most accurate book about the life of a football team ever published. 'His accuracy is sufficiently uncanny to be embarrassing,' wrote Bob Wilson in the *New Statesman*. 'Brilliant, vicious, unmerciful,' wrote *The Sun*. It caused great controversy at the time. Hunter Davies was the first writer to be allowed into the inner sanctums of a top football team, and his pen and his eyes spared nothing and no one. Now the main controversies have been forgotten. Or forgiven. Instead, his work has turned into a classic, probably the best book about football ever written.

> '*The Glory Game* engages the mind while revealing the soul of the beautiful game'
>
> – *The Herald*

THE GREATEST FOOTBALLER YOU NEVER SAW

The Robin Friday Story

by Paul McGuigan and Paolo Hewitt

ISBN 9781840181081
Now available as a Mainstream Sport Classic paperback (£7.99)
www.mainstreampublishing.com

Robin Friday was an exceptional footballer who should have played for England. He never did. Robin Friday was a brilliant player who could have played in the top flight. He never did. Why? Because Robin Friday was a man who would not bow down to anyone, who refused to take life seriously and who lived every moment as if it were his last. For anyone lucky enough to have seen him play, Robin Friday was up there with the greats. Take it from one who knows: 'There is no doubt in my mind that if someone had taken a chance on him he would have set the top division alight,' says the legendary Stan Bowles. 'He could have gone right to the top, but he just went off the rails a bit.' Loved and admired by everyone who saw him, Friday also had a dark side: troubled, strong-minded, reckless, he would end up destroying himself. Tragically, after years of alcohol and drug abuse, he died at the age of 38 without ever having fulfilled his potential. This book provides the first full appreciation of a man too long forgotten by the world of football, and will surely give him the cult status he deserves.

> 'There are times when you are profoundly affected by the things you read, when certain books are an inspiration. *The Robin Friday Story* is one such book. [Guigsy and Paolo] have turned out what will become one of the essential modern football books' *****
>
> – *FourFourTwo*

REBELS FOR THE CAUSE

The Alternative History of Arsenal Football Club

by Jon Spurling

ISBN 9781840189001
Now available as a Mainstream Sport Classic paperback (£7.99)
www.mainstreampublishing.com

Arsenal's on-field success has been well documented – from the golden era of Chapman's '30s teams to the modern-day triumphs of Wenger's cavaliers. But what has never been written before is the equally remarkable history of Arsenal's rebels, both on and off the pitch. Spanning almost 120 years, and set against a backdrop of turbulent social and political change, *Rebels for the Cause* assesses the legacy and impact of Arsenal's most controversial players, officials and matches.

From hard men like '30s player Wilf Copping to the reformed wild ones of recent years such as Tony Adams, Jon Spurling highlights the infamous figures whose refusal to conform has made them terrace legends.

Featuring extensive interviews with 15 former players, *Rebels for the Cause* is an indispensable guide to the alternative history of Arsenal Football Club, shedding new light on Arsenal's clash with Moscow Dynamos in '45, on the origins of the rivalry with Tottenham, on many of Highbury's cult heroes and on the struggle of several players to adapt to life outside the game.

> 'Fascinating stuff . . . reveals the story of the club's darker side . . . a good read'
>
> – *Shoot Monthly*

BENNY

The Life and Times of a Fighting Legend

by John Burrowes

ISBN 9781840186611
Now available as a Mainstream Sport Classic paperback (£7.99)
www.mainstreampublishing.com

Benny Lynch was Scotland's first World Boxing Champion and the most talked-about British sportsman of his generation. In fact, many consider him to be the finest fighter the country has ever produced.

Benny is the amazing account of how Lynch battled his way above and beyond the 'fifty-shilling men' of his home town of Glasgow to become the champion of Scotland, Britain, Europe and the world, earning a reputation as one of the greatest pugilists of all time. But this absorbing biography also details how his career sadly came to a premature halt because of Lynch's alcoholism, which destroyed his health and led to him being abandoned by his countless followers. It took his tragic death at the age of only 33 to restore the fallen idol to legendary status.

The gritty reality of the daily grind of life in the Depression-era Gorbals is captured vividly in this remarkable story of the rise and tragic fall of a fighting legend.

IN SEARCH OF TIGER

A Journey Through Golf with Tiger Woods

by Tom Callahan

ISBN 9781840187991
Now available as a Mainstream Sport Classic paperback (£7.99)
www.mainstreampublishing.com

Tom Callahan has written the seminal book on golfing great Tiger Woods. Woods, who has gone out of his way to protect his privacy, has never allowed himself to get close enough to a writer to be properly examined on the page. As a consequence, his fans know relatively little about him except what's divulged in quick tournament interviews or the scarce information passed out on occasion by one of his handlers.

Callahan followed Tiger around the world of golf for over seven years, enjoying a certain access to the man and his parents, Earl and Kultida Woods. His relationship with the family deepened when he undertook a remarkable journey to Vietnam to learn the fate of the South Vietnamese soldier who was Earl Woods' best friend during the war – and his son's namesake.

Tiger is a 20 year old when the book opens and 27 when it closes. During those years Callahan covered Woods at all the majors, including the Masters, the US Open and the British Open, culminating in Tiger's heart-stopping race to make history by clinching the string of majors nicknamed the 'Tiger Slam'. Along the way, Tom Callahan hears from everyone who is anyone in the world of Tiger Woods, including Phil Mickelson, Jack Nicklaus, David Duval, Butch Harmon, Ernie Els and of course, Tiger's ubiquitous mother and father. While learning about Tiger, we also enjoy a bird's eye view of golf, as it is now with Tiger on the scene, and as it was for centuries before.

> 'Deserves a place among the finest books ever written on golf or sports . . . the only Tiger book you ever need to read'
>
> – *Golf Digest*

A SEASON IN DORNOCH

Golf and Life in the Scottish Highlands

by Lorne Rubenstein

ISBN 9781840187052
Now available as a Mainstream Sport Classic paperback (£7.99)
www.mainstreampublishing.com

In 1977, Lorne Rubenstein, an avid golfer, first travelled to Dornoch in the Scottish Highlands. Young and adrift in life, he sought to uncover an authentic sense of self and turned instinctively to a place where his beloved game was purest. The experience had a profound effect on Rubenstein. As he writes, 'My week in Dornoch introduced me to a place with which I felt a connection. A week wasn't living there, but it was enough for Dornoch to imprint itself on my mind.' Twenty-three years later, in 2000, now an established golf writer, Rubenstein returned to Dornoch to spend an entire summer.

Rubenstein writes about the melancholy history of the Highland Clearances. He writes about the friendly and sometimes eccentric people who love their town, their golf and their single malt whisky, and delight in sharing them with visitors whom they recognise as kindred spirits. But most of all he writes about a summer lived around golf, in a community where golf is king.

A Season in Dornoch is an affectionate portrait of a place and the people who live there, a fascinating look at golf and the spirit and skills it calls forth, and a perceptive and ultimately moving memoir of one man's quest to experience again the pure love of sport that he knew in his youth.

> 'Rubenstein gives the reader a feel for what makes the appeal of the Highlands so enduring. He brings the place and its people to life'
>
> – Tom Watson

Ken Ferris is the author of *Football Fanatic*, an account of an odyssey that earned him a place in the *Guiness Book of Records*, and *Manchester United in Europe*. He has been a journalist for over 20 years and currently works for Reuters. He has also written books on economics, entitled *Market Movers* and *Reuters Guide to Official Interest Rates*.